TWENTIETH CENTURY VIEWS

The aim of this series is to present the best in contemporary critical opinion on major authors, providing a twentieth century perspective on their changing status in an era of profound revaluation.

Maynard Mack, *Series Editor*
Yale University

ROBERT LOWELL

ROBERT
LOWELL,

A COLLECTION OF CRITICAL ESSAYS,

Edited by

Thomas Parkinson

Prentice-Hall, Inc. *Englewood Cliffs, N. J.*

A SPECTRUM BOOK

Acknowledgments

For permission to reprint quotations from the poetry of Robert Lowell, acknowledgment is gratefully made to the following publishers: to Harcourt, Brace & World, Inc., for permission to use the passages from *Lord Weary's Castle*, copyright, 1944, 1946, by Robert Lowell; to Faber & Faber, Ltd., for permission to use the passages from *Poems 1938–1949*; to Harcourt, Brace & World, Inc., for the passages from *The Mills of the Kavanaughs*, copyright, 1948, by Robert Lowell; and to Farrar, Straus & Giroux, Inc., and Faber & Faber, Ltd., for permission to reprint passages from the following titles by Robert Lowell: *Life Studies*, copyright © 1956, 1959 by Robert Lowell; *For the Union Dead*, copyright © 1956, 1960, 1961, 1962, 1963, 1964 by Robert Lowell; *The Old Glory*, copyright © 1964, 1965 by Robert Lowell; and *Imitations*, copyright © 1958, 1959, 1960, 1961 by Robert Lowell.

Preface

The Introduction, using a discussion of Robert Lowell's poetry to represent the possible uses of modern literature in the university, follows a suggestion made by Maynard Mack, for which I am very grateful. Lowell is the first contemporary author to have a collection of essays on his work compiled for the series in Twentieth Century Views, so that this is a fitting occasion for such an essay.

Miss Martha Sternin aided me in the initial work on the book; Mrs. Roberta Reid Armstrong helped me bring it to completion and made many important suggestions. Other students in my graduate seminar brought me fresh perspectives on Lowell's poetry, and discussions with friends and colleagues were helpful, especially those with Josephine Miles. Miss Jean Hudson of the General Reference Service of the University Library at Berkeley was, as always, cheerful and tireless.

Berkeley, Calif.
July, 1967

Contents

ROBERT LOWELL

Introduction: Robert Lowell and the Uses of Modern Poetry in the University

by *Thomas Parkinson*

The Status of Poetry

The past twenty years in the United States have seen an enormous expansion of poetic activity, not only in the writing and printing of poetry but in the reading, the recording, the filming of poets as public figures. There exists no film of Yeats, Eliot, Pound, Stevens, or Williams; but National Educational Television has made faithful and eloquent films of Robert Lowell, Richard Wilbur, Gary Snyder, Robert Duncan, Denise Levertov, and despite his early death there is available a touching and vivid film of Frank O'Hara. The equipment existed in the twenties and thirties but was not used, and that is our loss. Ours, however, is an age of records, and the electronic equipment at once creates and answers to a deep need for stabilizing and fixing the processes of a life that moves threateningly out of control. Perhaps this obsession with records accounts for the fact that the most illuminating document on Robert Lowell to date is the *Paris Review* interview. There may be several names for the post-World War II period—the Age of Panic, the Age of Records—but it cannot be called an Age of Criticism. The energy that Burke, Winters, Blackmur, and Leavis put into critical writing now goes into poetry, fiction, or interviewing. And the number of young people with creative, especially poetic, concerns seems to be increasing; the sheer quantity of new magazines and books, many of them turned out on mimeograph machines, makes it hard to keep up with the current state and trend of the art.

Poetry in the United States is becoming an admired and even profitable art. Thanks to the good sense and energy of Betty Kray, nationwide poetry-readings now give many poets substantial incomes; some poets earn from fifteen to fifty thousand dollars a year from such readings, and the demand for poets to serve as teachers and geniuses-in-residence at colleges so exceeds the supply that at least one poet thinks himself worth a salary normally reserved for Nobel Prize-winners. I

put the matter in such crass commercial terms because the great surprise is not that in a society as capable of waste as ours so much energy
should go into an unrewarding enterprise, but rather that so high a
commercial and academic value should be placed on an activity that
was, only twenty years ago, the province of bohemians who had literally
to hire a hall in order to gather an audience. This shift in sensibility
has had profound effects on the study of literature in American universities, on graduate and undergraduate curricula, and on library poli-
cies. One major university library pays a retainer to an avant-garde
publisher in exchange for all correspondence he receives relating to his
publications. Libraries vigorously collect "little magazines," limited
editions of books, and original manuscripts, paying for them prices
comparable to those paid for material associated with standard classical authors. "Literature of the Twentieth Century" is the subject of
one in four doctoral dissertations in English. Journals are devoted
exclusively to articles on and bibliographies of twentieth-century
writers, poets, and novelists; and dramatists in their thirties or forties
with slim and undefined *oeuvres* are treated with the same seriousness
as Blake or Pope.

Graduate Study

The academic status of modern, even contemporary, literature has
radically altered as an aftermath of the pedagogical work of I. A. Richards, Cleanth Brooks, and others whose work was in turn a result of
the reexamination of the relation between the present and the tradition
growing out of classical modern writers such as Lawrence, Yeats, Eliot,
Pound, Joyce, Faulkner. The university has learned to live with these
revaluations and take a more convivial view of literature in the first
forty years of this century.[1] The increasing demand for holders of the
doctorate has expanded graduate-student populations to the point of
explosion and put such strain on library facilities as to make it very
tempting to work with authors whose works are in print and on whom
little preceding work has been done. To study Wordsworth or Milton,
it is necessary to read a body of secondary matter that is depressing
for the most part, but has at least the advantage of compelling the
student to a critical and analytical attitude toward literary study. Another book on such authors is justifiable only if it takes a fresh view
of the material or adds information not hitherto available. Neither
accomplishment can be undertaken lightly or attained with ease. Very
little intervenes, however, between the student and Robert Creeley; it

[1] Ong, Walter J., "Synchronic Present: The Academic Future of Modern Literature in America," *American Quarterly*, Vol. XIV, Number 2 (Summer, 1962).

is possible to say something original about Creeley because anything one says is bound to be new—nothing has been said about him, whereas Chaucer, Spenser, Shakespeare, Milton, Tennyson, Yeats. . . . Insofar as the graduate study of recent literature is encouraged by this tendency toward the untouched subject, the uncovered field, getting the dissertation done—insofar as it is an evasive action, it shows a certain biological good sense and self-protective shrewdness. The demand that every graduate student write a book-length argument about an important literary topic before he can be certified as a college teacher is usually dubious and often ridiculous.

Graduate study of modern literature suffers as a result, and my own sad conclusion is that books on modern literature, with few honorable exceptions, tend to be worse than the ordinary run of studies of earlier literatures. Many books on modern authors rely on contemporary clichés for their point of view, and on available books in print for their substance. They are enough to make one agree with Fred Millett and R. W. B. Lewis—despite the bizarre nature of their ideas of scholarship—that literature of the twentieth century is not a proper subject for study. Identifying scholarship with bibliography Millett has written:

> If it [scholarship] has any meaning in relation to contemporary English literature, it is a very different meaning from that it has in relation to the Renaissance, the eighteenth century, or even the Victorian period. The term *scholarship,* in the sense of a careful scientific manipulation of literary documents, is only rarely applicable here, although it may be exhibited by the best biographies of twentieth century literary figures.[2]

And Lewis accepts a less defined but equally exclusive idea of scholarship:

> The fact is, of course, that contemporary literature is not really a subject for scholarship. It can be a subject for criticism, though only of a provisional kind. . . . For in a deep and insuperable sense, contemporary literature must always be unfinished business, even if the writer studied has been dead for forty years. We are only just beginning to calculate— how could we have done it sooner?—the uncanny prophetic power in the later novels of Henry James, even as we are just catching up with the fearful accuracy of Henry Adams.[3]

It must be difficult to live on New Haven (or decade-saving) time, where a man dead forty years is a contemporary writer, perhaps in the sense

[2] Millett, Frederick, "Contemporary British Literature," pp. 187–88 in *Contemporary Literary Scholarship, A Critical Review*, ed. Lewis Leary (New York: Appleton-Century-Crofts, 1958).

[3] Lewis, R. W. B., "Contemporary American Literature," p. 203 in *Contemporary Literary Scholarship, A Critical Review*, ed. Lewis Leary (New York: Appleton-Century-Crofts, 1958).

that Shakespeare is our contemporary. All literature is unfinished business or graduate schools would long since have gone out of business. It is strange that it should be necessary to repeat platitudes as if they were weird novelties: the most recent literature is obviously in a state of change, and creative in the sense that it is altering itself, the world it exists in, and the literature that preceded it. The shift in sensibility since 1945 has given both Whitman and Shelley greater emphasis in the collective literary mind than they received when the New Criticism was new, and this shift was accelerated by the work of contemporary writers who handled material in the cumulative emotional manner of Shelley and Whitman. A poet of the stature of William Carlos Williams can give to Whitman's motives a new dignity; and the fact that Robert Duncan can seriously use the stanzaic form of Shelley's "Arethusa" gives fresh impulse to the study of Shelley among young poets and scholars. It doesn't matter whether Duncan and Williams are originators or beneficiaries of changes in the *Zeitgeist*; in their work we can see the implications and consequences of this change embodied in memorable and compelling form. As long as the human spirit grows— and it will continue to grow—the sense of the past will change.

This is a tempting vision. The very contemporaneity and creativity of literature now in the process of being written is extremely seductive. As a novelist once said when asked what his favorite literature was, "American literature, and I like it so much I write it myself." [4] There is a genuine similarity between artist and scientist, and the assertion is frequently made that the primary matter of literary study should be, as it is in the sciences, the contemporary for analytic study—and the creative for emulation and the practice of writing. But the natural sciences differ from the arts in that they are non-historical, even anti-historical; destructive in their acts of creation, building upon the past in order to make it irrelevant. Since many scientists are men of profound sensibility and grace of spirit, they maintain a pious and reverent attitude toward the great figures who have been inventive and creative in the past. But this admiration is directed toward heroic figures of the past as men while their inventions are regarded as magnificent, elegant, harmonious, inclusive—in short as purely aesthetic or moral rather than intellectual forces. The admiration that Walter Knight feels for Galileo and Faraday or that Charles Kittel [5] feels for Josiah Willard Gibbs is an admiration for human qualities of courage, independence, imaginative control, ingenuity; but each is perfectly aware of the intellectual limits of past work and would not consider it fruitful to go over the same ground and use equivalent methods.

[4] Donald Carpenter.

[5] Kittel, Charles, *Introduction to Solid State Physics*, 3rd ed. (New York: John Wiley & Sons, Inc., 1966).

Robert Lowell not only admires Rilke and Donne and Baudelaire but finds it useful to go over precisely the same ground and use equivalent methods, just as Robert Duncan does with Pindar, Ovid, and Whitman. For literature is both historical and ahistorical, so that the characteristic vision of the literary student, whether he is poet, scholar, or critic, is of all writers existing in his mind simultaneously, or of each writer existing within an elaborate social and intellectual and moral context extending into depths of time; and of ourselves, at our best, as existing in this large community as part of the historical and timeless. As far as the literary imagination is concerned, the human spirit grows without maturing.

The dichotomy that Millett and Lewis take for granted is nonexistent. When the differences between scholarship and criticism make for mutually exclusive areas of exploration, literary study is in a sad way. Then artificial compartmentalizing occurs that makes scholarship stuffy and criticism silly.

It is here that recent literature is most helpful, in graduate study. Such study should not be undertaken in order to evade the library problem or to indulge the sensibility, though both those enterprises are valid. As serious students of twentieth century literature know, theirs is not only the most difficult field of study but possibly the most prototypical. When properly done, work on twentieth century authors brings into play large bodies of secondary matter, intensive bibliographical study, research in magazines that existed only briefly in very limited editions, transcriptions of hitherto unexamined manuscripts. Much of the work that has been effectively done for authors of more remote periods must be done from scratch. When Richard Ellmann wrote his critical biography of Yeats, there was in print only one biography, and that a memoir by a man who, in Mrs. Yeats's phrase, had "a positive gift for confusing dates." There was no comprehensive bibliography, only a check-list of the books in William Roth's collection. A mere handful of the letters had been published, and there was no variorum edition of the poems. The manuscripts, then as now, were not catalogued and had not been arranged in any logical order. Preceding critical studies were negligible and plagued by forgivable ignorance.

Anyone who has worked on an author whose books and manuscripts have not been described learns quickly the relevance of the basic procedures of literary study. He must shape a bibliography and in some instances a variorum edition. He must make critical decisions and discriminations of style; fix to some measure the pattern of the author's intellectual, moral, and stylistic development; find his intellectual and literary sources; set him in the context of his contemporaries and in relation to the traditions of English and other literatures; assess his social position in relation to historical events that may themselves not yet have been assessed; and discover relevant biographical data. He is living in a world of conjecture, judgment, and qualitative discrimination, with very little to guide him.

This was the position that Richard Ellmann found himself in when he wrote *W. B. Yeats, the Man and the Masks,* and I appreciate his problem because when he was writing the first systematic biographic study at Yale, I was writing one of the first systematic critical studies of Yeats at Berkeley. Since that time a considerable light (though not smokeless) industry has grown out of the study of Yeats, so that he, like Wordsworth or Milton, can be used to exemplify various problems in the study of literature. He has become a standard literary classic, in the gloomy quantitative sense that more has been written about him than he wrote. Some of this work, like Russell Alspach's variorum edition of the lyric poems or Allan Wade's Soho Bibliography, is a model for students learning the basic tools of research. Surely every student should know how to use a first-rate bibliography—but it is no longer possible to learn by studying Yeats the process of constructing a bibliography or the equivalent of a variorum edition of a poem. The work has been done, and we have reached the point with this symptomatic modern classic where his value for a graduate student has become ritualized into patterns of study that are conventionally useful.

The advantage of studying recent literature is that in so doing one is forced to coordinate scholarly and critical methods. Instead of contemplating through secondary sources the design of a career or literary movement, the student is compelled to go through the process of establishing, however provisionally, design in material that he may be the very first to order. The discriminations made in treating the poetry of West Africa—or that of Robert Lowell—require a full engagement of taste and intelligence and bibliographical labor that in many ways exceeds the commitment required by the study of writers whose reputations have been relatively fixed and formulated by historical and critical judgment. It takes lonely courage to work on an unknown which may in turn reveal the unknown in ourselves. The graduate student who has not had that experience in any systematic form has not been fully trained. For when we look at literary study of any significance, it inhabits ". . . a world of conjecture, judgment, and qualitative discrimination." The student who would turn his back on such a world is not interested in literary study.

The Undergraduate College

It is difficult to think of the uses of modern literature in the liberal arts college when there is no definition of the use of the liberal arts college. Current undergraduate programs are in great disorder because the graduate programs of the great universities have become increasingly the norm by which liberal arts colleges assess and guide themselves. The problem has been accentuated by pressures from high schools that have increased the rigor of curricula and the amount of writing to a ridiculous degree. High school students are given assignments appropriate to people twenty years old, and twenty year olds are cast in pre-professional roles. Between the new high schools and the graduate schools, the liberal arts college is literally being flattened. Our entire educational system fosters false precocity, and the concept of maturity that it presents to the world is simple professionalism. One of the finest liberal arts colleges in the country wrote to the graduate office of my department recently and said that its graduates were complaining because their undergraduate education had not properly prepared them for graduate school—what should it do with its program? The chief irony was that my own department at the very moment was re-examining its undergraduate program because it had become too tightly linked to the doctoral program.

The questions raised by students about liberal education come under the rubric of "relevance," pertinence to current moral, social, and religious problems rather than utility in shaping a career. Their wisdom is to ask for wisdom, and in so doing they are facing up to the problems of liberal education more fully than those professors who think of undergraduate work as training for professional activity. Left to themselves, undergraduates drift toward contemporary literature, where they see their own problems embodied in the most immediately accessible and compelling form.

The most accessible, but not the most comprehensive. Current students can rouse despair in their teachers because of their often overt belief that the world began with their birth and that civilization is almost certain to end with their death. On the second point, they have some experience to guide them; you can't scare an entire generation to death with the atomic bomb and soothe them with commodities. It is also difficult to create any sense of human continuity in young Americans who have been so thoroughly indoctrinated in the expectation of immediate gratification. They are temporal provincials not through malice but through the example of their seniors. It is perhaps true that if students were left to their own concept of relevance they would read nothing but contemporary literature and write nothing but verse and fiction. Even if this were so, it would not have to be an unrelieved disaster.

Contemporary literature in English is unintelligible without knowledge of the history of literature in English and other languages and without study of many relevant fields of knowledge. There is an organic

continuity in the history of the novel that leads one from Mailer to
Dreiser to Dostoyevsky, and in poetry that compels one from Robert
Lowell through T. S. Eliot to Baudelaire, Donne, and Dante. This is
not a question of curriculum but of experienced relevance. It is inconceivable that any teacher could use *The Naked and the Dead* as
text without having the *Iliad*, *The Charterhouse of Parma*, and *The
Red Badge of Courage* crowd upon him. When students ask for moral
and religious relevance, any sensible teacher knows immediately that
his primary obligation is to show them that the fullest embodiment
of human destiny is in the great works of literature, that none of this
is outworn or superseded, and that any era, perhaps especially our own,
has only a partial and unsatisfactory grasp of human potentiality.

Robert Lowell

Lowell as much as any current poet deserves systematic study in universities. He is entwined in the great moral issues of our age with compelling fullness, reacting against the savagery and barbarism of great
and small wars, apprehending passionately the solitude and waste of
the individual caught in a world that, in Rilke's phrase, has "fallen
into the hands of men." He is in effect the poetic conscience tor-
mented by its perception of reality and its imagination of possibilities
in this most terrible of centuries, once spoken of with unconscious
irony as The American Century. And he sees this century within the
total web of the past and as a trouble to be seen in the major languages
of the world. He is neither a temporal nor a spatial provincial. American historical life is seen as an experienced whole, and the ancestral
voices of his poetry are familial, of New England, and at the same time
universal spirits. His work is not national in any sense, but local and
international, representing his identity as a New England writer and
his obligations as a member of the international poetic community. It
would be too much to ask that he embrace Oriental culture; his only
provincialism resides in his faithfully European affections, and surely
the legacy of Western Europe is rich—and relevant—enough to engage
the energies of a lifetime.

Lowell's movement from Roman Catholicism to general Christian
piety to a kind of agnostic existentialism is not only representative of
the religious options that have been successively viable for him but
also emblematic of the troubled religious spirit of Western Europeans
during the past twenty-five years. He is not totally inclusive, but only
a monster could fully represent all the currents of religious thought
that have moved through the spiritual chaos of contemporary thought.
The point about his religious obsessions, which have been widely

shared by thoughtful men, is that in his poetry those obsessions are tested by the excruciating demands of poetic discipline. Ideas are profound not in themselves but in the incisiveness of their impact; poetry, with music the most incisive of arts, works through its prosody and syntax a deepening impact on man's otherwise impervious mind. Lowell's poetry provides an embodiment of the religious condition that has the richness that comes only when heart, imagination, and intelligence are working together.

Poetry is also a test of religious and moral qualities. Lowell's early religious poetry displays the uneasiness with which Catholicism can be accommodated to the voice and method of his poetic sensibility. One of the dramas of Lowell's work resides in the poet's gradual recognition, through his poetry, of the incompatibility of his sense of Catholicism with his poetic technique. I am tempted to say that the failure rests not with the Catholicism but with the special technique; that the formulae of the poetry could not cope with the generosity of the Church and forced that many-mansioned house to a very restricted tenement. The breaking point comes with *The Mills of the Kavanaughs,* for with that book the specifically Catholic content of the poetry stops, as does the poetic style that is early Lowell. It is, in all senses, a divorce.

The relative silence that intervened between 1951 and 1959 reflects both the years of oppression during the most contemptible period of the cold war and Lowell's need, personal and poetic, to find a way of coping with experience without violating poetic demands. He himself ascribes the development of new capacities to a visit to the west coast, where he was opened to fresh poetic method; and the appearance of *Life Studies* accompanied a generally new approach—new at least to the national scene—that allowed Lowell a wider set of poetic permissions and demands than he had earlier granted himself. The style that emerges there is dramatic rather than symbolic and was accompanied by a fresh concern with theatre. That phase in his work is not yet completed, as the recent prose version of *Prometheus Bound* indicates.[6] My view of this development, quizzical to the point of being skeptical, appears in my essay (p. 143 below) and needs no elaboration here.

Accompanying this shift in his poetics was the appearance of a large body of translation, which, with the stage work, compelled a variegation of poetic voice. The most heartening element in Lowell's career is his refusal to rest secure in any limited mode of being, his constant quest for the poetic vocabulary of forms that will allow him to do his proper work. The imitations grant him both fixed plot and subject and modifying terms of phrase and movement. He forces upon himself the possibility of growth, and this requires courageous labor.

[6] *New York Review of Books,* Vol. IX, Number 1 (July 13, 1967), pp. 17–24.

The religious and moral problems poetically treated by Lowell should satisfy the most disaffiliated student's demand for relevance. And when the issues of this work are seen in the perspective that Lowell takes as his proper burden, the student is forced beyond the bounds of his own life and culture to see what informs human potentiality in the widest reference. D. H. Lawrence defined the novel as the point where the soul meets history, and Lowell is one of several current poets who want to reclaim that ground for the poetic imagination. In the process he raises major aesthetic as well as moral issues, forcing contemplation of the relationship between the conduct of phrase and the conduct of life.

In addition to his impact because of the direct human relevance of those problems he has elected as his own, Lowell presents aesthetic and historical difficulties. He is not a poet that one can accept without question; like Yeats or Lawrence, he forces the reader to grapple with his work. His surfaces are not beguiling or engaging *per se;* they are as challenging and disturbing as the problems they treat. Critical engagement with his poetry opens new battlegrounds within the reader's own spirit, compels self-awareness that can be painful and troubling. Exploring Lowell's world changes the landscape and fauna of one's own, so that one returns from the poetry to an altered condition of being.

This and no less is what should be asked of art. After the initial encounter between the work and the reader, further study is justified only in order to explain and estimate the consequences of such change. If there is a border-line between liberal and professional study of letters, it is to be found in this area, where the personal experience of art, the personal involvement, is transmuted into the need to inform others of that experience: by imitating the work in question in poetic form, by evaluating it in terms of one's own world view, by analyzing the elements that compose the work—all in the interests of instructing others. To make such instruction accurate and rational, information is required. There is, for instance, only one bibliography of Lowell, and that covering the work up to 1959. Numerous variants exist of some poems, and there is no variorum edition, nor could there be in any final sense. Still, a provisional collation of extant texts is necessary in the interests of temporal accuracy, and useful for insight into the motives of the poetry and the changing style. The poetry has much of the mosaic surface of Eliot or Pound, in which elements from previous poems are combined for wide allusive meaning; those sources or analogues are essential to full comprehension of the work. Dante, the Bible, Hawthorne, Melville, Latin and French poetry, particularly, and generally the poetic vocabulary of the entire European world, Donne, Herbert—Lowell's habit of mind is deeply and organically traditional, so that his work opens out on the great traditions of poetry and thought: The moral and social relevance of his own work reinforces the relevance of the entire poetic tradition to the very world in which we move and live and have our being.

To return to the uses of contemporary literature in the university, it has always seemed to me that one gross failing in formal literary study resides in its temporal discriminations that are only important when tested against the body of all literature. Increasingly in my own work I find the concept of "modern" literature is practically useless—there is only literature—so that in the reading list of my large lecture course in modern American literature appear Stendhal, Shakespeare, the Bible, as measures and complements to Mailer, Albee, and Eliot. The focus may remain on the writers of a particular period, but it is impossible to discriminate the particularity of that period without some present external norm. It is not unkindness to Albee that prompts me to assign *Macbeth* with *Who's Afraid of Virginia Woolf?* but a conviction that current students need desperately some sense of the time-bound nature of their own obsessions and the timelessness of art. And if I were teaching a course in Shakespeare, I should be strongly tempted to assign reading in Ionesco, Genet, Brecht, O'Neill, Strindberg, and Albee, in order to place Shakespeare in a perspective that may magnify as well as clarify his qualities. The danger in such an approach is clear; one has only to read Kott's *Shakespeare Our Contemporary* to realize what kinds of catastrophic nonsense can rise from the beatification of the contemporary. The proper use of contemporary literature requires tact, good sense, imagination, a knowledge of history, and a deep feeling for art. But then, the proper use of any literature requires those qualities.

Robert Lowell

interviewed by Frederick Seidel

Robert Lowell was born in Boston on 1 March 1917, great-grand-nephew of James Russell. He first attended St. Mark's School, and then Harvard, which he left after two years for Kenyon in order to study poetry, criticism, and the classics under John Crowe Ransom. He then attended Louisiana State University and afterwards worked for a short while with a New York publisher. During World War II he was a conscientious objector and served a prison sentence.

In 1947 and 1948 Mr. Lowell was Consultant in Poetry at the Library of Congress. He has held a Guggenheim fellowship and an Institute of Arts and Letters grant. He has lectured in poetry and creative writing at the State University of Iowa, the Kenyon School of English, and the Salzburg Seminar in American Studies in Austria; he has also taught at Boston University. In 1959 he was awarded a fellowship by the Ford Foundation to work as a poet-librettist in association with the Metropolitan Opera and the New York City Opera companies.

His first book of poems was *Land of Unlikeness*, published in 1944. Most of these poems were included in his second volume, *Lord Weary's Castle* (1946). In 1951 he published a third volume of poetry, *The Mills of the Kavanaughs*, and in 1959 *Life Studies*, consisting of new poems and an autobiographical fragment. He received the Pulitzer Prize for poetry in 1947 for *Lord Weary's Castle*.

Mr. Lowell is married to the writer Elizabeth Hardwick and has one child, a daughter, Harriet.

Robert Lowell

On one wall of Mr. Lowell's study was a large portrait of Ezra Pound, the tired, haughty outlines of the face concentrated as in the raised

"Robert Lowell" as interviewed by Frederick Seidel. From The Paris Review, No. 25 (Winter–Spring, 1961), 56–95. The interview has also been included in *Writers at Work: The Paris Review Interviews, Second Series* (New York: The Viking Press, Inc., 1963; London: Martin Secker & Warburg, Ltd., 1963). Copyright © 1963 by The Paris Review, Inc. Reprinted by permission of the publishers.

outlines of a ring seal in an enlargement. Also bearded, but on another wall, over the desk, James Russell Lowell looked down from a grey old-fashioned photograph on the apex of the triangle thus formed, where his great-grandnephew sat and answered questions.

Mr. Lowell had been talking about the classes he teaches at Boston University.

Four floors below the study window, cars whined through the early spring rain on Marlborough Street towards the Boston Public Garden.

INTERVIEWER: What are you teaching now?

LOWELL: I'm teaching one of these poetry-writing classes and a course in the novel. The course in the novel is called Practical Criticism. It's a course I teach every year, but the material changes. It could be anything from Russian short stories to Baudelaire, a study of the New Critics, or just fiction. I do whatever I happen to be working on myself.

INTERVIEWER: Has your teaching over the last few years meant anything to you as a writer?

LOWELL: It's meant a lot to me as a human being, I think. But my teaching is part-time and has neither the merits nor the burdens of real teaching. Teaching is entirely different from writing. You're always up to it, or more or less up to it; there's no question of its clogging, of its not coming. It's much less subjective, and it's a very pleasant pursuit in itself. In the kind of teaching I do, conversational classes, seminars, if the students are good, which they've been most of the time, it's extremely entertaining. Now, I don't know what it has to do with writing. You review a lot of things that you like, and you read things that you haven't read or haven't read closely, and read them aloud, go into them much more carefully than you would otherwise; and that must teach you a good deal. But there's such a jump from teaching to writing.

INTERVIEWER: Well, do you think the academic life is liable to block up the writer-professor's sensitivity to his own intuitions?

LOWELL: I think it's impossible to give a general answer. Almost all the poets of my generation, all the best ones, teach. I only know one, Elizabeth Bishop, who doesn't. They do it for a livelihood, but they also do it because you can't write poetry all the time. They do it to extend themselves, and I think it's undoubtedly been a gain to them. Now the question is whether something else might be more of a gain. Certainly the danger of teaching is that it's much too close to what you're doing—close and not close. You can get expert at teaching and be crude in pratice. The revision, the consciousness that tinkers with the poem—that has something to do with teaching and criticism. But the impulse that starts a poem and makes it of any importance is distinct from teaching.

INTERVIEWER: And protected, you think, from whatever you bring to bear in the scrutiny of parts of poems and aspects of novels, etc.?

LOWELL: I think you have to tear it apart from that. Teaching may make the poetry even more different, less academic than it would be otherwise. I'm sure that writing isn't a craft, that is, something for which you learn the skills and go on turning out. It must come from some deep impulse, deep inspiration. That can't be taught, it can't be what you use in teaching. And you may go further afield looking for that than you would if you didn't teach. I don't know, really; the teaching probably makes you more cautious, more self-conscious, makes you write less. It may make you bolder when you do write.

INTERVIEWER: You think the last may be so?

LOWELL: The boldness is ambiguous. It's not only teaching, it's growing up in this age of criticism which we're all so conscious of, whether we like it or don't like it, or practise it or don't practise it. You think three times before you put a word down, and ten times about taking it out. And that's related to boldness; if you put words down they must do something, you're not going to put clichés. But then it's related to caution; you write much less.

INTERVIEWER: You yourself have written very little criticism, haven't you? You did once contribute to a study of Hopkins.

LOWELL: Yes, and I've done a few omnibus reviews. I do a review or two a year.

INTERVIEWER: You did a wonderful one of Richards's poems.

LOWELL: I felt there was an occasion for that, and I had something to say about it. Sometimes I wish I did more, but I'm very anxious in criticism not to do the standard analytical essay. I'd like my essay to be much sloppier and more intuitive. But my friends are critics, and most of them poet-critics. When I was twenty and learning to write, Allen Tate, Eliot, Blackmur, and Winters, and all those people were very much news. You waited for their essays, and when a good critical essay came out it had the excitement of a new imaginative work.

INTERVIEWER: Which is really not the case with any of the critics writing today, do you think?

LOWELL: The good critics are almost all the old ones. The most brilliant critic of my generation, I think, was Jarrell, and he in a way connects with that older generation. But he's writing less criticism now than he used to.

INTERVIEWER: In your schooling at St. Mark's and Harvard—we can talk about Kenyon in a minute—were there teachers or friends who had an influence on your writing, not so much by the example of their own writing as by personal supervision or direction—by suggesting certain reading, for instance?

LOWELL: Well, my school had been given a Carnegie set of art books, and I had a friend, Frank Parker, who had great talent as a painter but who'd never done it systematically. We began reading the books and histories of art, looking at reproductions, tracing the Last Supper on tracing paper, studying dynamic symmetry, learning about Cézanne, and so on. I had no practical interest in painting, but that study seemed rather close to poetry. And from there I began. I think I read Elizabeth Drew or some such book on modern poetry. It had free verse in it, and that seemed very simple to do.

INTERVIEWER: What class were you in then?

LOWELL: It was my last year. I'd wanted to be a football player very much, and got my letter but didn't make the team. Well, that was satisfying but crushing too. I read a good deal, but had never written. So this was a recoil from that. Then I had some luck in that Richard Eberhart was teaching there.

INTERVIEWER: I'd thought he'd been a student there with you.

LOWELL: No, he was a young man about thirty. I never had him in class, but I used to go to him. He'd read aloud and we'd talk, he was very pleasant that way. He'd smoke honey-scented tobacco, and read Baudelaire and Shakespeare and Hopkins—it made the thing living— and he'd read his own poems. I wrote very badly at first, but he was encouraging and enthusiastic. That probably was decisive, that there was someone there whom I admired who was engaged in writing poetry.

INTERVIEWER: I heard that a very early draft of "The Drunken Fisherman" appeared in the St. Mark's magazine.

LOWELL: No, it was the Kenyon college magazine that published it. The poem was very different then. I'd been reading Winters, whose model was Robert Bridges, and what I wanted was a rather distant, quiet, classical poem without any symbolism. It was in four-foot couplets as smooth as I could write them. The *Kenyon Review* had published a poem of mine and then they'd stopped. This was the one time they said, if you'd submitted this we'd have taken it.

INTERVIEWER: Then you were submitting other poems to the Review?

LOWELL: Yes, and that poem was rather different from anything else I did. I was also reading Hart Crane and Thomas and Tate and Empson's *Seven Types of Ambiguity*; and each poem was more difficult than the one before, and had more ambiguities. Ransom, editing the *Kenyon Review*, was impressed, but didn't want to publish them. He felt they were forbidding and clotted.

INTERVIEWER: But finally he did come through.

LOWELL: Well, after I'd graduated. I published when I was a junior, then for about three years no magazine would take anything I did. I'd get sort of pleasant letters—"One poem in this group interests us, if you can get seven more." At that time it took me about a year to do two or three poems. Gradually I just stopped, and really sort of gave it up. I seemed to have reached a great impasse. The kind of poem I thought was interesting and would work on became so cluttered and overdone that it wasn't really poetry.

INTERVIEWER: I was struck on reading *Land of Unlikeness* by the difference between the poems you rejected for *Lord Weary's Castle* and the few poems and passages that you took over into the new book.

LOWELL: I think I took almost a third, but almost all of what I took was rewritten. But I wonder what struck you?

INTERVIEWER: One thing was that almost all the rejected poems seemed to me to be those that Tate, who in his introduction spoke about two kinds of poetry in the book, said were the more strictly religious and strictly symbolic poems, as against the poems he said were perhaps more powerful because more experienced or relying more on your sense of history. What you took seemed really superior to what you left behind.

LOWELL: Yes, I took out several that were paraphases of early Christian poems, and I rejected one rather dry abstraction, then whatever seemed to me to have a messy violence. All the poems have religious imagery, I think, but the ones I took were more concrete. That's what the book was moving towards: less symbolic imagery. And as I say, I tried to take some of the less fierce poems. There seemed to be too much twisting and disgust in the first book.

INTERVIEWER: I wondered how wide your reading had been at the time. I wondered, when I read in Tate's introduction that the stanza in one of your poems was based on the stanza in "The Virginian Voyages," whether someone had pointed out Drayton's poem to you.

LOWELL: Tate and I started to make an anthology together. It was a very interesting year I spent with Tate and his wife. He's a poet who writes in spurts, and he had about a third of a book. I was going to do a biography of Jonathan Edwards and he was going to write a novel, and our wives were going to write novels. Well, the wives just went humming away. "I've just finished three pages," they'd say at the end of the day; and their books mounted up. But ours never did, though one morning Allen wrote four pages to his novel, very brilliant. We were in a little study together separated by a screen. I was heaping up books on Jonathan Edwards and taking notes, and getting more and more numb on the subject, looking at old leather-bound volumes on freedom of the will and so on, and feeling less and less a calling. And there we stuck. And then we decided to make an anthology together. We both liked rather formal, difficult poems, and we were reading particularly the Sixteenth and Seventeenth centuries. In the evening we'd read aloud, and we started a card catalogue of what we'd make for the anthology. And then we started writing. It seems to me we took old models like Drayton's Ode—Tate wrote a poem called "The Young Proconsuls of the Air" in that stanza. I think there's a trick to formal poetry. Most poetry is very formal, but when a modern poet is formal he gets more attention for it than old poets did. Somehow we've tried to make it look difficult. For example, Shelley can just rattle off terza rima by the page, and it's very smooth, doesn't seem an obstruction to him—you sometimes wish it were more difficult. Well, someone does that today and in modern style it looks as though he's wrestling with every line and may be pushed into confusion, as though he's having a real struggle with form and content. Marks of that are in the finished poem. And I think both Tate and I felt that we wanted our formal patterns to seem a hardship and something that we couldn't rattle off easily.

INTERVIEWER: But in *Lord Weary's Castle* there were poems moving toward a sort of narrative calm, almost a prose calm—"Katherine's Dream," for example, or the two poems on texts by Edwards, or "The Ghost"—and then, on the other hand, poems in which the form was insisted upon and maybe shown off, and where the things that were characteristic of your poetry at that time—the kind of enjambments, the rhyming, the meters, of course—seem willed and forced, so that you have a terrific log jam of stresses, meanings, strains.

LOWELL: I know one contrast I've felt, and it takes different forms at different times. The ideal modern form seems to be the novel and certain short stories. Maybe Tolstoi would be the perfect example—his work is imagistic, it deals with all experience, and there seems to be no conflict of the form and content. So one thing is to get into poetry that kind of human richness in rather simple descriptive language. Then there's another side of poetry: compression, something highly rhythmical and perhaps wrenched into a small space. I've always been fascinated by both these things. But getting it all on one page in a few stanzas, getting it all done in as little space as possible, revising and revising so that each word and rhythm though not perfect is pondered and wrestled with—you can't do that in prose very well, you'd never get your book written. "Katherine's Dream" was a real dream. I found that I shaped it a bit, and cut it, and allegorized it, but still it was a dream someone had had. It was material that ordinarily, I think, would go into prose, yet it would have had to be much longer or part of something much longer.

INTERVIEWER: I think you can either look for forms, you can do specific reading for them, or the forms can be demanded by what you want to say. And when the material in poetry seems under almost unbearable pressure you wonder whether the form hasn't cookie-cut what the poet wanted to say. But you chose the couplet, didn't you, and some of your freest passages are in couplets.

LOWELL: The couplet I've used is very much like the couplet Browning uses in "My Last Duchess," in *Sordello,* run-on with its rhymes buried. I've always, when I've used it, tried to give the impression that I had as much freedom in choosing the rhyme word as I had in any of the other words. Yet they were almost all true rhymes, and maybe half the time there'd be a pause after the rhyme. I wanted something as fluid as prose; you wouldn't notice the form, yet looking back you'd find that great obstacles had been climbed. And the couplet is pleasant in this way—once you've got your two lines to rhyme, then that's done and you can go on to the next. You're not stuck with the whole stanza to round out and build to a climax. A couplet can be a couplet or can be split and left as one line, or it can go on for a hundred lines; any sort of compression or expansion is possible. And that's not so in a stanza. I think a couplet's much less lyrical than a stanza, closer to prose. Yet it's an honest form, its difficulties are in the open. It really is pretty hard to rhyme each line with the one that follows it.

INTERVIEWER: Did the change of style in *Life Studies* have something to do with working away from that compression and pressure by way of, say, the kind of prose clarity of "Katherine's Dream"?

LOWELL: Yes. By the time I came to *Life Studies* I'd been writing my autobiography and also writing poems that broke meter. I'd been doing a lot of reading aloud. I went on a trip to the West Coast and read at least once a day and sometimes twice for fourteen days, and more and more I found that I was simplifying my poems. If I had a Latin quotation I'd translate it into English. If adding a couple of syllables in a line made it clearer I'd add them, and I'd make little changes just impromptu as I read. That seemed to improve the reading.

INTERVIEWER: Can you think of a place where you added a syllable or two to an otherwise regular line?

LOWELL: It was usually articles and prepositions that I added, very slight little changes, and I didn't change the printed text. It was just done for the moment.

INTERVIEWER: Why did you do this? Just because you thought the most important thing was to get the poem over?

LOWELL: To get it over, yes. And I began to have a certain disrespect for the tight forms. If you could make it easier by adding syllables, why not? And then when I was writing *Life Studies,* a good number of the poems were started in very strict meter, and I found that, more than the rhymes, the regular beat was what I didn't want. I have a long poem in there about my father, called "Commander

Lowell," which actually is largely in couplets, but I originally wrote perfectly strict four-foot couplets. Well, with that form it's hard not to have echoes of Marvell. That regularity just seemed to ruin the honesty of sentiment, and became rhetorical; it said, "I'm a poem"—though it was a great help when I was revising having this original skeleton. I could keep the couplets where I wanted them and drop them where I didn't; there'd be a form to come back to.

INTERVIEWER: Had you originally intended to handle all that material in prose?

LOWELL: Yes. I found it got awfully tedious working out transitions and putting in things that didn't seem very important but were necessary to the prose continuity. Also, I found it hard to revise. Cutting it down into small bits, I could work on it much more carefully and make fast transitions. But there's another point about this mysterious business of prose and poetry, form and content, and the reasons for breaking forms. I don't think there's any very satisfactory answer. I seesaw back and forth between something highly metrical and something highly free; there isn't any one way to write. But it seems to me we've gotten into a sort of Alexandrian age. Poets of my generation and particularly younger ones have gotten terribly proficient at these forms. They write a very musical, difficult poem with tremendous skill, perhaps there's never been such skill. Yet the writing seems divorced from culture somehow. It's become too much something specialized that can't handle much experience. It's become a craft, purely a craft, and there must be some breakthrough back into life. Prose is in many ways better off than poetry. It's quite hard to think of a young poet who has the vitality, say, of Salinger or Saul Bellow. Yet prose tends to be very diffuse. The novel is really a much more difficult form than it seems; few people have the wind to write anything that long. Even a short story demands almost poetic perfection. Yet on the whole prose is less cut off from life than poetry is. Now, some of this Alexandrian poetry is very brilliant, you would not have it changed at all. But I thought it was getting increasingly stifling. I couldn't get my experience into tight metrical forms.

INTERVIEWER: So you felt this about your own poetry, your own technique, not just about the general condition of poetry?

LOWELL: Yes, I felt that the meter plastered difficulties and mannerisms on what I was trying to say to such an extent that it terribly hampered me.

INTERVIEWER: This then explains, in part anyway, your admiration for Elizabeth Bishop's poetry. I know that you've said the qualities and the abundance of its descriptive language reminded you of the Russian novel more than anything else.

LOWELL: Any number of people are guilty of writing a complicated poem that has a certain amount of symbolism in it and really difficult meaning, a wonderful poem to teach. Then you unwind it and you feel that the intelligence, the experience, whatever goes into it, is skin-deep. In Elizabeth Bishop's "Man-Moth" a whole new world is gotten out and you don't know what will come after any one line. It's exploring. And it's as original as Kafka. She's gotten a world, not just a way of writing. She seldom writes a poem that doesn't have that exploratory quality; yet it's very firm, it's not like beat poetry, it's all controlled.

INTERVIEWER: What about Snodgrass? What you were trying to do in *Life Studies* must have something to do with your admiration for his work.

LOWELL: He did these things before I did, though he's younger than I am and had been my student. He may have influenced me, though people have suggested the opposite. He spent ten years at the University of Iowa, going to writing classes, being an instructor; rather unworldly, making little money, and specializing in talking to other people writing poetry, obsessed you might say with minute technical problems and rather provincial experience—and then he wrote about just that. I mean, the poems are about his child, his divorce, and Iowa City, and his child is a Dr. Spock child—all handled in expert little stanzas. I believe that's a new kind of poetry. Other poems that are direct that way are slack and have no vibrance. His experience wouldn't be so interesting and valid if it weren't for the whimsy, the music, the balance, everything revised and placed and pondered. All that gives light to those poems on agonizing subjects comes from the craft.

INTERVIEWER: And yet his best poems are all on the verge of being slight and even sentimental.

LOWELL: I think a lot of the best poetry is. Laforgue—it's hard to think of a more delightful poet, and his prose is wonderful too. Well, it's on the verge of being sentimental, and if he hadn't dared to be sentimental he wouldn't have been a poet. I mean, his inspiration was that. There's some way of distinguishing between false sentimentality, which is blowing up a subject and giving emotions that you don't feel, and using whimsical, minute, tender, small emotions that most people don't feel but which Laforgue and Snodgrass do. So that I'd say he had pathos and fragility—but then that's a large subject too. He has fragility along the edges and a main artery of power going through the center.

INTERVIEWER: Some people were disappointed with *Life Studies* just because earlier you had written a kind of heroic poetry, an American version of heroic poetry, of which there had been none recently except your own. Is there any chance that you will go back to that?

LOWELL: I don't think that a personal history can go on forever, unless you're Walt Whitman and have a way with you. I feel I've done enough personal poetry. That doesn't mean I won't do more of it, but I don't want to do more now. I feel I haven't gotten down all my experience, or perhaps even the most important part, but I've said all I really have much inspiration to say, and more would just dilute. So that you need something more impersonal, and other things being equal it's better to get your emotions out in a Macbeth than in a confession. Macbeth must have tons of Shakespeare in him. We don't know where, nothing in Shakespeare's life was remotely like Macbeth, yet he somehow gives the feeling of going to the core of Shakespeare. You have much more freedom that way than you do when you write an autobiographical poem.

INTERVIEWER: These poems, I gather from what you said earlier, did take as much working over as the earlier ones.

LOWELL: They were just as hard to write. They're not always factually true. There's a good deal of tinkering with fact. You leave out a lot, and emphasize this and not that. Your actual experience is a complete flux. I've invented facts and changed things, and the whole balance of the poem was something invented. So there's a lot of artistry, I hope, in the poems. Yet there's this thing: if a poem is autobiographical—and this is true of any kind of autobiographical writing and of historical writing—you want the reader to say, this is true. In something like Macaulay's *History of England* you think you're really getting William III. That's as good as a good plot in a novel. And so there was always that standard of truth which you wouldn't ordinarily have in poetry—the reader was to believe he was getting the *real* Robert Lowell.

INTERVIEWER: I wanted to ask you about this business of taking over passages from earlier poems and rewriting them and putting them in new contexts. I'm thinking of the passage at the end of the "Cistercians in Germany," in *Land of Unlikeness,* which you rewrote into those wonderful lines that end "At the Indian Killer's Grave." I know that Hart Crane rewrote early scraps a great deal and used most of the rewrites. But doesn't doing this imply a theory of poetry that would talk much more about craft than about experience?

LOWELL: I don't know, it's such a miracle if you get lines that are half-way right; it's not just a technical problem. The lines must mean a good deal to you. All your poems are in a sense one poem, and there's always the struggle of getting something that balances and comes out right, in which all parts are good, and that has experience that you value. And so if you have a few lines that shine in a poem or are beginning to shine, and they fail and get covered over and drowned, maybe their real form is in another poem. Maybe you've mistaken the real inspiration in the original poem and they belong in something else entirely. I don't think that violates experience. The "Cistercians" wasn't very close to me, but the last lines seemed felt; I dropped the Cistercians and put a Boston graveyard in.

INTERVIEWER: But in Crane's "Ode to an Urn," a poem about a personal friend, there are lines which originally applied to something very different, and therefore, in one version or the other, at least can't be called personal.

LOWELL: I think we always bring over some unexplained obscurities by shifting lines. Something that was clear in the original just seems odd and unexplained in the final poem. That can be quite bad, of course; but you always want—and I think Chekhov talks about this— the detail that you can't explain. It's just there. It seems right to you, but you don't have to have it; you could have something else entirely. Now if everything's like that you'd just have chaos, but a few unexplained difficult things—they seem to be the life-blood of variety— they may work. What may have seemed a little odd, a little difficult in the original poem, gets a little more difficult in a new way in the new poem. And that's purely accidental, yet you may gain more than you lose—a new suggestiveness and magic.

INTERVIEWER: Do you revise a very great deal?

LOWELL: Endlessly.

INTERVIEWER: You often use an idiom or a very common phrase either for the sake of irony or to bear more meaning than it's customarily asked to bear—do these come late in the game, do you have to look around for them?

LOWELL: They come later because they don't prove much in themselves, and they often replace something that's much more formal and worked-up. Some of my later poetry does have this quality that the earlier doesn't: several lines can be almost what you'd say in conversation. And maybe talking with a friend or with my wife I'd say, "This doesn't sound quite right," and sort of reach in the air as I talked and change a few words. In that way the new style is easier to write; I sometimes fumble out a natural sequence of lines that will work. But a whole poem won't come that way; my seemingly relaxed poems are just about as hard as the very worked-up ones.

INTERVIEWER: That rightness and familiarity, though, is in "Between the Porch and the Altar" in several passages which are in couplets.

LOWELL: When I am writing in meter I find the simple lines never come right away. Nothing does. I don't believe I've ever written a poem in meter where I've kept a single one of the original lines. Usually when I was writing my old poems I'd write them out in blank verse and then put in the rhymes. And of course I'd change the rhymes a lot. The most I could hope for at first was that the rhymed version wouldn't be much inferior to the blank verse. Then the real work would begin, to make it something much better than the original out of the difficulties of the metre.

INTERVIEWER: Have you ever gone as far as Yeats and written out a prose argument and then set down the rhymes?

LOWELL: With some of the later poems I've written out prose versions, then cut the prose down and abbreviated it. A rapidly written prose draft of the poem doesn't seem to do much good, too little pain has gone into it; but one really worked on is bound to have phrases that are invaluable. And it's a nice technical problem: how can you keep phrases and get them into meter?

INTERVIEWER: Do you usually send off your work to friends before publishing it?

LOWELL: I do it less now. I always used to do it, to Jarrell and one or two other people. Last year I did a lot of reading with Stanley Kunitz.

INTERVIEWER: At the time you were writing the poems for *Lord Weary's Castle*, did it make a difference to you whether the poet to whom you were sending your work was Catholic?

LOWELL: I don't think I ever sent any poems to a Catholic. The person I was closest to then was Allen Tate, who wasn't a Catholic at the time; and then later it became Jarrell, who wasn't at all Catholic. My two close Catholic writer friends are prose writers, J. F. Powers and Flannery O'Connor, and they weren't interested in the technical problems of poems.

INTERVIEWER: So you feel that the religion is the business of the poem that it's in and not at all the business of the Church or the religious person.

LOWELL: It shouldn't be. I mean, a religion ought to have objective validity. But by the time it gets into a poem it's so mixed up with technical and imaginative problems that the theologian, the priest, the serious religious person isn't of too much use. The poem is too strange for him to feel at home and make any suggestions.

INTERVIEWER: What does this make of the religious poems as a religious exercise?

LOWELL: Well, it at least makes this: that the poem tries to be a poem and not a piece of artless religious testimony. There is a drawback. It seems to me that with any poem, but maybe particularly a religious one where there are common interests, the opinion of intelligent people who are not poets ought to be useful. There's an independence to this not getting advice from religious people and outsiders, but also there's a narrowness. Then there is a question whether my poems are religious, or whether they just use religious imagery. I haven't really any idea. My last poems don't use religious imagery, they don't use symbolism. In many ways they seem to me more religious than the early ones, which are full of symbols and references to Christ and God. I'm sure the symbols and the Catholic framework didn't make the poems religious experiences. Yet I don't feel my experience changed very much. It seems to me it's clearer to me now than it was then, but it's very much the same sort of thing that went into the religious poems —the same sort of struggle, light and darkness, the flux of experience. The morality seems much the same. But the symbolism is gone; you couldn't possibly say what creed I believed in. I've wondered myself often. Yet what made the earlier poems valuable seems to be some recording of experience, and that seems to be what makes the later ones.

INTERVIEWER: So you end up saying that the poem does have some integrity and can have some beauty apart from the beliefs expressed in the poem.

LOWELL: I think it can only have integrity apart from the beliefs; that no political position, religious position, position of generosity, or what have you, can make a poem good. It's all to the good if a poem *can* use politics, or theology, or gardening, or anything that has its own validity aside from poetry. But these things will never *per se* make a poem.

INTERVIEWER: The difficult question is whether when the beliefs expressed in a poem are obnoxious the poem as a whole can be considered to be beautiful—the probelm of the *Pisan Cantos*.

LOWELL: The *Pisan Cantos* are very uneven, aren't they? If you took what most people would agree are maybe the best hundred passages, would the beliefs in those passages be obnoxious? I think you'd get a very mixed answer. You could make quite a good case for Pound's good humor about his imprisonment, his absence of self-pity, his observant eye, his memories of literary friends, for all kinds of generous qualities and open qualities and lyrical qualities that anyone would think were good. And even when he does something like the death of Mussolini, in the passage that opens the *Pisan Cantos,* people debate about it. I've talked to Italians who were partisans, and who said that this is the only poem on Mussolini that's any good. Pound's quite wily often: Mussolini hung up like an ox—his brutal appearance. I don't know whether you could say the beliefs there are wrong or not. And there are other poems that come to mind: in Eliot, the Jew spelled with a small j in "Gerontion," is that anti-Semitism or not? Eliot's not anti-Semitic in any sense, but there's certainly a dislike of Jews in those early poems. Does he gain in the fierceness of writing his Jew with a small j? He says you write what you have to write and in criticism you can say what you think you should believe in. Very ugly emotions perhaps make a poem.

INTERVIEWER: You were on the Bollingen Committee at the time the award was made to Pound. What did you think of the great ruckus?

LOWELL: I thought it was a very simple problem of voting for the best book of the year; and it seemed to me Pound's was. I thought the *Pisan Cantos* was the best writing Pound had ever done, though it included some of his worst. It is a very mixed book: that was the question. But the consequences of not giving the best book of the year a prize for extraneous reasons, even terrible ones in a sense—I think that's the death of art. Then you have Pasternak suppressed and everything becomes stifling. Particularly in a strong country like ours you've got to award things objectively and not let the beliefs you'd like a man to have govern your choice. It was very close after the war, and anyone must feel that the poetry award was a trifling thing compared with the concentration camps. I actually think they were very distant from Pound. He had no political effect whatsoever and was quite eccentric and impractical. Pound's social credit, his Fascism, all these various things, were a tremendous gain to him; he'd be a very Parnassan poet without them. Even if they're bad beliefs—and some were bad, some weren't, and some were just terrible, of course—they made him more human and more to do with life, more to do with the times. They served him. Taking what interested him in these things gave a kind of realism and life to his poetry that it wouldn't have had otherwise.

INTERVIEWER: Did you become a translator to suit your own needs or because you wanted to get certain poems, most of them not before translated, into English? Or was it a matter of both, as I suppose it usually is, and as it was for Pound?

LOWELL: I think both. It always seemed to me that nothing very close to the poems I've translated existed in English; and on the other hand, there was some kind of closeness, I felt a kinship. I felt some sort of closeness to the Rilke and Rimbaud poems I've translated, yet they were doing things I couldn't do. They were both a continuation of my own bias and a release from myself.

INTERVIEWER: How did you come to translate Propertius—in fact, how did you come to have such a great interest in Roman history and Latin literature?

LOWELL: At Harvard my second year I took almost entirely English courses—the easiest sort of path. I think that would have been a disaster. But before going to Kenyon I talked to Ford Madox Ford and Ransom, and Ransom said you've just got to take philosophy and logic, which I did. The other thing he suggested was classics. Ford was rather flippant about it, said of course you've got to learn classics, you'll just cut yourself off from humanity if you don't. I think it's always given me some sort of yardstick for English. And then the literature was amazing, particularly the Greek; there's nothing like Greek in English at all. Our plays aren't formally at all like Aeschylus and Sophocles. Their whole inspiration was unbelievably different, and so different that you could hardly think of even the attempt to imitate them, great as their prestige was. That something like *Antigone* or *Oedipus* or the great Achilles moments in the *Iliad* would be at the core of a literature is incredible for anyone brought up in an English culture—Greek wildness and sophistication all different, the women different, everything. Latin's of course much closer. English is a half-Latin language, and we've done our best to absorb the Latin literature. But a Roman poet is much less intellectual than the Englishman, much less abstract. He's nearer nature somehow—somewhat what we feel about a Frenchman but more so still. And yet he's very sophisticated. He has his way of doing things, though the number of forms he explored is quite limited. The amount he could take from the Greeks and yet change is an extraordinary piece of firm discipline. Also, you take almost any really good Roman poet—Juvenal, or Vergil, or Propertius, Catullus—he's much more raw and direct than anything in English, and yet he has this block-like formality. The Roman frankness interests me. Until recently our literature hasn't been as raw as the Roman, translations had to have stars. And their history has a terrible human frankness that isn't customary with us—corrosive attacks on the establishment, comments on politics and the decay of morals, all felt terribly strongly, by poets as well as historians. The English writer who reads the classics is working at one thing, and his eye is on something else that can't be done. We will always have the Latin and Greek classics, and they'll never be absorbed. There's something very restful about that.

INTERVIEWER: But, more specifically, how did Latin poetry—your study of it, your translations—affect your measure of English poetry?

LOWELL: My favorite English poetry was the difficult Elizabethan plays and the Metaphysicals, then the nineteenth century, which I was aquiver about and disliked but which was closer to my writing than anything else. The Latin seemed very different from either of these. I immediately saw how Shelley wasn't like Horace and Vergil or Aeschylus—and the Latin was a mature poetry, a realistic poetry, which didn't have the contortions of the Metaphysicals. What a frail, bony, electric person Marvell is compared with Horace!

INTERVIEWER: What about your adaptation of Propertius?

LOWELL: I got him through Pound. When I read him in Latin I found a kind of Propertius you don't get in Pound at all. Pound's Propertius is a rather Ovidian figure with a great deal of Pound's fluency and humor and irony. The actual Propertius is a very excited, tense poet, rather desperate; his line is much more like parts of Marlowe's *Faustus*. And he's of all the Roman poets the most like a desperate Christian. His experiences, his love affair with Cynthia, are absolutely rending, destroying. He's like a fallen Christian.

INTERVIEWER: Have you done any other translations of Latin poems?

LOWELL: I did a monologue that started as a translation of Vergil and then was completely rewritten, and there are buried translations in several other poems. There's a poem called "To Speak of Woe That Is in Marriage" in my last book that started as a translation of Catullus. I don't know what traces are left, but it couldn't have been written without the Catullus.

INTERVIEWER: You've translated Pasternak. Do you know Russian?

LOWELL: No, I have rewritten other English translations, and seldom even checked with Russian experts. I want to get a book of translations together. I read in the originals, except for Russian, but I have felt quite free to alter things, and I don't know that Pasternak would look less close than the Italian, which I have studied closely. Before I publish, I want to check with a Russian expert.

INTERVIEWER: Can I get you back to Harvard for a minute? Is it true you tried out for the Harvard *Advocate,* did all the dirty work for your candidacy, and then were turned down?

LOWELL: I nailed a carpet down. I forget who the editor was then, but he was a man who wrote on Frost. At that time people who wrote on Frost were quite different from the ones who write on him now; they tended to be conservative, out of touch. I wasn't a very good writer then, perhaps I should have been turned down. I was trying to write like William Carlos Williams, very simple, free verse, imagistic poems. I had a little group I was very proud of which was set up in galleys; when I left Harvard it was turned down.

INTERVIEWER: Did you know any poets at the time?

LOWELL: I had a friend, Harry Brown, who writes dialogue for movies and has been in Hollywood for years. He was a terribly promising poet. He came to Harvard with a long correspondence with Harriet Monroe and was much more advanced than anyone else. He could write in the style of Auden or Webster or Eliot or Crane. He'd never graduated from high school, and wasn't a student, but he was the person I felt closest to. My other friends weren't writers.

INTERVIEWER: Had you met any older poets—Frost, for instance, who must have been around?

LOWELL: I'd gone to call on Frost with a huge epic on the First Crusade, all written out in clumsy longhand on lined paper. He read a page of that and said, "You have no compression." Then he read me a very short poem of Collins, "How Sleep the Brave," and said, "That's not a great poem, but it's not too long." He was very kindly about it. You know his point about the voice coming into poetry: he took a very unusual example of that, the opening of "Hyperion"; the line about the Naiad, something about her pressing a cold finger to her cold lips, which wouldn't seem like a voice passage at all. And he said, "Now Keats comes alive here." That was a revelation to me; what had impressed me was the big Miltonic imitation in "Hyperion."

I don't know what I did with that, but I recoiled and realized that I was diffuse and monotonous.

INTERVIEWER: What decided you to leave Harvard and go to Kenyon?

LOWELL: I'd made the acquaintance of Merrill Moore, who'd been at Vanderbilt and a Fugitive. He said that I ought to study with a man who was a poet. He was very close to Ransom, and the plan was that I'd go to Vanderbilt; and 1 would have, but Ransom changed to Kenyon.

INTERVIEWER: I understand you left much against the wishes of your family.

LOWELL: Well, I was getting quite morose and solitary, and they sort of settled for this move. They'd rather have had me a genial social Harvard student, but at least I'd be working hard this way. It seemed to them a queer but orderly step.

INTERVIEWER: Did it help you that you had had intellectual and literary figures in your family?

LOWELL: I really didn't know I'd had them till I went to the South. To my family, James Russell Lowell was the ambassador to England, not a writer. Amy seemed a bit peculiar to them. When I began writing I think it would have been unimaginable to take either Amy or James Russell Lowell as models.

INTERVIEWER: Was it through Ransom that you met Tate?

LOWELL: I met them at more or less the same time, but actually stayed with Tate before I knew Ransom very well.

INTERVIEWER: And Ford Madox Ford was there at some time, wasn't he?

LOWELL: I met Ford at a cocktail party in Boston and went to dinner with him at the Athens Olympia. He was going to visit the Tates, and said, "Come and see me down there, we're all going to Tennessee." So I drove down. He hadn't arrived, so I got to know the Tates quite well before his appearance.

INTERVIEWER: Staying in a pup-tent.

LOWELL: It's a terrible piece of youthful callousness. They had one Negro woman who came in and helped, but Mrs. Tate was doing all the housekeeping. She had three guests and her own family, and was doing the cooking and writing a novel. And this young man arrived, quite ardent and eccentric. I think I suggested that maybe I'd stay with them. And they said, "We really haven't any room, you'd have to pitch a tent on the lawn." So I went to Sears, Roebuck and got a tent and rigged it on their lawn. The Tates were too polite to tell me that what they'd said had been just a figure of speech. I stayed two months in my tent and ate with the Tates.

INTERVIEWER: And you were showing him your work all the while.

LOWELL: Oh, I became converted to formalism and changed my style from brilliant free verse, all in two months. And everything was in rhyme, and it still wasn't any good. But that was a great incentive. I poured out poems and went to writers' conferences.

INTERVIEWER: What about Ford?

LOWELL: I saw him out there and took dictation from him for a while. That was hell, because I didn't know how to type. I'd take the dictation down in longhand, and he rather mumbled. I'd ask him what he'd said, and he'd say, "Oh, you have no sense of prose rhythm," and mumble some more. I'd get most of his words, then I'd have to improvise on the typewriter.

INTERVIEWER: So for part of Ford's opus we're indebted to you.

LOWELL: A handful of phrases in *The March of Literature,* on the Provençal poets.

INTERVIEWER: That was the summer before you entered Kenyon; but most of the poems in *Land of Unlikeness* were written after you'd graduated, weren't they?

LOWELL: Yes, they were almost all written in a year I spent with the Tates, though some of them were earlier poems rewritten. I think becoming a Catholic convert had a good deal to do with writing again. I was much more interested in being a Catholic than in being a writer. I read Catholic writers but had no intention of writing myself. But somehow, when I started again, I won't say the Catholicism gave me subject matter, but it gave me some kind of form, and I could begin a poem and build it to a climax. It was quite different from what I'd been doing earlier.

INTERVIEWER: Why, then, did you choose to print your work in the small liberal magazines whose religious and political positions were very different from yours? Have you ever submitted to the *New Yorker* or the *Atlantic Monthly*?

LOWELL: I think I may have given something to the *Atlantic* on Santayana; the *New Yorker* I haven't given anything. I think the *New Yorker* does some of the best prose in the country, in many ways much more interesting than the quarterlies and little magazines. But poems are lost in it; there's no table of contents, and some of their poetry is light verse. There's no particular continuity of excellence. There just seems no point in printing there. For a while the little magazines, whose religious-political positions *were* very different from mine, were the only magazines that would publish me, and I feel like staying with them. I like magazines like the *New Statesman,* the *Nation,* the *New Republic*—something a little bit off the track.

INTERVIEWER: Just because they are off the track?

LOWELL: I think so. A political position I don't necessarily agree with which is a little bit adverse seems to me just more attractive than a time-serving, conventional position. And they tend to have good reviews, those magazines. I think you write for a small audience, an ardent critical audience. And you know Graves says that poets ought to take in each other's washing because they're the only responsible audience. There's a danger to that—you get too specialized—but I pretty much agree that's the audience you do write for. If it gets further, that's all fine.

INTERVIEWER: There is, though, a certain inbred, in-group anaemia to those magazines, at least to the literary quarterlies. For instance, it would have been almost inconceivable for *Partisan Review*, which is the best of them, I think, to give your last book a bad review or even a sharp review.

LOWELL: I think no magazine likes to slam one of its old contributors. *Partisan* has sometimes just not reviewed a book by someone they liked very much and their reviewer didn't. I know Shapiro has been attacked in *Partisan* and then published there, and other people have been unfavorably reviewed and made rather a point of sending them something afterwards. You want to feel there's a certain degree of poorer writing that wouldn't get published in the magazine your work appears in. The good small magazine may publish a lot of rather dry stuff, but at least it's serious, and if it's bad it's not bad by trying to be popular and put something over on the public. It's a wrenched personal ineptitude that will get published rather than a public slickness. I think that has something to do with good reviews coming out in the magazine. We were talking about *Partisan*'s not slamming one of its contributors, but *Partisan* has a pretty harsh, hard standard of reviewing, and they certainly wouldn't praise one of their contributors who'd gone to pot.

INTERVIEWER: What poets among your contemporaries do you most admire?

LOWELL: The two I've been closest to are Elizabeth Bishop—I spoke about her earlier—and Jarrell, and they're different. Jarrell's a great man of letters, a very informed man, and the best critic of my generation, the best professional poet. He's written the best war poems, and those poems are a tremendous product of our culture, I feel. Elizabeth Bishop's poems, as I said, are more personal, more something she did herself, and she's not a critic but has her own tastes, which may be very idiosyncratic. I enjoy her poems more than anybody else's. I like some of Shapiro very much, some of Roethke and Stanley Kunitz.

INTERVIEWER: What about Roethke, who tries to do just about everything you don't try to do?

LOWELL: We've read to each other and argued, and may be rather alike in temperament actually, but he wants a very musical poem and always would quarrel with my ear as I'd quarrel with his eye. He has love poems and childhood poems and startling surrealistic poems, rather simple experience done with a blaze of power. He rejoices in the rhetoric and the metrics, but there's something very disorderly working there. Sometimes it will smash a poem and sometimes it will make it. The things he knows about I feel I know nothing about, flowers and so on. What we share, I think, is the exultant moment, the blazing out. Whenever I've tried to do anything like his poems, I've felt helpless and realized his mastery.

INTERVIEWER: You were apparently a very close friend of Delmore Schwartz's.

LOWELL: Yes, and I think that I've never met anyone who has somehow as much seeped into me. It's a complicated personal thing to talk about. His reading was very varied, Marx and Freud and Russell, very catholic and not from a conservative position at all. He sort of grew up knowing those things and has a wonderful penetrating humorous way of talking about them. If he met T. S. Eliot his impressions of Eliot would be mixed up with his impressions of Freud and what he'd read about Eliot; all these things flowed back and forth in him. Most of my writer friends were more specialized and limited than Schwartz, most of them took against-the-grain positions which were also narrow. Schwartz was a revelation. He felt the poet who had experience was very much better than the poet with polish. Wordsworth would interest him much more than Keats—he wanted openness to direct experience. He said that if you got people talking in a poem you could do anything. And his own writing, *Coriolanus* and *Shenandoah,* is interesting for that.

INTERVIEWER: Isn't this much what you were saying about your own hopes for *Life Studies*?

LOWELL: Yes, but technically I think that Delmore and I are quite different. There have been very few poets I've been able to get very much from technically. Tate has been one of the closest to me. My early poems I think grew out of my admiration for his poems.

INTERVIEWER: What about poets in the past?

LOWELL: It's hard for me to imitate someone; I'm very self-conscious about it. That's an advantage perhaps—you don't become too imitative —but it's also a limitation. I tremble when I feel I'm being like someone else. If it's Rilke or Rimbaud or Propertius, you know the language is a big bar and that if you imitate you're doing something else. I've felt greater freedom that way. I think I've tried to write like some of the Elizabethans.

INTERVIEWER: And Crane? You said you had read a good deal of Crane.

LOWELL: Yes, but his difficult style is one I've never been able to do much with. He can be very obscure and yet write a much more inspired poem than I could by being obscure. There's a relationship between Crane and Tate, and for some reason Tate was much easier for me. I could see how Tate was done, though Tate has a rhythm that I've never been able to imitate. He's much more irregular than I am, and I don't know where the rhythm comes from, but I admire it very much. Crane said somewhere that he could write five or six good lines but Tate could write twelve that would hang together, and you'd see how the twelve were built. Tate was somehow more of a model: he had a lot of wildness and he had a lot of construction. And of course I knew him and never knew Crane. I think Crane is the great poet of that generation. He got out more than anybody else. Not only is it the tremendous power there, but he somehow got New York City; he was at the center of things in the way that no other poet was. All the chaos of his life missed getting sidetracked the way other poets' did, and he was less limited than any other poet of his generation. There was a fullness of experience; and without that, if you just had his mannerisms, and not his rather simple writing—which if done badly would be sentimental merely—or just his obscure writing, the whole thing would be merely verbal. It isn't with Crane. The push of the whole man is there. But his style never worked for me.

INTERVIEWER: But something of Crane does seem to have got into your work—or maybe it's just that sense of power thrashing about. I thought it had come from a close admiring reading of Crane.

LOWELL: Yes, some kind of wildness and power that appeals to me, I guess. But when I wrote difficult poems they weren't meant to be difficult, though I don't know that Crane meant his to be. I wanted to be loaded and rich, but I thought the poems were all perfectly logical. You can have a wonderful time explaining a great poem like "Voyages II," and it all can be explained, but in the end it's just a love poem with a great confusion of images that are emotionally clear; a prose paraphrase wouldn't give you any impression whatever of the poem. I couldn't do that kind of poem, I don't think; at least I've never been able to.

INTERVIEWER: You said that most of the writers you've known have been against the grain. What did you mean?

LOWELL: When I began writing most of the great writers were quite unpopular. They hadn't reached the universities yet, and their circulation was small. Even Eliot wasn't very popular then. But life seemed to be there. It seemed to be one of those periods when the lid was still being blown. The great period of blowing the lid was the time of Schönberg and Picasso and Joyce and the early Eliot, where a power came into the arts which we perhaps haven't had since. These people were all rather traditional, yet they were stifled by what was being done, and they almost wrecked things to do their great works —even rather minor but very good writers such as Williams or Mari-

anne Moore. Their kind of protest and queerness has hardly been
repeated. They're wonderful writers. You wouldn't see anyone as
strange as Marianne Moore again, not for a long while. Conservative
and Jamesian as she is, it was a terrible, private, and strange revolutionary poetry. There isn't the motive to do that now. Yet those
were the classics, and it seems to me they were all against the grain,
Marianne Moore as much as Crane. That's where life was for the
small audience. It would be a tremendous subject to say whether the
feelings were against the grain too, and whether they were purifying,
nihilistic, or both.

INTERVIEWER: Have you had much contact with Eliot?

LOWELL: I may have seen him a score of times in my life, and he's
always been very kind. Long before he published me he had some of
my poems in his files. There's some kind of New England connection.

INTERVIEWER: Has he helpfully criticized your work?

LOWELL: Just very general criticism. With the first book of mine
Faber did he had a lot of little questions about punctuation, but he
never said he liked this or disliked that. Then he said something
about the last book—"These are first-rate, I mean it"—something
like that that was very understated and gratifying. I feel Eliot's less
tied to form than a lot of people he's influenced, and there's a freedom
of the 'twenties in his work that I find very sympathetic. Certainly he
and Frost are the great New England poets. You hardly think of
Stevens as New England, but you have to think of Eliot and Frost as
deeply New England and puritanical. They're a continuation and a
criticism of the tradition, and they're probably equally great poets.
Frost somehow put life into a dead tradition. His kind of poetry must
have seemed almost unpublishable, it was so strange and fresh when
it was first written. But still it was old-fashioned poetry and really
had nothing to do with modern writing—except that he is one of the
greatest modern writers. Eliot was violently modern and unacceptable
to the traditionalist. Now he's spoken of as a literary dictator, but he's
handled his position with wonderful sharpness and grace, it seems to
me. It's a narrow position and it's not one I hold particularly, but I
think it's been held with extraordinary honesty and finish and development. Eliot has done what he said Shakespeare had done: all his poems
are one poem, a form of continuity that has grown and snowballed.

INTERVIEWER: I remember Jarrell in reviewing *Mills of the Kavanaughs* said that Frost had been doing narrative poems with ease for
years, and that nobody else had been able to catch up.

LOWELL: And what Jarrell said is true: nobody except Frost can do
a sort of Chaucerian narrative poem that's organized and clear. Well,
a lot of people do them, but the texture of their verse is so limp and
uninspired. Frost does them with great power. Most of them were

done early, in that *North of Boston* period. That was a miracle, because except for Robinson—and I think Frost is a very much greater
poet than Robinson—no one was doing that in England or America.

INTERVIEWER: But you hadn't simply wanted to tell a story in *Mills
of the Kavanaughs.*

LOWELL: No, I was writing an obscure, rather Elizabethan, dramatic
and melodramatic poem. I don't know quite how to describe this
business of direct experience. With Browning, for instance, for all his
gifts—and there is almost nothing Browning couldn't use—you feel
there's a glaze between what he writes and what really happened, you
feel the people are made up. In Frost you feel that's just what the
farmers and so on were like. It has the virtue of a photograph but
all the finish of art. That's an extraordinary thing; almost no other
poet can do that now.

INTERVIEWER: What do you suppose are the qualities that go into
that ability?

LOWELL: I don't know. Prose writers have it much more, and quite
a few prose writers have it. It's some kind of sympathy and observation
of people. It's the deep, rather tragic poems that I value most. Perhaps
it's been overdone with Frost, but there's an abundance and geniality
about those poems that isn't tragic. With this sense of rhythm and
words and composition, and getting into his lines language that is
very much like the language he speaks—which is also a work of art,
much better than other people's ordinary speech and yet natural to
him; he has that continuity with his ordinary self and his poetic self
—he's made what with anyone else would be just flat. A very good
prose writer can do this and make something of it. You get it quite
often in Faulkner. Though he's an Elizabethan sort of character,
rather unlike Frost, he can get this amazing immediacy and simplicity.
When it comes to verse the form is so hard that all of that gets drained
out. In a very conventional old-fashioned writer, or someone who's
trying to be realistic but also dramatic and inspired, though he may remain a good poet, most of that directness and realism goes. It's hard
for Eliot to be direct that way, though you get it in bits of *The Waste
Land,* that marvellous Cockney section. And he can be himself; I feel
Eliot's real all through the *Quartets.* He can be very intelligent or very
simple there, and *he's* there, but there are no other people in the
Quartets.

INTERVIEWER: Have many of your poems been taken from real people
and real events?

LOWELL: I think, except when I've used myself or occasionally
named actual people in poems, the characters are purely imaginary.
I've tried to buttress them by putting images I've actually seen and
in indirect ways getting things I've actually experienced into the poem.

If I'm writing about a Canadian nun the poem may have a hundred little bits of things I've looked at, but she's not remotely anyone I've ever known. And I don't believe anybody would think my nun was quite a real person. She has a heart and she's alive, I hope, and she has a lot of color to her and drama, and has some things that Frost's characters don't, but she doesn't have their wonderful quality of life. His Witch of Coös is absolutely there. I've gathered from talking to him that most of the *North of Boston* poems came from actual people he knew shuffled and put together. But then it's all-important that Frost's plots are so extraordinary, so carefully worked out though it almost seems that they're not there. Like some things in Chekhov, the art is very well hidden.

INTERVIEWER: Don't you think a large part of it is getting the right details, symbolic or not, around which to wind the poem tight and tighter?

LOWELL: Some bit of scenery or something you've felt. Almost the whole problem of writing poetry is to bring it back to what you really feel, and that takes an awful lot of manoeuvering. You may feel the door-knob more strongly than some big personal event, and the door-knob will open into something that you can use as your own. A lot of poetry seems to me very good in the tradition but just doesn't move me very much because it doesn't have personal vibrance to it. I probably exaggerate the value of it, but it's precious to me. Some little image, some detail you've noticed—you're writing about a little country shop, just describing it, and your poem ends up with an existentialist account of your experience. But it's the shop that started it off. You didn't know why it meant a lot to you. Often images and often the sense of the beginning and end of a poem are all you have—some journey to be gone through between those things; you know that, but you don't know the details. And that's marvellous; then you feel the poem will come out. It's a terrible struggle, because what you really feel hasn't got the form, it's not what you can put down in a poem. And the poem you're equipped to write concerns nothing that you care very much about or have much to say on. Then the great moment comes when there's enough resolution of your technical equipment, your way of constructing things, and what you can make a poem out of, to hit something you really want to say. You may not know you have it to say.

Introduction to *Land of Unlikeness*

by Allen Tate

There is no other poetry today quite like this. T. S. Eliot's recent prediction that we should soon see a return to formal and even intricate meters and stanzas was coming true, before he made it, in the verse of Robert Lowell. Every poem in this book has a formal pattern, either the poet's own or one borrowed, as the stanza of "Satan's Confession" is borrowed from Drayton's "The Virginian Voyage," and adapted to a personal rhythm of the poet's own.

But this is not, I think, a mere love of external form. Lowell is consciously a Catholic poet, and it is possible to see a close connection between his style and the formal pattern. The style is bold and powerful, and the symbolic language often has the effect of being *willed;* for it is an intellectual style compounded of brilliant puns and shifts of tone; and the willed effect is strengthened by the formal stanzas, to which the language is forced to conform.

A close reader of these poems will be able to see two general types, or extremes which it is the problem of the poet to unite, but which I believe are not yet united: this is not a fault, it merely defines the kind of poet that Lowell, at this early stage, seems to be. On the one hand, the Christian symbolism is intellectualized and frequently given a savage satirical direction; it points to the disappearance of the Christian experience from the modern world, and stands, perhaps, for the poet's own effort to recover it. On the other hand, certain shorter poems, like "A Suicidal Nightmare" and "Death from Cancer," are richer in immediate experience than the explicitly religious poems; they are more dramatic, the references being personal and historical and the symbolism less willed and explicit.

The history of poetry shows that good verse does not inevitably make its way; but unless, after the war, the small public for poetry shall exclude all except the democratic poets who enthusiastically greet the advent of the slave-society, Robert Lowell will have to be reckoned with. Christopher Dawson has shown in long historical perspective that material progress may mask social and spiritual decay. But the spiritual decay is not universal, and in a young man like Lowell, whether we like his Catholicism or not, there is at least a memory of the spiritual dignity of man, now sacrificed to mere secularization and a craving for mechanical order.

Review of *Land of Unlikeness*

by R. P. Blackmur

Robert Lowell's *Land of Unlikeness* makes a fairer foil for Miss Rukeyser than either Dryden or Fletcher, because it shows, not examples of high formal organization achieved, but poems that are deliberately moving in that direction and that have things put in to give the appearance of the movement of form when the movement itself was not secured. In fact, Lowell's verse is a beautiful case of citation in any argument in support of the belief in the formal inextricability of the various elements of poetry: meter is not meter by itself, any more than attitude or anecdote or perception, though any one of them can be practiced by itself at the expense of the others, when the tensions become mere fanaticism of spirit and of form: conditions, one would suppose, mutually mutilating. Something of that sort seems to be happening in Lowell's verse. It is as if he demanded to *know* (to judge, to master) both the substance apart from the form with which he handles it and the form apart from the substance handled in order to set them fighting. Much as Miss Rukeyser is confused about sex, Lowell is distraught about religion; he does not seem to have decided whether his Roman Catholic belief is the form of a force or the sentiment of a form. The result seems to be that in dealing with men his faith compels him to be fractiously vindictive, and in dealing with faith his experience of men compels him to be nearly blasphemous. By contrast, Dante loved his living Florence and the Florence to come and loved much that he was compelled to envisage in hell, and he wrote throughout in loving meters. In Lowell's *Land of Unlikeness* there is nothing loved unless it be its repellence; and there is not a loving meter in the book. What is thought of as Boston in him fights with what is thought of as Catholic; and the fight produces not a tension but a gritting. It is not the violence, the rage, the denial of this world that grits, but the failure of these to find *in verse* a tension of necessity; necessity has, when recognized, the quality of conflict

"Review of *Land of Unlikeness*" by R. P. Blackmur. From "Notes on Seven Poets" in *Language as Gesture* (New York: Harcourt, Brace & World, Inc., 1952; London: George Allen & Unwin, Ltd., 1952), pp. 334–36. Copyright 1945 by R. P. Blackmur. Reprinted by permission of the publishers.

accepted, not hated. To put a thing, or a quality, or an intimation, *in verse* is for the poet the same job as for the man not a poet the job of putting or holding a thing *in mind*. Mind and verse are mediums of response. If Lowell, like St. Bernard whom he quotes on his title page, conceives the world only as a place of banishment, and poetry (or theology) only as a means of calling up memories of life before banishment, he has the special problem of maturing a medium, both of mind and verse, in which vision and logic combine; and it is no wonder he has gone no further. *Inde anima dissimilis deo inde dissimilis est et sibi*[1] His title and his motto suggest that the problem is actual to him; the poems themselves suggest, at least to an alien mind, that he has so far been able to express only the violence of its difficulty. As it is now, logic lacerates the vision and vision turns logic to zealotry. I quote the last section of "The Drunken Fisherman" which seems to me the best-managed poem in the book.

> Is there no way to cast my hook
> Out of this dynamited brook?
> The Fisher's sons must cast about
> When shallow waters peter out.
> I will catch Christ with a greased worm,
> And when the Prince of Darkness stalks
> My bloodstream to its Stygian term . . .
> On water the Man-Fisher walks.[2]

[1] [A likeness which is no longer like its original is like itself no more—Ed.]
[2] From "The Drunken Fisherman" in *Lord Weary's Castle* (New York: Harcourt, Brace & World, Inc., 1946; London: Faber and Faber, Ltd., 1950).

From the Kingdom of Necessity

by Randall Jarrell

Many of the people who reviewed *Lord Weary's Castle* felt that it was as much of an event as Auden's first book; no one younger than Auden has written better poetry than the best of Robert Lowell's, it seems to me. Anyone who reads contemporary poetry will read it; perhaps people will understand the poetry more easily, and find it more congenial, if they see what the poems have developed out of, how they are related to each other, and why they say what they say.

Underneath all these poems "there is one story and one story only"; when this essential theme or subject is understood, the unity of attitudes and judgments underlying the variety of the poems becomes startlingly explicit. The poems understand the world as a sort of conflict of opposites. In this struggle one opposite is that cake of custom in which all of us lie embedded like lungfish—the stasis or inertia of the stubborn self, the obstinate persistence in evil that is damnation. Into this realm of necessity the poems push everything that is closed, turned inward, incestuous, that blinds or binds: the Old Law, imperialism, militarism, capitalism, Calvinism, Authority, the Father, the "proper Bostonians," the rich who will "do everything for the poor except get off their backs." But struggling within this like leaven, falling to it like light, is everything that is free or open, that grows or is willing to change: here is the generosity or openness or willingness that is itself salvation; here is "accessibility to experience"; this is the realm of freedom, of the Grace that has replaced the Law, of the perfect liberator whom the poet calls Christ.

Consequently the poems can have two possible movements or organizations: they can move from what is closed to what is open, or from what is open to what is closed. The second of these organizations— which corresponds to an "unhappy ending"—is less common, though there are many good examples of it: "The Exile's Return," with its menacing *Voi ch'entrate* that transforms the exile's old home into a place where even hope must be abandoned; the harsh and extraordinary "Between the Porch and the Altar," with its four parts each ending in constriction and frustration, and its hero who cannot get free of his mother, her punishments, and her world even by dying, but who sees both life and death in terms of her, and thinks at the end that, sword in hand, the Lord "watches me for Mother, and will turn/The bier and baby-carriage where I burn."

But normally the poems move into liberation. Even death is seen as liberation, a widening into darkness: that old closed system Grandfather Arthur Winslow, dying of cancer in his adjusted bed, at the last is the child Arthur whom the swanboats once rode through the Public Garden, whom now "the ghost of risen Jesus walks the waves to run/Upon a trumpeting black swan/Beyond Charles River and the Acheron/Where the wide waters and their voyager are one." (Compare the endings of "The Drunken Fisherman" and "Dea Roma.") "The Death of the Sheriff" moves from closure—the "ordered darkness" of the homicidal sheriff, the "loved sightless smother" of the incestuous lovers, the "unsearchable quicksilver heart/Where spiders stare their eyes out at their own/Spitting and knotted likeness"—up into the open sky, to those "light wanderers" the planets, to the "thirsty Dipper on the arc of night." Just so the cold, blundering, iron confusion of "Christmas Eve Under Hooker's Statue" ends in flowers, the wild fields, a Christ "once again turned wanderer and child." In "Rebellion" the son seals "an everlasting pact/With Dives to *contract*/The world that *spreads* in pain"; but at last he rebels against his father and his father's New England commercial theocracy, and "the world *spread*/When the clubbed flintlock broke my father's brain." The italicized words ought to demonstrate how explicitly, at times, these poems formulate the world in the terms that I have used.

"Where the Rainbow Ends" describes in apocalyptic terms the wintry, Calvinist, capitalist—Mr. Lowell has Weber's unconvincing belief in the necessary connection between capitalism and Calvinism —dead end of God's covenant with man, a frozen Boston where even the cold-blooded serpents "whistle at the cold." (The poems often use cold as a plain and physically correct symbol for what is constricted or static.) There "the scythers, Time and Death,/Helmed locusts, move upon the tree of breath," of the spirit of man; a bridge curves over Charles River like an ironic parody of the rainbow's covenant; both "the wild ingrafted olive and its root/Are withered" [these are Paul's terms for the Judaism of the Old Law and the Gentile Christianity grafted upon it]; "every dove [the Holy Ghost, the bringer of the olive leaf to the Ark] is sold" for a commercialized, legalized sacrifice. The whole system seems an abstract, rationalized "graph of Revelations," of the last accusation and judgment brought against man now that "the Chapel's sharp-shinned eagle shifts its hold/On serpent-Time, the rainbow's epitaph." This last line means what the last line in "The Quaker Graveyard"—"The Lord survives the rainbow of His will"—means; both are inexpressibly menacing, since they show the covenant as something that binds only us, as something abrogated merely by the passage of time, as a closed system opening not into liberation but into infinite and overwhelming possibility; they have something of the terror, but none of the pity, of Blake's "Time is the mercy of Eternity."

Then the worshipper, like a victim, climbs to the altar of the terrible *I* AM, to breathe there the rarefied and intolerable ether of his union with the divinity of the Apocalypse; he despairs even of the wings that beat against his cheek: "What can the dove of Jesus give/You now but wisdom, exile?" When the poem has reached this point of the most extreme closure, when the infinite grace that atones and liberates is seen as no more than the acid and useless wisdom of the exile, it opens with a rush of acceptant joy into: "Stand and live,/The dove has brought an olive branch to eat." The dove of Jesus brings to the worshipper the olive branch that shows him that the flood has receded, opening the whole earth for him; it is the olive branch of peace and reconciliation, the olive branch that he is "to eat" as a symbol of the eaten flesh of Christ, of atonement, identification, and liberation. Both the old covenant and the new still hold, nothing has changed: here as they were and will be—says the poem—are life and salvation.

Mr. Lowell's Christianity has very little to do with the familiar literary Christianity of *as if,* the belief in the necessity of belief; and it is a kind of photographic negative of the faith of the usual Catholic convert, who distrusts freedom as much as he needs bondage, and who sees the world as a liberal chaos which can be ordered and redeemed only by that rigid and final Authority to Whom men submit without question. Lowell reminds one of those heretical enthusiasts, often disciplined and occasionally sanctified or excommunicated, who are more at home in the Church Triumphant than in the church of this world, which is one more state. A phrase like Mr. Lowell's "St. Peter, the distorted key" is likely to be appreciated outside the church and overlooked inside it, *ad maiorem gloriam* of Catholic poetry. All Mr. Lowell's earliest poems would seem to suggest that he was, congenitally, the ideal follower of Barth or Calvin: one imagines him, a few years ago, supporting neither Franco nor the loyalists, but yearning to send a couple of clippers full of converted minute-men to wipe out the whole bunch—human, hence deserving. (I wish that he could cast a colder eye on minute-men; his treatment of the American Revolution is in the great tradition of Marx, Engels, and Parson Weems.) Freedom is something that he has wished to escape into, by a very strange route. In his poems the Son is pure liberation from the in-cestuous, complacent, inveterate evil of established society, of which the Law is a part—although the Father, Jehovah, has retained both the violence necessary to break up this inertia and a good deal of the menacing sternness of Authority as such, just as the poems themselves have. It is interesting to compare the figure of the Uncle in early Auden, who sanctifies rebellion by his authority; the authority of Mr. Lowell's Christ is sanctified by his rebellion or liberation.

Anyone who compares Mr. Lowell's earlier and later poems will see this movement from constriction to liberation at his work's ruling principle of growth. The grim, violent, sordid constriction of his earliest poems—most of them omitted from *Lord Weary's Castle*—seems to be temperamental, the Old Adam which the poet grew from and only partially transcends; and a good deal of what is excessive in the extraordinary rhetorical machine of a poem like "The Quaker Graveyard at Nantucket," which first traps and then wrings to pieces the helpless reader—who rather enjoys it—is gone from some of his later poems, or else dramatically justified and no longer excessive. "The Quaker Graveyard" is a baroque work, like *Paradise Lost,* but all the *extase* of baroque has disappeared—the coiling violence of its rhetoric, the harsh and stubborn intensity that accompanies all its verbs and verbals, the clustering stresses, learned from accentual verse, come from a man contracting every muscle, grinding his teeth together till his shut eyes ache. Some of Mr. Lowell's later work moved, for a while, in the direction of the poem's quiet contrast-section, "Walsing-ham"; the denunciatory prophetic tone disappeared, along with the savagely satiric effects that were one of the poet's weaknesses. Some of the later poems depend less on rhetorical description and more on dramatic speech; their wholes have escaped from the hypnotic bondage of the details. Often the elaborate stanzas have changed into a novel sort of dramatic or narrative couplet, run-on but with heavily stressed rhymes. A girl's nightmare, in the late "Katherine's Dream," is clear, open, and speech-like, compared to the poet's own descriptive medita-tion in an earlier work like "Christmas at Black Rock."

Mr. Lowell has a completely unscientific but thoroughly historical mind. It is literary and traditional as well; he can use the past so effectively because he thinks so much as it did. He seems to be con-demned both to read history and to repeat it. His present contains the past—especially Rome, the late Middle Ages, and a couple of centuries of New England—as an operative skeleton just under the skin. (This is rare among contemporary poets, who look at the past more as Blücher is supposed to have looked at London: "What a city to sack!") War, Trade, and Jehovah march side by side through all Mr. Lowell's ages: it is the fundamental likeness of the past and present, and not their disparity, which is insisted upon. "Cold/Snaps the bronze toes and fingers of the Christ/My father fetched from Florence, and the dead/Chatters to nothing in the thankless ground/His father screwed from Charlie Stark and sold/To the selectmen." Here is a good deal of the history of New England's nineteenth century in a sentence.

Of New England Mr. Lowell has the ambivalent knowledge one has of one's damned kin. The poems are crowded with the "fearful Witnesses" who "fenced their gardens with the Redman's bones"; the clippers and the slavers, their iron owners, and their old seamen knitting at the asylum; the Public Garden "where/The bread-stuffed ducks are brooding, where with tub/And strainer the mid-Sunday Irish scare/ The sun-struck shallows for the dusky chub"; the faith "that made the Pilgrim Makers take a lathe/To point their wooden steeples lest the Word be dumb." Here his harshest propositions flower out of facts. But some of his earlier satires of present-day politics and its continuation have a severe crudity that suggest Michael Wigglesworth rewriting the "Horatian Ode"; airplanes he treats as Allen Tate does, only more so—he gives the impression of having encountered them in Mother Shipton. But these excesses were temporary; what is permanently excessive is a sort of obstinate violence or violent obstinacy of temperament and perception—in a day when poets long to be irresistible forces, he is an inmovable object.

Mr. Lowell's period pieces are notable partly for their details—which are sometimes magically and professionally illusionary—and partly for the empathy, the historical identification, that underlie the details. These period pieces are intimately related to his adaptations of poems from other languages; both are valuable as ways of getting a varied, extensive, and alien experience into his work. Dismissing these adaptations as misguided "translations" is like dismissing "To Celia" or *Cathay,* and betrays an odd dislike or ignorance of an important and traditional procedure of poets.

Mr. Lowell is a thoroughly professional poet, and the degree of intensity of his poems is equalled by their degree of organization. Inside its elaborate stanzas the poem is put together like a mosaic: the shifts of movement, the varied pauses, the alternation in the length of sentences, and the counterpoint between lines and sentences are the outer form of a subject matter that has been given a dramatic, dialectical internal organization; and it is hard to exaggerate the strength and life, the constant richness and surprise of metaphor and sound and motion, of the language itself. The organization of the poems resembles that of a great deal of traditional English poetry— especially when compared to that type of semi-imagist modern organization in which the things of a poem seem to marshal themselves like

Dryden's atoms—but often this is complicated by stream-of-consciousness, dream, or dramatic-monologue types of structure. This makes the poems more difficult, but it is worth the price—many of the most valuable dramatic effects can hardly be attained inside a more logical or abstract organization. Mr. Lowell's poetry is a unique fusion of modernist and traditional poetry, and there exist side by side in it certain effects that one would have thought mutually exclusive; but it is essentially a post- or anti-modernist poetry, and as such is certain to be influential.

This poet is wonderfully good at discovering powerful, homely, grotesque, but exactly appropriate particulars for his poems. "Actuality is something brute," said Peirce. "There is no reason in it. I instance putting your shoulder against a door and trying to force it open against an unseen, silent, and unknown resistance." The things in Mr. Lowell's poems have, necessarily, been wrenched into formal shape, organized under terrific pressure, but they keep to an extraordinary degree their stubborn, unmoved toughness, their senseless originality and contingency: no poet is more notable for what, I have read, Duns Scotus calls *haeccitas*—the contrary, persisting, and singular thinginess of every being in the world; but this detailed factuality is particularly effective because it sets off, or is set off by, the elevation and rhetorical sweep characteristic of much earlier English poetry. Mr. Lowell is obviously a haptic rather than a visual type: a poem like "Colloquy in Black Rock" has some of the most successful kinaesthetic effects in English. It is impossible not to notice the weight and power of his lines, a strength that is sometimes mechanical or exaggerated, and sometimes overwhelming. But because of this strength the smooth, calm, and flowing ease of a few passages, the flat and colloquial ease of others, have even more effectiveness than they ordinarily would have: the dead mistress of Propertius, a black nail dangling from a finger, Lethe oozing from her nether lip, in the end can murmur to the "apple-sweetened Anio":

> . . . *Anio, you will please*
> *Me if you whisper upon sliding knees:*
> *"Propertius, Cynthia is here:*
> *She shakes her blossoms when my waters clear."*

Mr. Lowell, at his best and latest, is a dramatic poet: the poet's generalizations are usually implied, and the poem's explicit generalizations are there primarily because they are dramatically necessary—it is not simply the poet who means them. He does not present themes or generalizations but a world; the differences and similarities between it and ours bring home to us themes, generalizations, and the poet himself. It is partly because of this that atheists are vexed by his

Catholic views (and Catholics by his heretical ones) considerably less than they normally would be.

But there are other reasons. The poet's rather odd and imaginative Catholicism is thoroughly suitable to his mind, which is so traditional, theocentric, and anthropomorphic that no images from the sciences, next to none from philosophy, occur in his poems. Such a Catholicism is thoroughly suited to literature, since it *is* essentially literary, anthropomorphic, emotional. It is an advantage to a poet to have a frame of reference, terms of generalization, which are themselves human, affective, and effective as literature. *Bodily Changes in Fear, Rage, Pain, and Hunger* may let the poet know more about the anger of Achilles, but it is hard for him to have to talk about adrenalin and the thalamus; and when the arrows of Apollo are transformed into a "lack of adequate sanitary facilities," everything is lost but understanding. (This helps to explain the dependence of contemporary poetry on particulars, emotions, things—its generalizations, where they are most effective, are fantastic, though often traditionally so.) Naturally the terms of scientific explanation cannot have these poetic and emotional effects, since it is precisely by the exclusion of such effects that science has developed. (Many of the conclusions of the sciences are as poetic as anything in the world, but they have been of little use to poets— how can you use something you are delighted never to have heard of?) Mr. Lowell's Catholicism represents effective realities of human behavior and desire, regardless of whether it is true, false, or absurd; and, as everyone must realize, it is possible to tell part of the truth about the world in terms that are false, limited, and fantastic—else how should we have told it? There is admittedly no "correct" or "scientific" view of a great many things that a poet writes about, and he has to deal with them in dramatic and particular terms, if he has foregone the advantage of pre-scientific ideologies like Christianity or Marxism. Of course it seems to me an advantage that he can well forego; I remember writing about contemporary religious poems, "It is hard to enjoy the ambergris for thinking of all those suffering whales," and most people will feel this when they encounter a passage in Mr. Lowell's poetry telling them how Bernadette's miraculous vision of Our Lady "puts out reason's eyes." It does indeed.

It is unusually difficult to say which are the best poems in *Lord Weary's Castle*: several are realized past changing, successes that vary only in scope and intensity—others are poems that almost any living poet would be pleased to have written. But certainly some of the best things in the book are "Colloquy in Black Rock," "Between the Porch and the Altar," the first of the two poems that compose "The Death of the Sheriff," and "Where the Rainbow Ends"; "The Quaker Graveyard at Nantucket" and "At the Indian-Killer's Grave" have extremely good parts; some other moving, powerful, and unusual poems are "Death from Cancer," "The Exile's Return," "Mr. Edwards and the Spider," and "Mary Winslow"—and I hate to leave entirely unmentioned poems like "After the Surprising Conversions," "The Blind Leading the Blind," "The Drunken Fisherman," and "New Year's Day."

When I reviewed Mr. Lowell's first book I finished by saying, "Some of the best poems of the next years ought to be written by him." The appearance of *Lord Weary's Castle* makes me feel less like Adams or Leverrier than like a rain-maker who predicts rain and gets a flood which drowns everyone in the country. One or two of these poems, I think, will be read as long as men remember English.

Review of *Lord Weary's Castle*

by Richard Eberhart

A manuscript (1935) of Robert Lowell's early unpublished poems, numbering about sixty, showed that his mind was heavy, and that it was essentially religious. His course was already indicated in titles such as "Madonna," "Jericho," "New England," "Death," "Easter, an Ode," "Jonah," and "Phocion." The raw power was there. The forms were scarcely more complicated than the sonnet, which he yet employs, with variable rhyme schemes. And there was a heavy driving force and surd of prose which would bind the lyric flow in strict forms.

Early had begun the wrestling with the soul ("When Cotton Mather wrestled with the fiends from Hell"), the harsh struggle with the inner spirit against the outer world, the confrontation of intolerable opposites, the unresolvable realizations (resolved only in art) which are the crude and terrific fires that leap almost to madness in the mind, dancing with visions of poetic reality, the reality luring all sacrifice, all devotion, and the only power worth having. "Most wretched men/ Are cradled into poetry by wrong;/They learn in suffering what they/Teach in song," from the maniac's soliloquy in *Julian and Maddalo,* may be appropriate here. In the early unpublished poems I like best the lyrical strain. One poem began, "Perhaps I may not live for long/Or perhaps I'll never die" and had lines like "A sight of something after death/Bright angels dropping from the sky/ . . . I see them dancing in my eye/Their music often fills my ears/And I've been borne to heaven/In the tumult of their cry!"

Lowell's first book appeared in 1944, *Land of Unlikeness.* The title itself was expressive. The years had matured the wild early strains; much reading had been assumed; much experience had taken its toll. The result was an original type of writing, dense, somewhat crabbed, sincere, and harsh. It was the rugged, harsh, New England quality of the verse which stayed in the mind. These qualities were the opposites of gracefulness and sophistication. It is another world, the other world, latterly the Holy Word which have dominated and sustained

"Review of *Lord Weary's Castle*" by Richard Eberhart. From "Four Poets" in *Sewanee Review*, LV (1947), 324–36. Copyright 1947 by the University of the South. Reprinted by permission of the author and *Sewanee Review*.

Lowell. The verse was never vague or abstracted: it named the parts of Boston, Salem, Concord, "bread-stuffed ducks." Reading this book once again in California I felt an irritation with the limitation to the local scenes. One wanted the author to get out of New England, which he had done physically, but which he had not been able to accomplish intellectually. It was no doubt an unreasonable wish, but it prohibited a feeling of universality in the references to "Boston Common, or Beacon Hill." As well expect Sandburg to talk like a New Englander, or Jeffers like a Southerner. Satan and Christ were the realities, the Acheron was a short distance from the Charles. Jesus might as well walk on the waters of the Public Garden as anywhere. It was Lowell's refreshment to place Him there. The power of the book was spiritual. He brought Heaven very much down to earth, had most graphic presentations for ineffable concepts. It was the iron-forged will made a steel-tough poetry. It was a manacle-forged mind I heard. That was the power of the book, not whipping the British King, fighting the British lion to his knees, this late.

There seemed to be more direct, forthright passion in the first book than in the second, although ten poems are reprinted, sometimes with changes for the worse. The same type of passion inheres in the second book, but the consciousness of the artist has increased, blocking the prophetic flow with structural balances, presenting a matrix of verbal and phrasal niceties through which the initial thrusts must be felt. This change finds a minor equation in a sidelong consideration of the titles of the poems in the two volumes.

Lowell's poems are conventional in form. He has invented no new forms, employs a nicely devised nine-line stanza expertly—his very forms seem to show the restraints and formalities of his education. What is important is what is said within the lines and stanzas, the freshness he gives to them, the peculiar weights and daring shifts of his own personality. Also the seriousness of the intention of his work, its intense concentration, the steady maintenance of its own peculiarity, are important. We might look at the craftsman.

Poems reprinted from the first book have been changed in some particulars, sometimes incurring losses. It would be tedious to show the changes of each comma or dash, although collation provides a fascinating study. In "In Memory of Arthur Winslow, I," a stricter control has been aimed at in the new punctuation, but a loss sustained in omission of the sensuous "serge" in "on your serge yachting-blouse." A careful reading of No. II, "Dunbarton," in both versions, will show the conservatism of his changes: we lose "a mortician's Packard limousine," and for the explicit "Kinsolving" we are reduced to "the minister from Boston." In such changes we have the prudent mind at work, critical judgment restive against the freshness of its original impetus. The first powers are toned down. In III, "I come to bury you" becomes "I come to mourn you," but "Hosing out" for "Mining" is a gain to evocation. Even Cotton Mather's Hell in the new book is reduced to a small h. And in the last line "whipped the British King" becomes "whipped or backed the King?" Also, in II, "the slight coin-silver spoons/Some Winslow hammered thinner than Revere" seems better than its change to "the slight coin-silver spoons/The Sheriff beat to shame the gaunt Revere." In IV, direct quotation is reserved only for the second stanza; "To Trinity, Kinsolving's Church" is muted to "To Trinity, the costly Church."

"Salem" has only a slight change. "Concord," as if to be brought up to date, begins "Ten thousand Fords are idle here in search/Of a tradition" which had begun "Gold idles here in its inventor's search/For history." The reader is invited to compare the last five lines for preference; "where the Emersons/Washed out the blood-clots on my Master's robe" has become "where Thoreau/Named all the birds without a gun to probe," etc. "Napoleon Crosses the Berezina" has changes too, descriptive for problematical in the last line and a half. "The Slough of Despond" presents the same conservatism in alteration; in the last stanza "midden" is discarded and replaced by "wayward"; "Now how the Dead Sea waters swell" becomes the less graphic "Now how the weary waters swell"; and again Hell, in the last line, is reduced to a small h. The same intentions may be found in the manipulations of "The Crucifix," with gain in "Snapping at gobbets in my thumbless hand." In "Dea Roma" "Greek" cosmetics becomes "the king's" cosmetics; in stanzas two "But human torches lit the soldier home,/And victims dyed your purple crucifix:" has "But human torches lit the captains home/Where victims warped the royal crucifix:" The third stanza is omitted and with it one of Lowell's most masterful phrasings has been sacrificed due to what tone-deafness I do not know: "How many butchers and philosophers/Dirtied the Babylonian purple!" Austerity sometimes kills the very thing it seeks to preserve. In "The Drunken Fisherman" "are these fit terms/To mete the worm whose gilded rage/Havocs the in'ards of old age?" loses its spice to "are these fit terms/To mete the worm whose molten rage/Boils in the belly of old age?"

The changes in the poems show the artist as extremely critical of his material, which is necessary and good; but in my opinion the cold-headed tampering has in many cases dimmed the heat and originality of the prime utterance; in scarcely any cases have more striking or original phrases been discovered, a lesson in the dangers of changing poems once they are fused out of the heats and furies of first creation.

Lowell's poems are passionate, forceful, sometimes choking and bursting from the rigorous moulds of form they are poured into. Christ is his image—a fierce Christ, a complicated Christ. The poetry brims with life. Among so many excellent poems the reader will chose his own favorites. "Mr. Edwards and the Spider" is a wonderful piece: "What are we in the hands of the great God?"—somewhat Donnean in tone, with admirable shifts in rhythm in stanza 2, line 1, and in stanza 4, line 2, line 4, and with a neat transition at the end of stanza 3. "New Year's Day," "Rebellion," "In the Cage," "The Quaker Grave-yard in Nantucket," "After the Surprising Conversions" I would name, but each reader will select his own for favor. The title page has a Look-We-Have-Come-Through sort of drawing by Frank Parker, an old schoolmate of the author's.

Part of the magnificence of Hopkins is that even the most spiritual poems are composed with such concious art ("who knows how?") that you want to savor them as sensual contexts apart from their spiritual meaning. Merton (I mean no direct value-comparison with Hopkins) is unconscious of such a type of artistry in the pervasive spiritual consciousness which overwhelms him. I have tried to divorce his later poems from the spiritual impact as things of his spirit intimately related to his Catholicism, but with failure. So divorced, they seem to lose much of their poetry. But they cannot, or at any rate cannot easily be so divorced, and their goodness as poetry is inextricably bound up in the force of the spiritual charge.

In the face of a message so purely projected, with such innocence, it is difficult to see the point in tearing down the verse to look at the parts. The words are only the vehicle for a flame. It might not have been words, but paint, or stone, or deeds only. The flame is his spiritual consciousness. If you will allow a protest about the innocence I would make up a paradox that innocence is innocence only when knowledge-able; to put it more bluntly, there must be in it the certainty that much or all evil has been known or perceived imaginatively, there must be the harsh assurance of struggle, a total awareness of a totality of experience.

What I find in Merton is an innocence that takes you in (perhaps that is what it is supposed to do); the poetry takes you in; it rushes you along and lifts you up; it excites and it pleases. But later the feeling persists, at least in a non-Catholic, that this innocence is shallow, that it is in some respect inhuman, without congruence with a certain type of humility.

In Lowell I find a different kind of spirituality. He has achieved some innocence through apparently much suffering or acuteness of perception of evil, of sin, of hardly resolvable tensions. His poems cry out with the struggle and effort of them; their sometime inharmonious-ness, their lack of easy flow, their turgid and lumbering gaits show his own praise of the Lord in his own terms. In Merton it is the Lord's terms. In one sense the two poets are striking at the same goal, a universal hymn of praise, the glory of the Lord. When Merton is unconvincing it is because he is so sure, when Lowell is unconvincing it is because he is so unsure. Lowell's mind still allows of doubt, perplexities, the depths of human taint, the imperfect; these he evokes, and their religious resolutions, in rather bleak, discordant, particular, concrete images. The coldness and torsion still show the struggle: but there is humanity in it. Lowell is not altogether out of Hell; he convinces us that he is human, bodied.

Whom Seek Ye?:
A Note on Robert Lowell's Poetry

by Will C. Jumper

Quem quaeritis in sepulchro, O Christicolae?
—Iesum Nazarenum crucifixum, O Coelicola.
—The English *Quem Quaeritis*

Robert Lowell, who won the Pulitzer Prize for Poetry in 1946 with the volume *Lord Weary's Castle*,[1] is viewed by a number of contemporary critics as the present best hope of American poetry; and, since critical interest in his work has been high for more than ten years, he warrants consideration by the serious student. This discussion will be concerned with some aspects of the Pulitzer Prize volume, a fact which obviously limits the range of the poetry examined; but such a procedure is not unfair to the poet, for the collection is a representative sampling of his best work. Except for a greater interest in the narrative built upon the dramatic monologue—an interest already evident in at least two poems in *Lord Weary's Castle*—the work appearing subsequent to the prize volume shows no marked characteristics not found in the 1946 book. Indeed, the later poems demonstrate the weaknesses rather than the strong points of the earlier work.

Critical interest has concerned itself largely with four aspects of Lowell's writing: thematically, his Catholicism and his radicalism; technically, his traditionalism and his violence. But the terms are misleading. The Catholicism—which is at least three-quarters anti-Calvinism —is certainly ubiquitous; the radicalism is a curious mixture of Jeremiah, St. Francis of Assisi, and Karl Marx; the traditionalism resides

[1] Robert Lowell. *Lord Weary's Castle* (Harcourt, Brace).

largely in technical detail—and that with a difference—; and the violence is both thematic and technical to an explosive degree.

For an understanding of the collection we have, aside from the poems themselves, two clues furnished by Lowell. In a note[2] he tells us that the title—which is not the title of any poem in the book—comes from an old ballad:

> *It's lambkin was a mason good*
> *As ever built wi' stane:*
> *He built Lord Wearie's castle*
> *But payment gat he nane . . ,*

In a prescript[3] he prays:

> Suscipe, Domine, munera pro tuorum commemoratione Sanctorum: ut, sicut illos passio gloriosos effecit; ita nos devotio reddat innocuos.*

In view of the emphasis of the book and the sentiment of the Latin quotation, it seems possible that Lowell means Lambkin to be Christ, Lord Weary to be mankind smothered in *acedia,* and the castle to be the structure of salvation. But, of course, other logical meanings can not be overlooked. The exploitation of the poor by the rich is a recurrent theme in the book, and the stanza fits the idea. Also, for Lowell, the inertia of habitual sinful behavior—built by the individual man, as it were, stone by stone—is the donjon-keep of damnation, and one of the major evils against which he inveighs. In a more self-pitying and personal poet, one might suspect the stanza to be the poet's cry against an unappreciative audience; but this construction applies to Lowell only if he is being ironic. Presumably the volume is both commemorative and didactic; but the saints are hard to find—except in intaglio—, and the *passio*—in both senses—is far more prominent than the *devotio.*

One avenue of investigation which may be fruitful for the understanding of a comparatively young poet is the influence exerted upon his work by other writers. In specific poems—titled as "after" various poets—the tribute of imitation is paid to Rimbaud, Valery, Rilke, and Sextus Propertius.[4] In his introductory note he mentions that he has borrowed a line from C. F. MacIntyre (whose name he misspells), an

---

* ["Receive, O Lord, these gifts for the commemoration of Thy Saints, that just as their passion made them glorious, so may our devotion free us of sin." The line is from the Secret of the Mass for the finding of the body of St. Stephen Protomartyr, which is celebrated on August 3—Ed.]

[2] *Ibid.,* p. vii.

[3] *Ibid.,* p. 1.

[4] Strictly speaking, these are not "imitations." They range from fairly close paraphrases, like the Rilke, to loose adaptations like the Rimbaud.

ardent proselyter for T. E. Hulme, Laforgue, Baudelaire, and Rilke. Other poems name or implicate, in an approving sense, Vergil, Dante, Hawthorne, and Melville; in a pejorative sense, Bunyan, the American Puritans, Unitarianism, and transcendentalism. Other influences, less specific but equally definite, can be found. "The Quaker Graveyard in Nantucket," if it leans heavily on Melville for both matter and manner, also looks to Milton for its rhetorical effects. The trick of deliberate ambiguity, the Janus-word, though deriving originally from Donne, probably arrives at Lowell through Pound, Eliot, and Auden. The interest in Propertius and Dante and the copious use of phrases and full lines in Latin and Italian also point to Pound and Eliot, though the non-English quotations in Lowell are thoroughly integrated into the prose sense. Crashaw almost certainly lurks behind meditations like "As a Plane Tree by the Water," and the couplet that Lowell employs for narrative and for satire seems closer to Crashaw (for example, in "For Hope") than to any other poet, especially in the violent enjambements in mid-phrase and the free use of short lines. The social protest stems from many sources, though Cobbett is the only specific mention that Lowell makes. The Catholicism comes from Church tradition, the Vulgate Bible (especially the Old Testament), and the huge body of Latin and vernacular writing which the Church has accumulated, but it comes as well from Dante and Crashaw. Its corollary is the anti-Calvinism which motivates, I think, Lowell's interest in Hawthorne and Melville and which certainly defines his attitude toward Bunyan, Mather, Hooker, and Edwards as well as toward Unitarianism and its pantheistic offspring.

Randall Jarrell [5] says of Lowell's poetry:

> The organization of the poems resembles that of a great deal of traditional English poetry . . . , but often this is complicated by stream-of-consciousness, dream, or dramatic-monologue types of structure.

This is true, as we shall see, but the complication is far commoner than the simon-pure form. Elsewhere in his essay, in a passage which is intended to be complimentary and which was approved by Lowell for publication in the Ciardi volume, Jarrell says:

> The things in Mr. Lowell's poems, have, necessarily, been wrenched into formal shape, organized under terrific pressure, but they keep to an extraordinary degree their stubborn, unmoved toughness, their senseless originality and contingency.

[5] John Ciardi, ed. *Mid-Century American Poets*. (New York: Twain Publishers, Inc., 1950), p. 164. All the quotations from Jarrell will be found in this volume, pp. 158–67. Rather than writing his own prose introduction, Lowell suggested the reprinting of Jarrell's discussion.

This statement is remarkable for more than the punctuation—which has been carefully reproduced. If we remove the first comma, replace the fifth comma by a semicolon, and understand that "formal shape" refers only to structural details, we have in the words of a warm admirer of Mr. Lowell most of what we should want to say in criticism of his techniques. And, obligingly, Mr. Jarrell has also furnished us with the text for the other major objection when he says,

> What is permanently excessive is a sort of obstinate violence or violent obstinacy of temperament and perception. In a day when poets wish to be irresistible forces, he is an immovable object.

This violence is exemplified by the sonnet "The Soldier," in which Lowell lifts the predicament of Buonconte of Dante's *Purgatorio* from its context and, by means of odd juxtaposition, fallacious theology, and building rhetorical tension, creates a diatribe against war that is brutal, poetically shocking, and metaphysically violent to the extent of lacking unity as a poem.

In "The North Sea Undertaker's Complaint" the problem is a different one. The poem suffers partially from the employment of a non-existent plot—or at least a plot not existent in the poem itself. But the big problem lies in the use of private language at crucial points in the poem:

> *Now south and south and south the mallard heads,*
> *His green-blue bony hood echoes the green*
> *Flats of the Weser, and the mussel beds*
> *Are sluggish where the webbed feet spanked the lean*
> *Eel grass to tinder in the take-off. South*
> *Is what I think of. It seems yesterday*
> *I slid my hearse across the river mouth*
> *And pitched the first iced mouse into the hay.*

Up to this last line, although there is too much repetition, some idiosyncratic enjambement, and occasional overly-conversational diction, the poem has employed excellent detail for recreating the scene. But what does the eighth line mean? It may mean "and buried the first dead priest," but there is no way of proving it; and the line seems unduly slangy if that is the meaning. It continues, clearly in a somewhat Laforguian vein:

> *Thirty below it is. I hear our dumb*
> *Club-footed orphan ring the Angelus*
> *And clank the bell-chain for St. Gertrude's choir*
> *To wail with the dead bell the martyrdom*
> *Of one more blue-lipped priest; the phosphorus*
> *Melted the hammer of his heart to fire.*

Again, what does the last line and a half mean? Up to this point we can assume that the dramatic monologue presents the undertaker's anti-clericalism and his blasé view toward death as opposed to the "normal" and perhaps sentimental view. But why "phosphorus"? Why the strange concluding figure? Is he still equating the priest to a mouse? Is the phosphorus to be taken as the common poison for rodents? If so, how does it fit into the plot of which we have only a fragmentary glimpse? Even if, as has been suggested, the phosphorus is to be identified with the phosphorescence of the *aurora borealis,* and therefore with the killing cold of the North Sea, how does it fit into the poem? The all-important—for a sonnet—final line has shot off in a completely unrelated direction and shattered the unity of the poem. Whether obscurity or obscurantism, it is bad writing.

These two sonnets show some of the ways in which Lowell employs the "psychological organization" of his experimentalist mentors as opposed to the "logical organization" of traditional poetry. However minutely one may wish to break down structural methods of poetry for purposes of clarification and classification, it is obvious that repetition with variation, rational progression of argument, and narrative (or balanced combinations of these) are basically and traditionally "logical" modes of construction. It is equally obvious that what Yvor Winters calls pseudo-reference, qualitative progression, and the double mood (when it is truly double rather than consciously employed for controlled contrast) are basically "illogical." Defenders of the latter types of organization have seized upon the valid researches of psychologists into the irrational aspects of human behavior—*for the purpose of more complete rational understanding*—and have made these data the basis of a justification of irrationality on the grounds that, if illogical, such organization is psychological, that is, true to the structure of uncontrolled sensory-emotional experience. If poetry is to be no more than an attempt at reproducing sensory-emotional experience, then the method is perfectly justified. But if poetry is to be a rational evaluation of both intellectual and sensory-emotional experience, the method is inadequate to the poetic purpose.

We take away from "The Soldier" a memory of violence, that is, both poetic shock and emotional shock, and a memory of skilled metrical and aural effects. From "The North Sea Undertaker's Complaint" we take away a memory of purposeful obscurity and a somewhat cheap irony. The metrical structure is accurate, if unsubtle, but the suggestion lingers that the final lines say what they do partly because "phosphorus" and "fire" rime with "Angelus" and "choir."

The poem "After the Surprising Conversions," on the other hand, works with logical and frightening clarity from beginning to end. It uses narrative as its framework in a monologue of letter form. The

material derives from a *post script* which Jonathan Edwards appended
to a letter on the "surprising conversion" occurring in the mid-eight-
eenth century. The recipient was Reverend Benjamin Colman, and
the added note tells him of the suicide of a "man of some renown,"
actually the uncle of Edwards. Lowell picks up the phrases and psy-
chology of Edwards and expands with material derived from the narrative proper and from his own imagination. He has Edwards report the
deplorable wave of defections from the Church set off by the suicide. As
spiritual adviser, he seeks for all the plausible reasons he can find: "He
came from melancholy parents," he had "too much or little wit," he
took to reading Scripture for himself, "meditated terror, and he
seemed/Beyond advice or reason." But finally the minister admits
what he considers to be the real cause of the trouble, a *privatio Dei*:
"The breath of God had carried out a planned/And sensible with-
drawal from this land." The poem ends with the minute and characteristic, but essentially meaningless, scrutiny of nature for symbolic
insights which we find in much Puritan writing:

> September twenty-second, Sir, the bough
> Cracks with the unpicked apples, and at dawn
> The small-mouth bass breaks water, gorged with spawn.

The apples are unpicked because the whole town has begun to neglect
the Puritan imperative to labor; what the bass means is purely in the
realm of metaphysical speculation. The real point of the poem is, of
course, that there is no room in the theocracy of New England for the
person who takes the tenets of Calvinism seriously—that the man who
perseveres in pure Calvinistic meditation ends either as a suicide or as
a heretic. The form of the poem is the Crashaw couplet—without the
irregular line length. At line ends phrases break over violently, and
strong masculine rimes are used to define the form despite the run-
over. This latter quality at times becomes annoying as a conscious
device, but otherwise the structure is firm and the poem as a whole
most successful in its revelation of character and theme. Here Lowell
employs the means of traditional poetry to achieve a logical and
satisfying result.

It would be misleading, however, to leave the impression that in
the volume one poem in three is logical and traditional. In the whole
volume of forty-two poems, only "Salem," "Children of Light," "At a
Bible House," "Charles the Fifth and the Peasant, 1790," "The
Ghosts," and "The Fens" can be classified with "After the Surprising
Conversions" as largely free from various kinds of obscurity and
thoroughly logical in construction. It may be significant that, with
one exception, these eight poems are concerned either with anti-
Calvinism or with socio-political protest, themes with which Lowell

is deeply concerned as a polemicist. Other poems, to be sure, like "As a Plane Tree by the Water," have only a small area of willful obscurantism, or at least of the exploitation of not discernibly logical relationships. But many of the poems are marred to a greater or less degree by the extremely private nature of the concepts employed.

To be fair to Lowell, we must take note, moreover, of the excellence of not a small part of the writing in *Lord Weary's Castle*. A number of poems are, in whole or in part, brilliantly realized. Whole poems which fall into this classification are "The Ghost," a monologue spoken by a dead mistress and derived from Sextus Propertius; "Salem," an *ubi sunt* sonnet that errs only slightly in overdoing its onomatopoeia; "At a Bible House," the portrait of a dying Calvinist; "Mr. Edwards and the Spider," a pyrotechnical handling of a Jonathan Edwards sermon which might be the best poem in the book but for occasional idiosyncrasies; "After the Surprising Conversions," already commented upon; and "Where the Rainbow Ends," an amazing piece of rhetoric which sells itself despite its confusions. Very few of the poems lack some redeeming lines, and sections of other poems are worth mentioning. Whether or not it is derived from W. C. Williams, the second stanza of "New Year's Day" is imposing even when it loses itself in obscurity. Sections IV and VI of "The Quaker Graveyard" are completely successful in what they set out to do. In "Between the Porch and the Altar," a confusing treatment of the Oedipus theme, section III ("Katherine's Dream"), though marred by some abrupt shifts in progression, is a highly effective dramatic monologue which gathers commanding power as it works to the end.

Of his technique, we can say that Lowell has, when he chooses to employ it, an effective command of traditional poetic disciplines. Generally, however, he uses traditional rhetorical and verse forms within an experimental structure. He is addicted to violent material, violent juxtaposition, and erratic imagery and figure, all of which often make the relationship between the "what" and the "how" of his poems difficult to discover.

What of the themes? Randall Jarrell says quite accurately that the poems revolt against:

> the Old Law, imperialism, militarism, capitalism, Calvinism, Authority, the Father, the "proper Bostonians," the rich. . . .

What Jarrell does not say is that Lowell's Catholicism is almost entirely equated with this revolt. For Lowell, Catholicism is the negative of every one of these bogeymen except authority—and he is extremely ambivalent in his attitude toward the authority of the Church. Specifically he refers to "the church whose double locks,/Wait for St. Peter, the distorted key." One can hardly avoid the conclusion that Lowell

chose the Catholic Church as much to outrage his Calvinistic heritage
as for any other reason. He prays to Mary:

> *Mother, for these three hundred years or more*
> *Neither our clippers nor our slavers reached*
> *The haven of your peace in this Bay State:*
> *Neither my father nor his father. . . .*

He is violent and specific in the poem "Children of Light":

> *Our fathers wrung their bread from stocks and stones*
> *And fenced their gardens with the Redman's bones;*
> *Embarking from the Nether Land of Holland,*
> *Pilgrims unhoused by Geneva's night,*
> *They planted here the Serpent's seeds of light;*
> *And here the pivoting searchlights probe to shock*
> *The riotous glass houses built on rock,*
> *And candles gutter by an empty altar,*
> *And light is where the landless blood of Cain*
> *Is burning, burning the unburied grain.*

"Nether Land of Holland," "unhoused by Geneva's night," and
"Serpent's seeds of light" are all specific and unmistakable identifica-
tions of Calvinism with Satan. "Empty altar" denies the validity of
the Protestant dispensation; and the two closing lines, still using the
light in an ironic sense, indicate that only the power to destroy their
own potentiality remains of their once great driving force. A complete
revulsion from such a concept of Calvinism would involve either ab-
solute irreligion or Catholicism. For Lowell's mind, steeped in Christian humanistic values, the only possible choice was Catholicism.[6]

There is evidence to support this analysis. When we turn to the
poems treating directly with religious subjects, we are stuck by the
negativism of the poetry. Here are the concluding lines of three meditations.

> *O Christ, the spiralling years*
> *Slither with child and manger to a ball*
> *Of ice; and what is man? We tear our rags*
> *To hang the furies by their itching ears,*
> *And the green needles nail us to the wall.*

---

[6] Jarrell's explanation is simpler: "The poet's rather odd and imaginative Catholicism is thoroughly suitable to his mind, which is so traditional, theocentric, and
anthropomorphic that no images from the sciences, next to none from philosophy,
occur in his poems. Such a Catholicism is thoroughly suited to literature, since it is
essentially literary, anthropomorphic, emotional." This seems unfair to Lowell,
Catholicism, and literature.

*

And lion-taming Satan bows and loops
His cracking tail into a hangman's noose;
He is the only happy man in Lent.
He laughs into my face until I cry.

*

On Ninth Street, through the Hallowe'en's soaped glass,
I picked at an old bone on two crossed sticks
And found, to Via et Vita et Veritas
A stray dog's signpost is a crucifix.

These come respectively, from "Christmas in Black Rock," "The First Sunday in Lent," and "The Crucifix." Jarrell states that the poems are all built upon the basic struggle between what is "closed, turned inward, incestuous, that blinds or binds," and what is "free and open, that grows or is willing to change . . . , the realm of freedom, of the Grace that has replaced the Law, of the perfect liberator whom the poet calls Christ." Jarrell is basically correct in this analysis, but he overdoes his conclusion that Lowell's emphasis is on the "open" rather than the "closed." The prophet of man's imminent doom speaks more loudly than the guide to the new light. Even the poems which attempt a positive solution do it less than half-heartedly. "Christmas Eve under Hooker's Statue," a most effective Jeremiad, piles up bitterness upon bitterness: "How the long horn of plenty broke like glass/In Hooker's gauntlets," "I ask for bread, my father gives me mould," "Where is the summer garden? In its bed/The ancient speckled serpent will appear." All it can offer at the end is: "But we are old, our fields are running wild:/Till Christ again turn wanderer and child." "Where the Rainbow Ends," the concluding and summarizing poem, gathers together almost all the major themes and points them to the question: "What can the dove of Jesus give/You now but wisdom, exile?" The answer is the nearest thing to a positive statement that Lowell can make: "Stand and live,/The dove has brought an olive branch to eat." Jarrell interprets this:

> The dove of Jesus brings to the worshipper the olive branch that shows him that the flood has receded, opening the whole earth for him; it is the olive branch of peace and reconciliation, the olive branch that he is "to eat" as a symbol of the eaten flesh of Christ, of atonement, identification, and liberation.

Even if this hyperbolic expansion of the figure is indicated, it does not balance the deadly weight of the particulars of the whole poem—and it is hard to believe that Lowell does not know that olives eaten from the branch are painfully bitter.

Lowell is a serious, intelligent, gifted, and powerful—albeit sometimes misguided—poet. He is basically a poet of revolt, and that revolt is specifically directed against the Calvinism of his heritage, which he identifies with the Old Law of the Hebraic dispensation, and against all the historical, social, political, and economic patterns of a New-England-led America. But, like the Saxon who could denounce the conquerors only by learning the Norman language—and thereby began to be Normanized—, Lowell adopts the "poetic vocabulary" and the habits of mind of the opposition. He leans toward organization by reverie and association, the acceptance of a solipsistic universe, which is the ultimate product of the disappearance of God from the Ockhamist-Calvinist conception of being. In his denial of Calvinistic total depravity, predestinarianism, and faith without works, he does not reach the affirmation of Aristotelian-Thomistic reason, freedom, and individual responsibility. He does not find the joy of the risen Christ, nor the emancipation of rational Christianity. He has not escaped the tragic Christ and the voluntaristic universe of Calvin.

To the "whom seek ye in the sepulchre" of the angel, he has answered, "Jesus of Nazareth who was crucified." But he has not yet heard the message of the angel nor yet learned to sing the "Alleluia, resurrexit Dominus!"

"The Quaker Graveyard in Nantucket"

by Hugh B. Staples

During World War II, the naval vessel on which Lowell's cousin, Warren Winslow, was serving disappeared and no Ishmael survived to explain her fate. Lowell's reaction to this catastrophe, "The Quaker Graveyard in Nantucket," is the elegiac expression of some of his most urgent preoccupations: the nature of God, the possibility of salvation, the destructive effects of spiritual alienation, the Heracleitean flux of warring elements in the phenomenal world, and man's ultimate impotence in the grip of natural forces and the hands of the great God.

The parallels to the situation that occasioned "Lycidas" (the death of a young man to whom the poet has a more than casual yet less than intimate relationship; death by drowning; the unrecovered body) must have suggested themselves; and while at first glance it may seem presumptuous to compare the two elegies, it is clear that Lowell implicitly invites just such a comparison in the poem itself. For example, the nine sections of the poem (as originally printed in the *Partisan Review*) contain 194 lines, divided, like the 193 lines of "Lycidas," into a loose stanzaic structure of pentameter lines, varied by an occasional trimeter. Similarly, the stanzas vary a good deal in length. Each stanza has its own highly intricate rhyme scheme, repeated in only two cases (stanzas II and VII in the *Lord Weary's Castle* version), yet differing from each other only slightly. Like Milton, then, Lowell adapts the *canzone* form to his own uses; like Milton, he continues the elegiac tradition by going beyond his lament to a larger consideration of contemporary and universal issues. Like his predecessors, Lowell proposes an answer to the apparent futility of a young man's death, but in terms of Catholic mysticism rather than through the more or less orthodox Protestant solution of Milton or the Neo-Platonic reassurances of Shelley in "Adonais."

These and other considerations, to be discussed below, place "The Quaker Graveyard" in the great tradition of the English elegy, but Lowell has made his own unique contributions to it. Like Milton and

Shelley, and in keeping with his own earlier practice, he has drawn upon both classical and Biblical sources for his patterns of imagery, but in addition he has borrowed descriptive passages and motifs from two great figures in his own native tradition—Thoreau and Melville. In this way he is able to pay indirect homage to his own literary heroes, as Milton does to Theocritus, Bion and Virgil, as Shelley does to Milton in "Adonais," and to infuse his elegy with an added richness and a dimension of universality that would otherwise be lacking. Like Milton, Lowell shows his adroitness in using place-names to evoke the *genius loci;* for the Hebrides, Namancos and Bayona he substitutes Nantucket, Martha's Vineyard, and Walsingham—all names freighted with literary and philosophical connotation. His gift for harsh, grating, powerfully disruptive kinaesthetic diction reaches its fullest expression in this poem. His indignation at the Quakers' barbarous cruelty in such lines as:

> *The death-lance churns into the sanctuary, tears*
> *The gun-blue swingle, heaving like a flail,*
> *And hacks the coiling life out: it works and drags*
> *And rips the sperm-whale's midriff into rags,*
> *Gobbets of blubber spill to wind and weather . . .*

are at least as shocking an intrusion into the elegiac mood as Shelley's diatribes against the reviewers or any of Milton's angry strictures at the "blind mouthes." Yet they serve the same purpose—a criticism of the pettiness of human nature—and the movement from a mood of anger and desolation to one of at least hopeful resignation follows the pattern of "Lycidas" and "Adonais"; the discordant moods of the first five movements are a careful preparation for the contrasting harmonious *largo* of stanza VI—"Our Lady of Walsingham" and for the resolution in the section which follows.

Aside from discarding the decorative trappings of the conventional pastoral elegy (the shepherds, nymphs and personifications—who may be seen, however, somewhat darkly, as the Quakers, the sea-gulls, and the statue of the Virgin), Lowell had made only one radical departure from the old tradition: he has omitted any expression of personal grief and he has made no allusion to his personal career as poet. This is the more surprising when it is remembered that Lowell, like Shelley and Milton, was just under thirty when he composed his elegy—at an age when poets have traditionally felt compelled to re-examine and restate their poetic principles. There is no need, however, to seek for biographical explanations for this departure; the answer lies within the central meaning of the poem itself. For Lowell's conclusion is that the human desire to preserve the sense of self-identity runs counter to the Will of God, and is equally in opposition to the transcendental wisdom of the Virgin, who

> *knows what God knows,*
> *Not Calvary's Cross nor crib at Bethlehem*

—not the anthropomorphism of this world, but the Divine Revelation of the next. And thus the poet's career, like the sailor's death, and the extinction of individual consciousness for which that death is a generic symbol, are not necessarily relevant to the larger purpose of God. For the statue of the Virgin is at the heart of the poem—she stands opposed to the context of decay and corruption, natural, spiritual, and physical, in which her image is placed in the poem, and it is only in these terms that the crucial last line of the elegy:

> *The Lord survives the rainbow of His Will*

can be understood.

The first twelve lines of the poem, dealing with the imagined recovery of the dead sailor's body, are taken almost directly from Thoreau's description of a shipwreck victim.* The lines:

> *We weight the body, close*
> *Its eyes and heave it seaward whence it came*

have a meaning beyond the literal, for Lowell introduces here the theme of human evolution, considered as a part of God's plan. The process of creation has begun in the sea; it is fitting for it to end there. The remote early origins of human life in the sea are adumbrated in the lines in stanza III:

> *All you recovered from Poseidon died*
> *With you, my cousin*

and the same theme is finally summarized in the closing lines of the poem:

> *You could cut the brackish winds with a knife*
> *Here in Nantucket, and cast up the time*
> *When the Lord God formed man from the sea's slime*
> *And breathed into his face the breath of life,*
> *And blue-lung'd combers lumbered to the kill.*

The evolutionary process, then, is reversible; creation implies destruction, and if man "formed from the sea's slime" immerses himself merely in the physical world, he must—as Lowell has argued before

* See Appendix I, p. 70.

in "Colloquy in Black Rock"—become subject to its inevitable dissolution. So the drowned sailor has, in this opening stanza, in common with the master of the *Pequod,* only a "hell-bent deity," and his submarine peregrinations remind us of Milton's hero in those regions:

> *Where thou perhaps under the whelming tide*
> *Visit'st the bottom of the monstrous world*

This is the world presided over by Poseidon, the earth-shaker—an epithet that in itself reflects the Heracleitean formula: "Fire lives in the death of air; and air in the death of fire; water lives in the death of earth, and earth in the death of water."

Instead of Milton's wished-for dolphins, however, only

> *the heel-headed dogfish barks its nose*
> *On Ahab's void and forehead.*

And even the ritual of acknowledging the power of the sea cannot placate Poseidon, cannot save the drowned sailor or his comrades, when they are "powerless to sandbag this Atlantic bulwark," and the naval salute of the "steeled fleet" is a confession of such impotence. Thus, in accordance with the elegiac tradition, the opening section of "The Quaker Graveyard" is a tribute to the power of death and to the remorseless operation of the Heracleitean flux. The mood is sombre; the attitude hopeless.

This mood is deepened in the succeeding stanzas, and the violence of the metaphors becomes nearly unbearable in their intensity, as if to provided a more dramatic contrast to the calm of stanza VI, and to the peace that only mystical contemplation can afford. But meanwhile, Lowell is concerned to introduce his social and political criticism (in the widest sense), which is intimately woven into the texture of the poem that it may be overlooked altogether by the unwary reader. In this respect, Lowell's practice is quite divergent from Milton's: in "Lycidas," the excoriation of a corrupt clergy amounts almost to a digression; here, the Quakers and their pursuit of Mammon seem to be suggested naturally by the locale and circumstances of Warren Winslow's death.

For Lowell, the Quakers symbolized inhuman cruelty—which has for its cause spiritual alienation and for its motive economic greed.[1]

---

[1] Lowell in this respect is again following Melville's conception of the Nantucket Quakers, who appear to belie their religion's reputation for pacifism. See, for example, the whole of Chapter Sixteen, "The Ship," in *Moby Dick,* from which the following quotation is taken:

"Now, Bildad, like Peleg, and indeed many other Nantucketers, was a Quaker, the island having been originally settled by that sect; and to this day its inhabitants in general retain in an uncommon measure the peculiarities of the Quaker, only

The "mad scramble of their lives"—the exploitation and destruction of God's creatures, the whales (coupled in the case of Ahab with the un-Christian lust for vengeance and an open defiance of God), forms an implied analogue to the spectacle of man's inhumanity to man in modern warfare. We have here, in other words, an extension of the same kind of parallel drawn earlier in such poems as "Children of Light" and "Christmas Eve Under Hooker's Statue," the satire is thus, like Milton's, at once pungent and indirect. But in place of the "two-handed engine," Lowell substitutes the inexorable force of the elements—a destructive reaction in the natural order that can be viewed as an expression of the Wrath of God.

In this sense, the poem's epigraph from *Genesis*:

> Let man have dominion over the fishes of the sea and the fowls of the air and the beasts and the whole earth, and every creeping creature that moveth upon the earth.

takes on a special irony. The "God-fearing" Quakers have taken this passage as a warrant for their rapacity and greed. They have forgotten not only the ancient penalties of *hybris* in their defiance of Poseidon, but they have also divorced themselves from the central meaning of Christianity, thereby depriving themselves of the possibilities of grace. "What it cost them is their secret," but the implication is that it cost them nothing less than their own salvation. There is a similar irony involved in their plaintive, self-righteous cry,

> *'If God himself had not been on our side,*
> *When the Atlantic rose against us, why,*
> *Then it swallowed us up quick.'*

Better for them if they *had* been swallowed up quick, like Jonah, but like the peasants in Breughel's picture, they remain to the end blind to their dilemma. Their blindness, however, is in no respect different from that of contemporary combatants, their supplications are as meaningless as modern un-Christian prayers for success in the war. Evil can only beget evil, and Lowell's vision of the time:

> *When the whale's viscera go and the roll*
> *Of its corruption overruns this world*
> *Beyond tree-swept Nantucket and Wood's Hole*
> *And Martha's Vineyard*

symbolizes the corrosive spiritual effects of the act of killing, whether

---

variously and anomalously modified by things altogether alien and heterogeneous. For some of these same Quakers are the most sanguinary of all sailors and whale-hunters. They are fighting Quakers; they are Quakers with a vengeance."

for economic profit, or by sanction of contemporary society; the ocean is not mocked, only "fouled with blue sailors."

Lowell explores two ways out of this predicament, though the two ways are perhaps essentially only different aspects of The Way. Concerning the first, salvation through the intercession of Christ (Milton's answer), Lowell appears to be ambivalent, although stanza V ends with the prayer:

> *Hide,*
> *Our steel, Jonas Messias, in Thy side.*

a metaphorical complex almost Metaphysical in its associations of Christ as the Lamb of God who bears away the sins of this world, Jonah, who is mysteriously resurrected, the centurion with his spear at the Crucifixion, the harpoon and the whale. But instantly, as if in answer to this invocation, the whole tone of the poem changes from one of death and destruction in the disturbed Atlantic to the meditative peace and calm of the shrine of Our Lady of Walsingham:

> *There once the penitents took off their shoes*
> *And then walked barefoot the remaining mile:*
> *And the small trees, a stream and hedgerows file*
> *Slowly along the munching English lane,*
> *Like cows to the old shrine, until you lose*
> *Track of your dragging pain.*
> *The stream flows down under the druid tree,*
> *Shiloah's whirlpools gurgle and make glad*
> *The castle of God. Sailor, you were glad*
> *And whistled Sion by that stream. But see:*

The first half of stanza VI, then, describes a tranquil pastoral scene; the water imagery, hitherto so fraught with danger, is tamed—Deluge has become Baptism. Here Lowell goes beyond his acknowledged source (E. I. Watkin's description of the English countryside surrounding the shrine at Walsingham) with the introduction of the Sailor in line 9. Suddenly we realize that this passage is a rendering of a conventional conception of Heaven—one held, perhaps, by the dead cousin, and similar to his grandfather's "painted paradise of harps and lutes," depicted in "In Memory of Arthur Winslow." It recalls, too, the vision of Heaven in Milton's elegy:

> *So Lycidas sunk low, but mounted high*
> *Through the dear might of him that walk'd the waves*
> *Where other groves, and other streams along,*
> *With Nectar pure his oozy Lock's he laves,*
> *And hears the unexpressive nuptiall song*
> *In the blest Kingdoms meek of joy and love.*

The parallel is reinforced not only in terms of an individual consciousness preserved in transcendent regions but also in terms of the imagery of pleasant groves, calmed waters, and the joy of Salvation expressed in song. This is one way of thinking about immortality, Lowell suggests, but, characteristically, he rejects the simple and the merely conventional; ominously, the operative words in the stanza are the last two: "But see . . ." And in the vision that follows:

> *Our Lady, too small for her canopy,*
> *Sits near the altar. There's no comeliness*
> *At all, or charm in that expressionless*
> *Face with its heavy eyelids. As before,*
> *This face, for centuries a memory,*
> Non est species, neque decor,
> *Expressionless, expresses God: it goes*
> *Past castled Sion. She knows what God knows,*
> *Not Calvary's Cross nor crib at Bethlehem*
> *Now, and the world shall come to Walsingham.*

Lowell seems to be rejecting the anthropomorphic notion of Heaven, as "the castle of God," and the human desire for personal immortality, which, because it *is* human is somehow inferior to the vision which the Virgin shares with God. Significantly, her image in this shrine is strangely dehumanized: "There's no comeliness at all," her face is "expressionless" because it "expresses God." Evidently she is a part of the Peace that passeth men's understanding—a concept at which Milton hints in the phrase from "Lycidas": "the *unexpressive* nuptiall Song." At any rate, this is a loftier interpretation of the Godhead; one that—as Lowell points out—"goes *past* castled Sion." It is a state in which all human aspirations and concerns must be left behind: both the joy of birth ("the crib at Bethlehem") and the suffering of death ("Calvary's Cross"). As the whalers' priest, Father Mapple, says in the conclusion to his sermon on Jonah, the final prayer of the true Christian should be:

> I have striven to be Thine, more than to be this world's, or mine own. Yet this is nothing; I leave eternity to Thee; for what is man that he should live out the lifetime of his God? [2]

In other words, Lowell's view is that of the traditional Christian mystic, a view that accommodates an anthropomorphic theology only because it is necessary to have such an extended metaphor to bring those who are not capable of the higher mystical union with God to an approximation of the truth. It is for this reason that Plato relies

[2] *Moby Dick,* Chapter IX.

on myth and Jesus on parable. It is a transcendental conception of immortality very close to the climactic resolution of the antagonism of the Many and the One in "Adonais":

> *Life, like a dome of many-coloured glass*
> *Stains the white radiance of Eternity,*
> *Until Death tramples it to fragments.*

Or as Lowell himself puts it in the final line of the elegy:

> *The Lord survives the rainbow of His will.*

Appendix I

The Quaker Graveyard in Nantucket.

I.

The sea was still breaking . . .

Much of the imagery of the first dozen lines are taken from "The Shipwreck," which is the opening chapter of Thoreau's *Cape Cod*. The relevant passage reads as follows:

> The brig *St. John*, from Galway, Ireland, laden with emigrants, was wrecked on Sunday morning; it was now Tuesday morning, and the sea was still breaking violently on the rocks. There were eighteen or twenty of the same large boxes that I have mentioned, lying on a green hillside, a few rods from the water, and surrounded by a crowd. . . . I saw many marble feet and matted heads as the clothes were raised, and one livid, swollen, and mangled body of a drowned girl,—who probably had intended to go out to service in some American family,—to which some rags still adhered, with a string, half concealed by the flesh, about its swollen neck; the coiled-up wreck of a human hulk, gashed by the rocks or fishes, so that the bone and muscle were exposed, but quite bloodless,—merely red and white,—with wide-open and staring eyes, yet lustreless, dead lights; or like the cabin windows of a stranded vessel, filled with sand . . ."
>
> —Henry David Thoreau, *Cape Cod,* Boston,
> Houghton Mifflin, 1898, pp. 5–6.

III.

Nantucket's westward haven . . .

"Westward" here appears to be a mistake for "eastward."

IS the whited monster . . .

The symbolic function of the white whale in "The Quaker Graveyard" has all the ambiguity of its prototype in *Moby Dick*. On a
literal level, it is of course the object of the Quakers, materialistic
greed. On the level of religious symbolism, Lowell has combined in
the whale both Old and New Testament conceptions of God; that is,
as Jehovah—inscrutable, wrathful and vengeful and as Christ, the
means of salvation. Here, for example, Lowell, in the phrase "IS, the
whited monster" has in mind such a formulation as that in *Exodus*
iii, 14:

"And God said unto Moses, I AM THAT I AM: and he said, Thus
shalt thou say unto the children of Israel, I AM hath sent me to you."

This is a reading which itself reflects a confusion in the mind of
early translators as to the meaning of the Tetragrammaton, and also
contains the idea of God as Essence. At the same time, however, I
think Lowell also means to retain by the word "IS" a reference to
Christ (*Iesus Salvator*). In this way, the Quaker whalers can be seen as
opposing themselves to the Will of God, represented as Jehovah, and
also by destroying the body of the whale, they are, as it were, repeating
the role of the Roman soldiers in the drama of the Crucifixion.

Note that Lowell uses this term ("IS") in a similar way in "Where
the Rainbow Ends."

IV.

Clamavinus, O depths . . .

Cf. *Psalms* cxxx, 1:
"Out of the depths have I cried unto thee, O Lord."

Let the sea-gulls wail/For water, etc. *. . .*

The idea here seems very close to Thoreau's reaction to the scene
of shipwreck, described in the same chapter as above:

> On the whole, it was not so impressive a scene as I might have ex-
> pected. If I had found one body cast upon the beach in lonely place,
> it would have affected me more. I sympathized rather with the winds
> and waves, as if to toss and mangle these poor human bodies was the
> order of the day. If this was the law of Nature, why waste any time
> in awe and pity? If the last day were come, we should not think so much
> about the separation of friends or the blighted prospects of indi-
> viduals . . .

(*Cape Cod,* p. 11.)

Who will dance/The mast-lashed master of Leviathans . . .

The reference is to Ahab, who, however, becomes finally lashed to
the white whale itself. Lowell is also combining here two other allusions: (1) to Odysseus, a wiser man than Ahab, who had himself
lashed to the mast in order to avoid certain destruction in his pursuit
of knowledge (symbolized by the Sirens); and (2) the myth of Orpheus,
whose attempt to recover Eurydice from Hades ended in failure. The
point here is the same as that stated in stanza I—"Ask for no Orphean
lute/To pluck life back."—i.e., the power of the sea (and of God) is
invincible and irrevocable.

the great ash-pit of Jehoshaphat . . .

Friar and Brinnin, in their *Modern Poetry,* quote Lowell as identifying this phrase with "The day of judgment. The world, according
to some prophets, will end in fire." In the third chapter of *Joel,* as
Walter B. Rideout has pointed out, there is a description of God's
judgment at the last day taking place in the valley of Jehoshaphat.

the death-lance churns into the sanctuary

Some of the imagery of this passage seems to be adapted from
Chapter 61 of *Moby Dick*—"Stubb Kills a Whale," just as the description of the sinking ship later in this stanza is taken from the
final chapter, which portrays the destruction of the Pequod.

VI.

As Lowell indicates in a prefatory note to *LWC,* " 'Our Lady of
Walsingham' is an adaptation of several paragraphs from E. I. Watkin's *Catholic Art and Culture.*" The central passage is:

> For centuries the shrine of Our Lady of Walsingham has been an
> historical memory. Now once again pilgrims visit her image erected in a
> mediaeval chapel, where, it is said, they took off their shoes to walk
> barefoot the remaining mile to the shrine and to which, there is some
> reason to think, a hermitage was attached. The shrine has been spared
> the tawdry ornament and commercialised vulgarity which made Huys-
> mans conclude that the devil, the lord of ugliness, had been permitted
> to take possession of the architecture and ornaments of Lourdes. The
> road to the chapel is a quiet country lane shaded with trees, and lined
> on one side by a hedgerow. On the other, a stream flows down beneath
> the trees, the water symbol of the Holy Spirit, "the waters of Shiloah
> that go softly," the "flow of the river making glad the city of God."
> Within the chapel, an attractive example of Decorated architecture, near
> an altar of mediaeval fashion, is seated Our Lady's image. It is too small

for its canopy, and is not superficially beautiful. "Non est species neque decor," there is no comeliness of charm in that expressionless face with heavy eyelids. But let us look carefully, and allow the image, as every work of art should be allowed, to speak to us in its own language. We become aware of an inner beauty more impressive than outward grace. That expressionless countenance expresses what is beyond expression. It is the countenance of one whose spirit dwells in a region beyond emotion and thought, the centre of which mystical writers speak. Mary is beyond joy and sorrow. For her spirit is in God, and she knows as He knows, receiving His knowledge. No longer the Mother of Sorrows nor yet the human joy of the crib, she understands the secret counsel of God to whose accomplishment Calvary and Bethlehem alike ministered. Therefore her peace, the central peace of God, is beyond the changes of earthly experience. And the inscrutability of that illegible countenance is the inscrutability of the Divine Will made known to her.

—E. I. Watkin, *Catholic Art and Culture,* London, Hollis and Carter, 1947 (Revised edition—first published 1942), p. 177.

VI.

Shiloah . . . Sion

Watkin's mention of Shiloah evidently suggested to Lowell another Miltonic association—with the opening lines of *Paradise Lost*:

'or if *Sion* Hill
Delight thee more, and *Siloa's* Brook that flow'd
Fast by the Oracle of God . . .'

VI.

Similarly, the desecration of the Ark by the presence of the false god, Dagon (I Samuel v) reminds Lowell of the "Atlantic . . . fouled with blue sailors" leading him to describe the corpses who have died for Mammon in Miltonic terms: "Sea-monsters, upward angel, downward fish": an adaptation of *Paradise Lost*, I, 462-3.

The Age of Lowell

by Irvin Ehrenpreis

For an age of world wars and prison states, when the Faustian myth of science produces the grotesquerie of fall-out shelters, the decorous emotion seems a fascinated disgust. After outrage has exhausted itself in contempt, after the mind has got the habit of Dallas and South Africa, the shudder of curiosity remains. Every morning we think, something new and insufferable is about to happen: what is it? Among living poets writing in English nobody has expressed this emotion with the force and subtley of Robert Lowell. In an undergraduate poem Lowell described himself as longing for the life of straightforward beliefs and deeds, of simple lust, conventional faith and boyish sports. But "sirens sucked me in," he said; and painful, feverish contemplation was his fate:

> On me harsh birches, nursing dew,
> Showered their warm humidity.
>
> ("The Dandelion Girls")

Like Baudelaire, he saw things so disturbing that they almost kept him from making them into poetry.

Yet the confident life of public action might have seemed young Lowell's certain destiny. For his family line ran about as high as an American genealogy could go. His mother was descended from Edward Winslow, a Pilgrim Father who came to America on the *Mayflower*. Edward's son was a mighty Indian killer and a governor of Plymouth Colony. Lowell's mother also traced herself to the New Hampshire frontiersman John Stark, who was made a colonel at Bunker Hill and a general in the Revolutionary War. Lowell's father, though trained as a naval officer, belonged to the intellectual family that produced teachers and clergymen as well as fighters. The original R. T. S. Lowell, five generations ago, was also a naval officer. Another namesake,

"The Age of Lowell" by Irvin Ehrenpreis. From *Stratford upon Avon Studies 7* ed. John Russell Brown and Bernard Harris. Copyright © 1965 by Edward Arnold (Publishers) Ltd. Reprinted by permission of the author and Edward Arnold (Publishers) Ltd.

Lowell's great-grandfather, "delicate, sensitive, strangely rarefied," was a poet best known for a ballad on the relief of Lucknow, and spent four years as headmaster of St. Mark's, one of the most fashionable boys' schools in the United States. Lowell's great-great-uncle, James Russell Lowell, a Harvard professor and one of the famous poets of his era, became ambassador to the court of St. James's. For most of the memories on which Lowell was bred, Puritan New England, especially Boston, provided the setting; and in the history of the Massachusetts Bay Colony he could find his Tree of Jesse.

It was on these very elements that he was to turn his first great storm of poetic disgust. They supplied the object of a clamorous repudiation. The shape the outburst took, however, depended less on ancestry than on a set of experiences that seem to have determined Lowell's original literary color: his meeting with the circle of John Crowe Ransom and Allen Tate, his conversion to Roman Catholicism and his dramatic response to the second world war.

At St. Mark's School, Lowell found his interest in poetry encouraged by the poet Richard Eberhart, one of the teachers. He began experimenting with free verse but soon switched to stanzaic forms. As an undergraduate at Harvard he went to see Robert Frost, bearing a "huge epic" on the First Crusade. The great man perused a page, told the visitor that he lacked "compression," and read him Collins's "How Sleep the Brave" as an example of something "not too long." For a period Lowell tried to write simple, imagistic poems like those of W. C. Williams; but the university around him seemed less than a nest of singing birds, and he heeded a recommendation that he should study under John Crowe Ransom. In the middle of his undergraduate career, after a summer spent with Allen Tate, he left Harvard altogether and went to Kenyon College, in rural Ohio, where Ransom was teaching.

For a while now, Lowell even lived in Ransom's house, and later shared lodgings with two other young writers, one of whom, Peter Taylor, has published a short story based on their college friendship ("1939"). During these years, the critic Randall Jarrell taught English at Kenyon, and he too lived a while with the Ransoms. It seems obvious that the network of literary affiliations gave the young student, who had been growing "morose and solitary" at home, a welcome substitute for blood relations who felt small sympathy with his talent. Lowell often describes himself as belonging to the "second generation" of the Fugitives; he spent long periods in a quasi-filial or fraternal connection with three or four of the authors he met in the years before the war, and he speaks of them with the sort of loyalty one extends to kin. The conservative politics, strong but orthodox religious faith, and high literary standards to which these Southerners were attached must have

seemed to him seductive alternatives to the commonplace Repub-
licanism, mechanical church-going and materialist aspirations that
characterized a "Boston" formed (as he saw it) by successive lines of
Puritans, Unitarians and low-church Episcopalians. To Lowell the
home of his forebears stood for a rootless but immobile sterility.

In 1940, when he took a step towards establishing a family of his
own, Lowell not surprisingly married another writer, the novelist
Jean Stafford, whose "flaming insight" he commemorates in a recent
poem. He was also converted to Roman Catholicism, the church peculiarly associated in Boston with the large population descended from
humble Irish immigrants, natural enemies, in politics and culture, of
his own class. But the poet already felt committed to a kind of moral
vitality that could for only a limited time be expressed in Roman
terms. During the period when his new-found church was something
defiant of the Boston he had repudiated, and so long as the language,
symbols, and ritual represented materials to be conquered and employed for explosive purposes, he could use Catholicism as an ingredient of poetry. But when it was only the faith he had to accept, the
church came to seem as oppressive and self-contradictory as the code of
his native class.

It was during the years of his first marriage and his adherence to the
church that Lowell's earliest books of poetry appeared. Apart from
what had come out in an undergraduate magazine, the first poems he
published were a pair in the *Kenyon Review* 1939. But years went by
before any successors could be seen in print, partly because the few he
wrote were rejected when he sent them out. Then in 1943 about a
dozen of his poems turned up in the literary quarterlies, to be followed
the next year by a collection, *Land of Unlikeness*. This gathering, with-
holding and sudden releasing of his work is typical of the poet's
method; for he labors over his poems continually and plans each collection as a sequence, the opening and closing poems in each making a
distinct introduction and conclusion, and the movement between them
tending from past to present, from question to resolution, from
ambiguous negation to hesitant affirmative.

Above the influences of Ransom and Tate, or the steady use of
Catholic religious imagery, or the many motifs drawn from Boston
and New England, the most glaring feature of Lowell's two earliest
volumes was a preoccupation with the second world war. Not long
after the United States joined that war, he committed the most dramatic public act of his life. Characteristically, this act seemed at once
violent and passive, and was calculated to make his parents very un-
comfortable. In what turned out to be no more than preliminary
steps, he twice tried to enlist in the navy but was rejected. Soon, however, the mass bombing of non-combatants shocked his moral prin-

ciples; and when he was called up under the Selective Service Act, he declared himself a conscientious objector. Rather than simply appear before the responsible board and declare his convictions, he refused to report at all, and thus compelled the authorities to prosecute him.

In order to give his deed the widest possible significance, he released to the press a thousand-word open letter to President Roosevelt. Here Lowell drew repeated attention to the historic eminence of his ancestors. He described himself as belonging to a family that had "served in all our wars, since the Declaration of Independence"; he told the President that the Lowell family traditions, "like your own, have always found their fulfillment in maintaining, through responsible participation in both civil and military services, our country's freedom and honor." He said that he had tried to enlist when the country was in danger of invasion but that this danger was past, and the intention of bombing Japan and Germany into submission went against the nation's established ideals. He could not participate in a war, Lowell said, that might leave Europe and China "to the mercy of the U.S.S.R., a totalitarian tyranny committed to world revolution."

Twenty years later he was still signing open letters of protest to newspapers; and although his opinions had altered, their direction had not shifted. "No nation should possess, use, or retaliate with its bombs," he wrote in a 1962 symposium. "I believe we should rather die than drop our own bombs." It is suggestive of the poet's sensibility that he should link suicide with mass murder, as though the way to prevent the second might be to commit the first. The themes of self-destruction and assassination are often joined in his work, the one apparently redeeming or proving the altruism of the other. Yet parricide becomes a mythical, guilt-ridden route to justice and liberty; for by throwing over the traditional family pieties, the young Lowell seems to have felt he was destroying his begetters and oppressors.

* * *

The poems that appeared in *Land of Unlikeness* (1944) were mostly written during a year Lowell spent with the Tates after leaving Kenyon College. In them he devoted himself mainly to a pair of themes reflecting recent history. One was the un-Christian character of the Allies' role in the second world war; the other was the causal connection between the doctrines of America's founders and the desolate condition, spiritual and material, of the country in the thirties. Looking back, Lowell saw in the ideals and motives of his ancestors the same contradictions, the same denial of a Christ they professed to worship, that made his own world a land of unlikeness, i.e. a place obliterating the image of divinity, a culture where the old metaphors that made created beings recall their creator, no longer operated. Those who

had flown from persecution came here to persecute the red men; those
who hated war made war on nature, plundering whales and neighbours
for unspiritual profit.

In order to dramatize and generalize this view, he drew parallels between divine and human history: between the war and Doomsday,
between the dust bowl sharecroppers and Cain. And he set up an-
titheses: between profits and mercy, between political slogans and
charity. To the second world war he opposed Christ. In the social and
political theories of the Fugitives, Lowell found support for his tendency to identify degeneracy with the city, the machine, and Roosevelt's centralized democracy, even as he associated true civilization with
rural, aristocratic society. And since the South itself was yielding to
the rapid movement from one set of conditions to the other, Lowell
could apply his argument to humanity in general, through parallels
drawn from *Genesis* and *Revelation,* from the myth of Troy, and from
history. Thus the advent of cosmopolitan industrialism becomes a sign
that we are all descended from Cain; the first Eden becomes a symbol
of that ante-bellum, ostensibly Augustan society which the North supposedly destroyed; the fall of Troy becomes the analogue of the defeat
of the South. Since the new war had the effect of speeding the hated
process, it was easily drawn into this aspect of Lowell's rhetoric.

By the time he composed these poems, Lowell had given up free
verse and was writing obscure poems in metre in a style of his own.
Most of those in *Land of Unlikeness* are savagely ironical. Besides
employing puns or conceits repeatedly and with great earnestness, he
brought in hackneyed phrases and common tags of quotations, giving
sarcastic new directions to their meaning. He invented grotesque
metaphors, such as "Christ kicks in the womb's hearse." Although the
stanzas of most of the poems are elaborate, the rhythms are heavy, the
sounds are cluttered, alliteration occurs often and unsubtly.

Into such verses he pressed enough violence of feeling to stun a sensitive ear. Certain dramatic monologues and visionary pieces on religious themes make the greatest uproar. The tighter the stanza forms,
the wilder the bitterness: erratic rhythms, blasphemous images, deliberately hollow rhetoric erupt over the objects of his onslaught. But
instead of the tight form providing an ironic contrast or intensifying
counterpoint to the violent tone, it seems arbitrary. The mind that
follows the form seems cut off from the mouth that screams the
sacrilege:

> In Greenwich Village, Christ the Drunkard brews
> Gall, or spiked bone-vat, siphons His bilged blood
> Into weak brain-pans and unseasons wood. . . .

("Christ for Sale")

In another poem the speaker is a slum mother apostrophizing the corpse of her baby, who has died on Christmas Day, 1942 (soon after the sinking of the British aircraft carrier *Ark Royal*):

> So, child, unclasp your fists,
> And clap for Freedom and Democracy;
> No matter, child, if Ark Royal lists
>   Into the sea;
>   Soon the Leviathan
>   Will spout American.
>
> ("The Boston Nativity")

In this kind of satire the irony sounds so wild that most readers ignore the poet's meaning while observing his frenzy. The caricature of the nativity scene does not succeed in mocking America's moral pretensions during the war. It only forces upon one's perceptions the distorted religiosity of the writer. After all, by Lowell's own argument, there could be no real heroes in history apart from Christ. As in Tate's "Aeneas at Washington," the Southern gentleman comes finally to seem less like Hotspur than like Richard II, standing for ideals he did not die to defend.

Yet not every speech is a tantrum. In a few of the poems Lowell's detachment suggests that his churnings, in the others, are an effort to produce a heat wave in a naturally cold climate. Observation, dry and wry commentary, fascinated disgust—these are the marks of his subtler self, and these are what appear, for example, in "The Park Street Cemetery." This poem, a survey of the tombstones in a Boston graveyard, has less violence than distaste in its tone. Lowell treats the site as a repository of those Puritan colonists who bequeathed to the America they founded their own confusion of grace with fortune. The form is appropriately relaxed: three stanzas, each of seven unrhymed, irregular lines; and the poet ends not with a scream but a deadnote:

> The graveyard's face is painted with facts
> And filagreed swaths of forget-me-nots.

The positive doctrines of *Land of Unlikeness* seem less significant than the negative directions. Whether Lowell espouses Southern agrarianism or Roman Catholicism, his principles attract him less as ideals of aspiration than as possibilities disdained by his ancestors. Against early New England the real charge he makes is that it failed to meet its own ultimate standards; for Lowell is after all another sober moralist with a Puritan's severity. He scolds Boston as Blake scolded London: for the death of vision and the death of conscience. Nowhere does he imply that dogma bestows serenity, or that, as some Southerners

would argue, the integrity of a ceremonious traditionalism outweighs
the human misery on which it may rest.

For the poet, finally, the real problem remained unsolved. In most
of this volume his best-integrated poems were his understatements;
those that showed the highest technical ambition were bathetic. He had
to find a style that would reconcile his interest in technique with his
interest in justice, that would identify private with public disturbances.
For such a style the elements lay not in the regularity of his stanzas,
not in the depth of his piety, and not in his political judgments. It lay
in Lowell's preoccupation with tone, in his humanitarian conscience,
and in his sense of history. When he employed these to enlarge the
meaning of an immediate personal experience, he produced the best
poems in *Land of Unlikeness*: "The Park Street Cemetery," "In
Memory of Arthur Winslow," "Concord," and "Salem."

*   *   *

Not only the older writers belonging to the circle of Ransom and
Tate but also several other critics gave unusual attention to *Land of
Unlikeness*. It was praised briefly but intensely by F. W. Dupee and
Arthur Mizener. There was a careful review by Blackmur and a
eulogy by J. F. Nims. But when Lowell's next book *Lord Weary's
Castle* appeared (1946), the critical reception became a thunder of
welcome.

As usual, there is a link between the old work and the new. In the
last poem of *Land of Unlikeness* the poet had mentioned the curse of
"exile" as the alternative to the blessing of Canaan: God offered Israel
the choice, says the poet; and when Israel chose to turn away from
God's "wise fellowship," the outcome was Exile. The opening poem of
Lord Weary's Castle is called "The Exile's Return," suggesting a common theme for both books. But the theme has broadened. In the new
collection the poet implies that nothing was or could be settled by the
war. In rejecting divine leadership, it is moral justice, the creative principle bringing order out of chaos, that we have banished from its self-
made home. Thus if the expatriate is taken to mean Christ, the lord
still waits for the world he built to pay him his due homage. He still
menaces us with the judgment that the war prefigured. As a creator,
however, the Exile is also the poet or artist; and in this sense he wants
to be paid for the truthful visions with which he has blessed an ungrate-
ful world. For he holds out the threat of a poet's curse, and his isolation remains the mark of society's misdirection. In a private extension
of this sense the Exile is Lowell himself, released from jail after serving
about five months of the year and a day to which he had been sentenced. Coming back to ordinary routines, he meets in new forms the
same moral issues he had wrestled with before his imprisonment.

All these implications are in "The Exile's Return." Here, an émigré comes back to his German home after the war, under the protection of American garrisons. But the shattered place looks the opposite of Eden; and if the first springtime brings lilies, it brings as well the agony of responsibility. To suggest the aspect of the neglected artist, Lowell crowds the poem with allusions to Mann's Tonio Kröger, who stood "between two worlds" without feeling at home among either the bourgeoisie or the artists. To suggest the themes of heaven and hell, he has seasonal references to an infernal winter, a spring of rebirth, the "fall" of autumn, and the entrance to Dante's hell. For the motifs of imprisonment and release he uses a jail-like hôtel-de-ville, a Yankee "commandant" and a parcel of "liberators" who are as yet innocent or "unseasoned."

In direct contrast, the closing poem of the book, "Where the Rainbow Ends," deals with an American city, Boston, that has never been bombed but that faces the dissolution caused by decay of conscience. Not war but winter devastates this city. Not as a refugee but as a voluntary exile from worldliness, the poet-prophet offers his people the alternative to the Judgment prefigured by the cold season:

> What can the dove of Jesus give
> You now but wisdom, exile? Stand and live,
> The dove has brought an olive branch to eat.
>   ("Where the Rainbow Ends")

Repeatedly in this book, Lowell shows an understanding of how his elemental powers might be fused, how his unnatural calmness of tone in dealing with horrifying material might be supported by an apparent casualness of style screening a meticulous exactness of underlying structure. His sense of the past justifies ironically the calmness of tone. For to the degree that one considers human misery and cruelty as the reflection of permanent instinct—rather than transient ignorance—one will view one's own corruption and one's neighbor's not with scandalized outbursts but with comprehending calm. Furthermore, through the distancing effect of history, as through the shaping effect of complex form, one can even achieve a coherent grasp of one's own deepest, most secret anguish. With these several powers Lowell also made good use of a set of influences that he had earlier felt only at some remove, as they were present in the work of Tate, Eliot, and Ransom. These influences emanate from the great line of French Symbolists and post-Symbolists, to whom the "modern" experimental movement in poetry owes its orgin. When Lowell turned to Rimbaud, Valéry, and Rilke for models, he was accepting the cosmopolitan conception of literature that American poets as diverse as Whitman and Pound have worked with.

The defect of *Lord Weary's Castle* is the same as that of *Land of Unlikeness*. In Whitman, Tate, and Hart Crane, one cannot help noticing a habit of substituting rhetoric, in the form of self-conscious sublimity, for poetry. If Lowell, their heir, yields to this habit, it is because, like them, he has the highest conception of the poet's task. But the mere posture of soaring, the air of prophecy, does not make a speech either noble or prophetic. In Lowell's most commonly over-praised work, "The Quaker Graveyard," the use of rhetoric joins with a denseness of symbolism to make a poem that seems more impressive for aspiration than for accomplishment.

Throughout this poem he contrasts two views of saving grace: the idea of a special gift to the elect, and the idea of something that infuses not merely all men but all creatures. The in-group's com-placency Lowell attaches to the Protestant sects of colonial New Eng-land and to his patriotic cousin, who died at sea for a cause Lowell rejected. As a measure of the limitations of this ethic, which he associ-ates with war-loving capitalism, Lowell invokes the great evolutionary chain of created beings. The world, he keeps saying, exists as a moral order in which separate men are not masters but participants: both the sea slime from which we rose and the whale that we plunder lie be-neath the same law that subsumes humanity. To sectarian arrogance he opposes the innocence of the humbler orders of creation, for whom cruelty is an accident of their nature. As the solvent of arrogance he offers the Catholic compassion of Christ embodied in Mary his mother.

In Lowell's usual manner, the end of the poem recalls the beginning. We move back to the Quaker graveyard on Nantucket Island off the coast of Massachusetts. But where the initial scene was of violent death in a great war, the closing gives us the lifeless cemetery of wind and stone and tree. Now the poet glances back to the very start of the evolutionary process and contrasts that moment, when life and death were born together, with the present outlook of a corpse-littered sea. And suddenly the capacious cemetery of the Atlantic becomes a sym-bolic contrast to the filled graveyard of the Quakers: God has more room than this; the old covenant has given way to the new gospel.

In this fascinating work the failure of the rhetoric grows obvious if we notice the weakness of the poem's penultimate section. Here Lowell puts the snug, familiar salvation that his cousin might aspire to beside the Catholic vision of the universal but quite unknowable God reflected in the image of Our Lady of Walsingham. Though this pas-sage is a deliberate understatement, the effect is not powerful by implication; rather, it sounds bathetic. Beyond human griefs or joys, says the poet, the Virgin

> knows what God knows,
> Not Calvary's Cross nor crib at Bethlehem
> Now, and the world shall come to Walsingham.

If we compare Lowell's two stanzas, in their attempt to express the inexpressible, with similar passages in Eliot's "Dry Salvages" (which is, with *Lycidas,* one of the models for this poem), we must admit that there is a posed air, a willed simplicity, in Lowell's lines that never appears in, say, "Lady, whose shrine stands on the promontory," etc. This forced tone seems the more regrettable because Lowell's passage is meant to deliver the positive alternative to the errors he denounces with such thoroughness. It is in the overcharged stretches of churning sounds, eruptive rhythm, and violent imagery that we seem to hear the authentic voice of the poet:

> In the great ash-pit of Jehoshaphat
> The bones cry for the blood of the white whale,
> The fat flukes arch and whack about its ears. . . .

We cannot help feeling that he enjoys his destructive vision in a way not compatible with his role as prophet, moralist, or recipient of wisdom.

In another long poem, "At the Indian-Killer's Grave," Lowell gives a more appropriate display of his powers. The history of its composition reminds us of his habitual alteration of his own work; for much of the poem comes out of the "Park Street Cemetery," and the closing lines are a magnificent adaptation of verses from another early poem. Moreover, as he transforms these materials, the poet enlarges their meaning. Like the speaker in Tate's "Ode to the Confederate Dead," the poet here contemplates a graveyard where his direct or spiritual ancestors are buried among their peers. Unlike Tate's speaker, however, he searches for the meaning of their sins, not their virtues. Staring about at the figures carved on the gravestones among the vegetation, he contrasts the Puritan dead with the living Irish who now hold political power in Boston. The sound of a train stopping underground makes him think of time stopping and of the Judgment to come; and he wonders about the fate of the Pilgrims' souls. He imagines the spirit of the Red Indian chief, King Philip, addressing the Puritan Indian-killers and reminding them that all their pretensions to being the chosen of God have left them only the corrupted bodies that now serve as carrion for sea-gulls. He looks at the toothed railing, thinks of dragon's teeth, and ponders the double source, natural (i.e. Cadmean) and spiritual (i.e. Adamic), of our instinct for evil. Then in a sudden, astonishing close, the poet turns from the old law to the new, from Adam to Christ; and he calls on the four evangelists to guide

him towards the inclusive faith of the Roman Catholic church, to a
vision of salvation that more than admits the Indian chief; for it
promises Philip that the blessed Virgin herself will deck out his head
with flowers:

> John, Matthew, Luke and Mark,
> Gospel me to the Garden, let me come
> Where Mary twists the warlock with her flowers—
> Her soul a bridal chamber fresh with flowers
> And her whole body an ecstatic womb,
> As through the trellis peers the sudden Bridegroom.

And there, in a fine identification of his private conversion with both
the history of Massachusetts and the religious or mythical account of
all human history, Lowell brings his poem to a close.

Generally, the poet sounds a tone of self-restraint, of calm but en-
grossed repugnance, that reminds one of Ransom's poems "Necro-
logical" and "Armageddon." This tone he drops appropriately in two
counterbalanced passages: the outburst of Philip, who speaks with a
savage violence of sound and image, and the lyric close and climax,
when calm is replaced by rapture. The apparently loose-knit free associations rest on a carefully adjusted underpinning. Even the setting
of the poet's meditation belongs to his subject, because the Puritan
colonists brooded hourly upon death and the grave. They dressed in
black and regarded the beauties of animate nature as bad diversions
from the proper study of man, viz. death and judgment, heaven and
hell. Nevertheless, they proudly gave themselves the title of the elect
of God, promoting themselves to Paradise. It is a tremendous historical
irony that their haughty Calvinism should have given way, in Boston,
to the avowedly humble, Catholic faith of the Irish—to the church that
in colonial times proselytized among the Indians instead of beheading
them. In effect, the whore of Rome waltzes over the Puritan graves:
"the trollop dances on your skulls."

A shimmering elaboration of imagery in the Symbolist manner connects the past and the present, the beginning of the poem with the end,
the surface and the meaning. As the poet questions the spectacle
before him, he wonders whether the fate of the dead is knowable or
whether the pagan idea of vengeance may not be carried out, so that
Philip may eternally scalp the self-styled righteous men (Blake's "just
man") who killed his people. This scalp-head-skull image appears
again and again in the poem, reaching its most brilliant transformation at the end, when the Virgin is pictured as twisting Philip's "war-
lock" or pigtail with flowers. Between these points the head becomes
the English crown, responsible for building King's Chapel—a motif
that opposes King Charles to King Philip. It then turns into the

"dome" of the Statehouse that replaced the royal authority. Next, Philip's head reappears on a "platter" or gravestone. The phrasing recalls St. John and therefore the apostle or evangelist Philip. As a prophet now, the Indian can address his damned enemies and point out that the Catholics are raised over their heads. The dome becomes a globe that is the natural world, rejected (so says the poet) by the Puritans as they "hurled/Anathemas at nature." The head reappears in the headstones of the graves and finally in Mary's handling of Philip's head.

Parallel to these metamorphoses move the images of the garden. We start in the desolate garden of the cemetery, which the Puritans have reached in place of Paradise. Shrubs and sculpture remind one of similar scenes. So the view expands into both the Public Garden, where the Beacon Hill brahmins walked, and the Boston Common, which was more likely the playground of the Irish. Lowell toys with the ironies implicit in "garden" and "common," and with the further irony that though fashionable Beacon Hill is where his own class live, it is topped by the Statehouse that in effect belongs to the Irish. Under the Common, meanwhile, runs the subway, analogue of hell, with its serpentine green trains, symbolic of time. Easily enough, the Garden and the Common expand into the whole "land" that the Puritans denounced and despoiled. This contracts at once into the mud that buries them now. The buildings around the Common are like palisades around the early settlements, intended, however, not to keep the wilderness from swallowing the villages but to keep, as it were, the remnant of natural ground from spreading. Finally, the motif reminds the poet of the ground in which Cadmus sowed the dragon's teeth, emblematic of original sin.

* * *

It seems remarkable that while some of the best poems in *Lord Weary's Castle* were imitations, or free English versions, of works in other languages, some of the least effective were dramatic monologues. In a poem like "The Ghost," based upon Sextus Propertius, Lowell performed a superb job of giving his own voice to another poet. But in the double-monologue "The Death of the Sheriff," the structure of which depends upon changes of voice and shifts in point of view, the speaker's smothered, crowded, dull murmur hardly alters from beginning to end. It's as though Lowell had too much to say to be able to submerge himself in an imaginary personality, and for that very reason found it easy to submerge a sympathetic author's character in his own.

His next book, *Mills of the Kavanaughs* (1951), brought these complementary tendencies to a crisis. The unqualified successes in it are a

dazzling pastiche of Virgil and an adaptation of Werfel. But the long-
est and most ambitious works are five attempts at narrative dramatized
through monologue. In four of these one feels that the poet has contrived situations offering the greatest opportunities for allusiveness and
symbolism, and has sacrificed to such opportunities the absolutely
essential narrative line upon which any dramatic monologue depends.
He had obviously worked with immense pains over the title poem,
running to more than five hundred lines, many of them beautiful
evocations of the Maine landscape that gives the piece its setting.
Nevertheless, although the plot would sound irresistibly sensational in
summary—dealing with the madness and suicide of a patrician Catholic who married his sister by adoption—the poem is so hemmed in by
cross-references and correspondences as to be wholly static. At one
point Lowell goes so far as to match the number of a figure on a bird
guide, once memorized by the protagonist, to the number of the stanza
in which the man tries to recall the bird's name. The same substitution
of arbitrary parallelism for narrative drama almost makes an impasse
out of the last poem in the book, "Thanksgiving's Over." Here Lowell
sends his main characters to a church on Thirty-First Street in New
York, and situates their home next to the Third Avenue elevated train
("El"), in order to supply allusions to the Trinity.

Yet "Thanksgiving's Over" is one of the most revealing of Lowell's
poems. Published two years after his divorce from Jean Stafford and
the year after his marriage to the essayist Elizabeth Hardwick, it comes
from a time when he no longer felt buoyed up by the church. Louise
Bogan called the book *Mills of the Kavanaughs* a "dark midpoint" in
his development, "which must in some way be transcended." In this
closing poem Lowell shows that he was passing the midpoint and
going on. All the ingredients of his false rhetorical style are here: the
monologue, the nightmare, madness, murder, suicide, and blasphemy.
But the implications are not the old ones.

To the speaker of the poem Lowell gives the voice of a man who
has lost the struggle to maintain his Christian faith and now ponders
the events that culminated in his failure. He is a Roman Catholic, a
New Yorker, and a widower, whose young, demented wife had believed
herself impregnated by the Holy Ghost. After she tried to kill herself
by jumping from a window, he sent her to a sanatorium in the mountains of Vermont, where she died. It is now Thanksgiving Day, 1942,
and Michael the widower half remembers, half dreams of his dead wife.
As he tries to make sense out of the monstrous experiences, he thinks
he hears her talking.

The themes of the wife's increasingly disconnected chatter are love
and peace, her assumption being that these are united in the church.
But as her incoherence deepens, it becomes clear that the serenity she

offers is available only to those who are as credulous as children. Within the wife's character, therefore, the themes are split so as to suggest the opposition between religious doctrines and human nature. She would like to feel love as spiritual charity, and therefore denies her passionate impulses. She would like morality to issue from the passive acceptance of authority, and so she denies the need for a struggle between the good and evil in our constitution. Through suppression, her hidden passions become adulterous lusts projected on other persons. Towards Michael her affection turns to jealousy, and she feels like killing him. When this wish is thwarted, the hate turns inward, and she tries to kill herself.

The poet implies that by giving up religion one might resolve some of these conflicts, but one would then have to face the pain of a life without ultimate meaning. Michael must choose between abandoning God and abandoning his rational conscience. As the peculiarly shocking symbol of his dilemma the poet focuses on the doctrine of the Trinity. Thus the action of the poem is set at the very end of the Trinity season, the week before Advent Sunday. Since the third person of the Trinity appears iconographically as a dove, there is a profusion of sacrilegious bird imagery. In order to involve other aspects of doctrine or ritual, the poet complicates the central theme with allusions to the Eucharist (etymologically "thanksgiving"), the Incarnation (as enacted in the Annunciation), and so forth. As a kind of parody of each, he produces natural analogues. Within the fantasy of the girl's unconscious the Trinity takes the form of a love triangle. She confuses the Dove with a celluloid parrot and imagines herself pregnant with birds. Since the conventional dish at an American Thanksgiving dinner is a turkey, the poet can introduce grotesque ambiguities signifying the sterility of the Holy Ghost or the end of Michael's belief: "My fowl was soupbones."

In flying from adultery to death, the girl was impelled by a guilt due to religion. So against the ideal of sexless conception displayed in paintings of the Annunciation, the poet sets the pagan fertility of "St. Venus" in Botticelli's Primavera. Against the child's sexless world of faith (evoked by allusions to Mother Goose rhymes, nursery tales and Peter Pan) he sets the world of parenthood. In a distortion of phrases from the *Messiah* we hear the solution that Michael cannot yet accept: birds singing, "Come unto us, our burden's light"—not the Dove but the birds of nature, of light and Lucifer and reason.

Over such themes the poet builds his characteristic sort of towering edifice; for the poem stands on an amazing reticulation of allusions. *Paradise Lost,* for obvious reasons, is continually evoked. The wretched couple are identified with Faust and Gretchen or with Hamlet and Ophelia. From her asylum window the wife sees the harpies of Baude-

laire's "Cythère." Yet the essential image and meaning of the poem
do not hinge on such clues. Michael sits and listens at the end of the
poem, but he does not pray or receive a sign. It seems certain that
when he boards a train, it will take him away from "this deaf and
dumb/Breadline for children"—as the wife unintentionally describes
Roman Catholicism for the poet.

In Michael we confront again those linked themes of passive observation and wild impulse to travel that underlie so much of the nightmare violence in Lowell's poems. The wife's confinement in a cell
reflects Michael's emotional seclusion. For the faithful Christian, life is
a cage from which he escapes to Life; for the fallen Christian the
limits of mere life make another kind of cage. Afraid to stir, for fear
of wrecking the object of his stirring, the poet repeatedly speaks as a
walled-off voyeur frantically watching the lives of others. Like a traveller in a sealed railway car, he passes over the earth, looking but never
doing, always on the move and never in motion: he has replaced action
by vision.

*   *   *

Lowell has said it was hard for him to find a subject and a language
of his own. He can describe himself as writing a rather formal style
coming out of Tate, Hart Crane, Ransom, and Eliot. But when he composed the brilliant, influential poems that were collected in *Life Studies*
(1959), he took a line less reminiscent of those masters than of Pound.
At last he had discovered his language and subject.

By the time this book appeared, Lowell had received enough prizes
and awards to ease most men's desire for public recognition. He was
the father of an infant daughter (born January, 1957); he was a member of the Boston University Department of English; and he held the
honorary degree of Doctor of Letters. Yet he had suffered a deeply
disturbing experience when his mother died (February, 1954); and the
emotional pressures evident in his poetry had undermined his health
until he was forced to turn for aid to hospital treatments.

The continuance of the emotional strains, tempered by domestic
amenities and balanced by extraordinary marks of success in his career,
seem to have enabled Lowell to discover the best uses for his talent.
Superficially the transformation appeared in the lightening of his
style. Lowell has said that soon after the *Mills of the Kavanaughs* came
out, the pace of his writing slowed almost to a halt, and his allusive,
rhetorical manner came to seem "distant, symbol-ridden and wilfully
difficult." He felt that his old poems too often hid what they were
about, presenting a "stiff, humourless and even impenetrable surface."
So he began paraphrasing Latin quotations when he used them, and
adding extra syllables to lines in order to make them clearer or more

colloquial. With such a poem as the short, perfect "In the Cage" (1946)—a tetrameter sonnet recapturing the grimness of the months he spent in jail—he had already shown the strength of a comparatively unadorned language, free from obscurities but suffused with irony. This manner now became not the exception but the rule. Line after line, in poem after poem, reads like a well-turned but easily spoken remark made by a fastidious, self-critical speaker who is at home with slang.

But the ease of language was only the outer sign of Lowell's new attitude towards his own nature. Without losing the tone of fascinated disgust, he now found it possible not only to treat himself as part of history but to treat history as part of himself. The course of his life became the analogue of the life of his era; the sufferings of the poet became a mirror of the sufferings of whole classes and nations. It was not as a judge that he now claimed his authority: it was as the heroic artist, the man capable of turning vision into act. Through the title of his book Lowell gave himself the status of a craftsman who reveals life in general by the rendering of his own life.

Appropriately enough, *Life Studies* opens with a train journey from the city of priests to the city of artists, Rome to Paris. But the speaker is neither a character in a dramatic monologue nor an impersonal commentator. He is the poet talking about his own experiences. Here as generally in the book, Lowell has of course invented facts and altered truths. Yet the reader feels himself in touch with the real author and not with a mask. Similarly, the entrance into the poem is deliberately casual, with what look like random associations suggesting the real flow of a unique consciousness.

If the formal frame is thus a common earthly journey, the object presented is a miraculous one: the bodily assumption of the Virgin, proclaimed as dogma in the jubilee year 1950. So the title "Beyond the Alps" means not only a trip towards France but also its opposite, "ultramontane," or the old epithet for supporters of papal infallibility. Lowell is using that doctrine, which the proclamation of the new dogma pressed to a record-breaking extreme, as the emblem of vulgar human credulity—the decay of imagination into superstition—a principle embodied in the pope. To escape from such tempting corruptions, the poet struggles within himself, during the night of his train journey, emerging at dawn into a sense of rebirth, a commitment to the creative imagination. Turning towards the intellect and the arts—towards Athene and Apollo—he rejects Mary and Pius. The pope is depicted, with grotesque irony, between a purring electric razor in one hand (the cat of rational science) and a canary in the other (the dove of faith).

In keeping with the opposition between religion and art, Lowell treats the mountains that appear in his poem as versions of Parnassus. So the journey recalls the celebrated simile, in Pope's *Essay on Criticism,* comparing the Alps to the challenge that art sets before the ambition of genius: "Hills peep o'er hills, and Alps on Alps arise." It is thus appropriate that at the time the poem opens, the inartistic Swiss should just have failed to climb Everest.

Violence, as usual in Lowell's work, accompanies the polarity of stillness and movement. By mentioning the Swiss (historic mercenary soldiers), the poet hints at the third principle of human nature which the poem deals with, i.e. destructive violence, personified by the warrior-king. The success of Caesarean terror in chaining the mind differs only in mode from the success of the magician-priest: Mussolini is as Roman as Pius. For an ideal culture, that could make violence, magic, and reason work together, Lowell offers not Rome but inimitable Hellas; and while the morning sun, like the imagination, transforms the bleak moonlit peaks into dazzling Parthenons, the reborn poet thinks of another traveller, Odysseus, escaping symbolically from the dark cave of Polyphemus by blinding the cyclops with a dazzling firebrand. Athene, the guide of Odysseus, easily united in herself all the roles to which popes and dictators aspire; the reader recalls that she was also *parthenos* or virgin, born miraculously without a mother, inspirer of a temple outshining St. Peter's; and Lowell reminds us that she sprang not from the flesh but from the intellect of Jove. To this white height the poet dare not attempt to climb. Only Paris is left, the "black classic" city of our own disintegrating culture; for our age seems unable to give direction and purpose to the primeval, irrational violence of human nature.

The intellectual design of this exhilarating poem has little system about it. Yet the texture, phrasing and versification offer immediate pleasures to the ear. It consists of three sonnets with slightly irregular rhyme schemes, the last of the three ending in a couplet that also serves as epigrammatic close to the whole work.[2] This pattern is enriched by a fullness of alliteration, assonance and internal rhyme that, so far from obtruding upon the offhand casualness of phrasing, only seems to deliver an ironical counter-thrust to it. Puns and other witticisms supply an elegant distance from which the poet can regard his own discomfort:

> I envy the conspicuous
> waste of our grandparents on their grand tours—
> long-haired Victorian sages accepted the universe, ˌ
> while breezing on their trust funds through the world.

[2] When Lowell revised this poem for his most recent collection, he also restored a fourth stanza which was judiciously omitted from the text in *Life Studies.*

The imagery has the same sort of forceful inconsequence: mountains and birds, tyrants and feet reappear in startling transformations as the wonderfully managed tone deepens from humor to bitterness to sublimity. The elaborate manipulations of height and depth, white and black, the four elements, are old habits of the poet. But the similar treatment of tiny details turns accidents into beauties. Thus the train stewards' tiptoe walk (while they ritually bang on their dinner gongs in a startling allusion to the Mass) becomes, in the second stanza, the toe of St. Peter, superstitiously kissed by pilgrims; and then, in the third, the splendor of the dawn of our culture as the poet sees

> Apollo plant his heels
> on terra firma through the morning's thigh.

It is not easy to overpraise *Life Studies*. I suppose the most startling ingredient in the book was the new direction taken by the poet's conscience. In place of either direct protest or the fusion of his own morality with that of a Christian community, Lowell attached himself to several classes of heroic victims: children, artists, imprisoned criminals, and the mentally ill. Though these have always been linked in the Romantic tradition, most poets dealing with them risk the dangers of posturing and sentimentality. Precisely through making his own case the central case, Lowell avoids either fault. Instead of merely seeing him, we see his view of his peers.

Thus by reviewing his early memories not as they point inward but as they revolve about this or that pathetic adult, he gives a toughening perspective to the sufferings of the child; for these are balanced by the sufferings the child either causes or ironically ignores in the adult. Dealing with poets, he secures a similar distance by balancing the ignominies of the external life against the victories of the imagination. When he handles his most recalcitrant material, the humiliating lives of psychotics, he can allow himself a comical irony that would sound intolerable coming from anyone but the inmate of an institution:

> There are no Mayflower
> screwballs in the Catholic Church.
> ("Waking in the Blue")

Of course, each of these figures also stands as a measure of the disorder in society: the unrewarded artist, the corrupted child, the madhouse that mirrors the world. Each further becomes an extension of the past: thanks in part to the mere movement of decades, Lowell can bestow on personal recollections the dignity of history:

> These are the tranquilized *Fifties*,
> And I am forty.
> ("Memories of West Street")

Not through the public aspect of his ancestry but through the independent private experiences of the struggling poet, he can serve as the record of his age, and connect that age with the sweep of earlier epochs.

In all these accomplishments the controlling factor is a matter of tone. If Lowell had not managed to infuse the despair of his disgust with the humor of his irony, he could not have established the framework that screens the reader from the simple pathos of most confessional verse. In the production of this tone, the use of slang, resharpened clichés and witticisms is crucial: instead of straining, as in Lowell's earlier work, to give the banalities of life a moral urgency (often without succeeding), they now suggest the speaker's mastery of his experience. It is this saving irony, energized by disgust, that carries him across his most difficult, self-destructive nights. When he emerges from the darkness of "Skunk Hour," the penultimate (originally the last) and almost the finest poem in this almost uniformly splendid book, what supports him and us is surely the power of his tolerance and humor, shoved smack up against a hideous crisis.

*   *   *

In tracing Lowell's career up to 1960, one may describe it as following two successive motions. When he wrote his earlier works, the poet tried to give them importance by starting from the great moral issues or crises of history and then matching those with themes derived from his private ordeals. After *Mills of the Kavanaughs,* however, he was willing to start from his private experiences and project these upon history and public life. Since the effect of the change was a fresh and distinctive kind of poetry, Lowell seems to have felt impelled to push his explorations further. Preoccupied as he was with the continuity of his own work, and educated as he was in Eliot's idea of literature as a body of classics that the innovator alters and enlarges, Lowell naturally looked around among established masters to find either foreshadowings of his discoveries or parallels to his themes and tone.

From the very beginning he had in a sense been doing this. When he incorporated other men's lines into his own verses, when he made a Latin, French, or German author's words the basis for a new poem in American English, he was suggesting that at least in certain corners of their *œuvre* the strangers shared his moods. As if to show there were no limits to his ambition, Lowell now set about discovering his own qualities in the whole range of European literature. Having projected his experiences as a human being upon the history of the twentieth century, he now projected his identity as an artist upon the meaning of "poetry"; for he began producing free adaptations or "imitations" of the work of a dozen and a half poets from Homer to Montale. Even before they were reprinted in the collection entitled *Imitations* (1961), these poems were received with a surprising degree of incomprehension, which was aggravated rather than lightened when the whole book came out. Only the rare reader either observed that the arrangement of the book was not chronological, or accepted the author's statement that the contents were a sequence rather than a miscellaneous collection.

In fact, of course, *Imitations* is Lowell's attempt to find his voice in the high places of literature, to fashion retrospectively a tradition for his accomplishment. He is legitimizing his progeny, replacing the Lowells and Winslows by Baudelaire, Rimbaud, and Rilke. In drawing up such a genealogical tree, Lowell again implies that he has found his essential identity not in a social class or in a religious communion but in his character as a writer. So it seems appropriate that the bulk of the models belong to the Symbolist tradition. For Symbolism is the movement that defined the creative mind as the supreme object of poetic contemplation.

Once again, the opening and closing poems have special significance. Lowell begins with a startling extract from the *Iliad,* which picks up the motif of his "For the Union Dead"—the last poem (under a different title) in the revised edition of *Life Studies.* "For the Union Dead" had dealt with the mystery of heroism, in which a human life reaches nobility by the manner of death: "man's lovely/peculiar power to choose life and die." To open *Imitations,* Lowell gives us "The Killing of Lykaon." Suddenly Homer is not the Olympian whose view shifts with dignified ease from Greek side to Trojan, or from man to God; but he is the singer of the "mania" of Achilles. "Mania" rather than the conventional "wrath," says Lowell in his version of the epic invocation. No doubt he is punning on *mênin,* the first word in the first of all our poems. However, he is also, and quite fairly, discovering in the ancient poet his own tendency to regard any irresistible passion as a sort of madness. The extract that follows the bit from the invocation comes from Book XXI of the *Iliad,* and contrasts heroic murder with ignominious death: Achilles insists on despatching the vanquished Lykaon and spurns his victim with a tirade on the killing of Trojans. The hero, foreseeing the dissolution of his enemies' corpses, suggests that the reduction to nothingness eliminates their value as persons. Lowell makes the speech his own by infusing it with a love-hate hysteria that sounds feverish and self-conscious but possesses a marvellously nervous vitality:

> You too must die, my dear. Why do you care?
>
> . . . .
>
> the dark shadows of the fish will shiver,
> lunging to snap Lykaon's silver fat.

The answer to Achilles' debasement of the human spirit is the final
work in *Imitations,* "The Pigeons," from Rilke. In the middle of this
poem we meet a band of Greek warriors about to die. But here they
personify the poet's army of creative impulses, destroyed through being
realized. The word "mania" appears too, in the last line of the poem
and the book. Yet it is no longer Achilles' rage to annihilate; it is now
the resistance of reality to the artist's drive towards perfection; for
the imagination of course opposes itself to nothingness and aspires to
eternity. So the metaphor changes, and a poem becomes a ball flung
from "all-being" towards eternity, "almost out of bounds," but gain-
ing a tragic intensity, or "body and gravity," from the pull that draws
it back towards non-existence. In the exquisitely phrased first half of
this fine work, Lowell-Rilke employs not a ball or an army but the
flight and return of pigeons as a metaphor for the artist's impulses.
Each bird is like a creative vision seeking independent life. So the
most beautiful pigeon is always the one that has never left the coop,
the pure conception not yet embodied; for to be fixed is to be finished.
Nevertheless, says Lowell,

> only by suffering the rat-race in the arena
> can the heart learn to beat.

The soaring unity, in such lines, of slang, passion, and insight reveals
the strength of Lowell's talent.

The progress from the death-bounded battles of Achilles to the
tragic campaigns of the artist reaches its peripety in the poems from
Baudelaire, placed ironically after Hugo's tributes to the defeated
warrior Napoleon and the dead artist Gautier. In Baudelaire the great
themes of *Imitations* surge together: death, love, and art. Lowell has
selected poems that carry us from the revulsion of the artist against
passion to the welcome the artist gives death. If his style sounds drier
than Baudelaire's and less felicitous in rhythm than Pound's, it has a
decorous violence of language and imagery that no other American
poet can produce. Yet not intensity of expression alone but strength
of intellect, the consciousness enveloping the intensity, draws the
disruptive forces together. Lowell's confident meters, the bold, catchy
phrases, express not simply what Baudelaire felt but what we still
want: a power to transcend lust and decay by the imagination that
digests them:

> reptilian Circe with her junk and wand. . . .
> Desire, that great elm fertilized by lust. . . .
> It's time. Old Captain, Death, lift anchor, sink!

If in artistic sensibility Lowell seems peculiarly at home with Baudelaire, he seems as a person still more at ease with Rimbaud, whose

work is placed at the exact center of the book. With both poets he finds continual opportunities for employing his own tone and his imagery of passivity eager for motion. But Rimbaud brings out attitudes towards childhood and corrupted innocence that remind us at once of *Life Studies*. Mme. Rimbaud as "Mother" inexorably recalls Mrs. Lowell:

> she thought they were losing caste. This was good—
> she had the true blue look that lied.

So also the isolated "poète de sept ans" brings back the "last afternoon with Uncle Devereux Winslow." Yet in revealing what he shares with Rimbaud, Lowell also reveals what the rest of us share with them both. The double image here has the distancing but clarifying effect that irony produces in *Life Studies*. When he gives us his amazingly fresh, rich version of "The Lice-Hunters"—with its symmetry of disgusting perceptions, its complexity of assonance or rhyme, and its steadiness of rhythm—Lowell evokes the whole tendency of our nagging generation to inspect, regret, and enjoy emotional crises:

> He heard their eyebrows beating in the dark
> whenever an electric finger struck to crush
> a bloated louse, and blood would pop and mark
> the indolence of their disdainful touch.

*   *   *

From a glance at Lowell's most recent work, coming out in periodicals, one can prophecy that his next book will establish his name as that normally thought of for "the" American poet. It will be a wide shift from the fame of Robert Frost, whom so many non-readers of poetry were able to admire along with the literary audience. Frost did many things that Lowell does not. Though unsuccessful as a farmer, he could celebrate aspects of rural life that Lowell never touches. He knew how to tell a story. He was the last important American poet to use the old forms and the old language convincingly. If Frost endured, in the fate of his family, more frightful disasters than Lowell, he was blessed with the power of maintaining his ego against them. Yet he stood for few extraordinary or wayward ideas. His connection with literature outside the conventional English and American models was slight. It is remarkable how often his early poems are indistinguishable from the early poems of Graves or Ransom. He opened few roads that other writers could travel. No one could call Frost a poet's poet.

Lowell, on the contrary, seems determined to maintain his intellectual distinction, his subtlety, his rigorous complexity of form. What appears most astonishing about the recent work is the way old motifs persist in new transformations with deepening significance. There are the city garden, the parallels of beast with man, the bitter pathos of memory working on the fixed character. But in the new poems of private recollection Lowell inclines to emphasize the hold that history has on the present, the powerlessness of the self to resist the determination of open or hidden memories. The insatiable consciousness of the poet comments sardonically on the very self-censuring auto-analysis that produced *Life Studies*.

At the opposite extreme from the private self the poet can now draw human as well as Symbolist analogies between the terrible numbers of suffering people and his own unique experiences. "Buenos Aires," one of his finest new "public" poems, has the wit and clever phrasing that make lines attractive on a first reading: "old men denied apotheosis" (i.e. equestrian statues of defunct dictators); "Peron,/the nymphets' Don Giovanni." The poet's games with expressive sound have unusual vigour—for example, a crescendo of echoes of "air" towards the end, preparing for the name of the city that is the subject of the poem. This "air" becomes a sarcastic pun; for foul air, miasma, "hot air," cold fog, emptiness, seem what the place betokens. In the final line the last word, "crowds," echoes the last word of the first stanza, "herds," and reminds one of the likeness drawn throughout the poem between cattle and people; for it is the suffering and passivity of the humblest class that connect them with the author.

As usual, the images are what make the poem work. This time they depend on the old partners, love and war, Venus and Mars, united here by means of Peron's name *Juan*, which suggests the Don Juan legend. Lowell, disgusted by the official façade of the city, treats it as a depopulated, over-furnished opera set, which he contrasts with the offstage crowds of the real Argentina. The opera is of course *Don Giovanni*; and the center of the poem recapitulates history with dead generals in white marble recalling Mozart's Commendatore. Instead of the file of Don Juan's abandoned mistresses, we meet marble goddesses mourning deceased heroes; or sex and death joined in a skull-like obelisk. Instead of the great lover in hell, we hear Peron bellowing from exile, the seducer of his people.

Among these scenes the poet moves on foot in a circular path, as spectator or sufferer. He starts from and returns to his hotel, caressing inanimate statues (his muses) en route but speaking to nobody. Instead of virile love, he encounters homosexuals in a park; but like Donna Anna, though unlike Argentina, he fights off seduction. Fascinated as so often by what repels him, he sees the truth behind the scrim and delivers it to us by way of his conscience.

A similar solidity of structure and depth of implication pervade the best of the new poems of introspection, "Eye and Tooth" and the superb tribute to his wife, "Night Sweat." "Eye and Tooth," a skilful extraction of humor from despair, illustrates a truism about middle age: viz. that so far from bringing us serenity, the years leave us naked; only we learn, not without some disgust, that the self can survive even the shabbiest humiliation. The poem depends on a brilliant use of the *eye-I* pun. Treating vision as memory or id, Lowell presents the voyeur poet's eye as an unwreckable showcase of displeasing memories that both shape and torment the person. The dominating metaphor is, so to speak, "I've got something in my I and can't get it out." Towards the end Lowell neatly ties the public to the domestic by implying that just as his readers observe his gestures with the unease provoked by their own recollections, so his familiars must in the routines of living find his condition hardly more bearable than he does:

> Nothing! No oil
> for the eye, nothing to pour
> on those waters or flames.
> I am tired. Everyone's tired of my turmoil.

Ransom once played with the idea of Lowell's becoming the Ovid or Virgil of America. But if Lowell feels drawn to themes of epic scope, his mode is neither narrative nor celebratory. For a closer parallel we must look at another epoch in another nation, at the difficult life and disquieting art of Baudelaire. Besides the fundamental similarities of their childhoods, Beaudelaire during adolescence inclined like Lowell to a lonely, morose disposition; and it was in the community of artists that he found a lasting family. He was attracted to painting but not to music. As an adult he responded more intensely to city scenes than to country landscapes. In his personality he combined deep passivity with an eagerness to keep working and moving. Though he had begun writing poetry while at school, he always procrastinated about publication, working over his poems with perfectionist ardor. When he produced a book, it was no miscellaneous gathering but an organization of separate poems into a general scheme reflecting his peculiar outlook.

Still more persuasive are the similarities in the works. Both men have the posture of a fallen Christian. Both deal rather with the horrors of passion than the pleasures of love, and treat death as more seductive than frightening. For both of them, art emerges from profound intellection, from labor, suffering, self-disgust. They build their best poems around complex images linked by connotation, and not around arguments or events. They introduce coarse, distasteful words into a style that is rich and serious. Their poems follow circular movements, with the end touching the beginning.

Their differences are obvious. Lowell's use of history is deliberate; Baudelaire clings to immediate reality. The development of Lowell's characteristic successes depends on an impression of haphazardness at the start turning into a highly wrought climax, whereas Baudelaire's surface has elegance of workmanship throughout. Lowell relies overwhelmingly on visual imagery, whereas Baudelaire appeals elaborately to sounds, and is remarkable for a synaesthetic use of smells. Rhythmically, Lowell sounds less interesting than Baudelaire.

Yet if we search still further, if we place "Le Cygne" beside "For the Union Dead," the two sensibilities reveal still more intimate kinship. There is the same sympathy with the wretched, the same disgust with the life that imposes wretchedness upon them, the same transformation of the city-pent poet into an emblem of the human spirit exiled from its original home. Finally, it seems important that Lowell and Baudelaire take so much of the matter of their poems from the most secret rooms of their private lives; for the true biography of them both emerges not from a tale of their friendships or families or external careers but from their works alone. The real Lowell, like the real Baudelaire, is met with in the poetry to which he has given himself altogether.

Review of *The Mills of the Kavanaughs*

by Randall Jarrell

Since Robert Lowell's *The Mills of the Kavanaughs* consists of only seven poems—one tremendously long, four quite sizeable—I can treat them one by one. "The Fat Man in the Mirror" makes a better impression on you if you haven't read the strange and beautiful Werfel poem on which it is based; this "imitation after Werfel!"— never was anything less imitative!—is a baroque, febrile, Horowitz-Variations-on-*The-Stars-and-Stripes-Forever* affair. Part I of "Her Dead Brother" is a restrained, sinister, and extremely effective poem; the suicide-by-gas-stove Part II is effective in some portions, but is mannered and violent—Part I seems better off as the separate poem that it originally was. It would be hard to write, read, or imagine a more nightmarish poem than "Thanksgiving's Over." On one level it is a complete success, and it is almost with a sigh of relief that one concludes that it does not quite succeed on another level, that all this is the possible with which art does not have to deal, not the probable with which it must. Still, it is a frightening and impressive—and in parts very moving—poem which anybody will want to read. The organization and whole conception of "David and Bathsheba in the Public Garden" are so mannered and idiosyncratic, so peculiar to Mr. Lowell, that the poem is spoiled, in spite of parts as beautiful as that about the harvest moon. Someone is sure to say about this poem that you can't tell David from Bathsheba without a program: they both (like the majority of Mr. Lowell's characters) talk just like Mr. Lowell.

I cannot think of any objection at all to "Mother Marie Therese" and "Falling Asleep over the Aeneid," and if I could I would be too overawed to make it. "Mother Marie Therese" is the best poem Mr. Lowell has ever written, and "Falling Asleep over the Aeneid" is— is better; *very* few living poets have written poems that surpass these. "Mother Marie Therese" is the most human and tender, the least specialized, of all Mr. Lowell's poems; it is warped neither by Doctrine nor by that doctrine which each of us becomes for himself; in it, for

once, Mr. Lowell really gets out of himself. Sometimes the New Bruns-
wick nun who is talking does sound like a not-too-distant connection
of the Lowells, but generally she seems as much herself as porpoise-
bellied Father Turbot, "his bald spot tapestried by colored glass,"
seems himself when he squeaks: "N-n-nothing is so d-dead/As a dead
S-s-sister." Certainly Father Turbot is real; the drowned Mother Superior ("reading Rabelais from her chaise,/Or parroting the *Action
Française"; she who "half-renounced by Candle, Book, and Bell,/Her
flowers and fowling-pieces for the church"; she who saw that our
world is passing, but "whose trust/Was in its princes") is real; and
the sixty-year-old nun who speaks the poem in grief for her is most
real of all. One can judge something of her reality and of the quality
of the poem simply by looking at the long passage with which the
poem ends:

> *The bell-buoy, whom she called the Cardinal,*
> *Dances upon her. If she hears at all,*
> *She only hears it tolling to this shore,*
> *Where our frost-bitten sisters know the roar*
> *Of water, inching, always on the move*
> *For virgins, when they wish the times were love,*
> *And their hysterical hosannahs rouse*
> *The loveless harems of the buck ruffed grouse*
> *Who drums, untroubled now, beside the sea—*
> *As if he found our stern virginity*
> Contra naturam. *We are ruinous;*
> *God's Providence through time has mastered* us:
> *Now all the bells are tongueless, now we freeze,*
> *A later Advent, pruner of warped trees,*
> *Whistles about our nunnery slabs, and yells,*
> *And water oozes from us into wells;*
> *A new year swells and stirs. Our narrow Bay*
> *Freezes itself and us. We cannot say*
> *Christ even sees us, when the ice floes toss*
> *His statue, made by Hurons, on the cross*
> *That Father Turbot sank on Mother's mound—*
> *A whirligig! Mother, we must give ground,*
> *Little by little; but it does no good.*
> *Tonight, while I am piling on more driftwood,*
> *And stooping with the poker, you are here,*
> *Telling your beads; and breathing in my ear,*
> *You watch your orphan swording at her fears.*
> *I feel you twitch my shoulder. No one hears*
> *Us mock the sisters, as we used to, years*

> *And years behind us, when we heard the spheres*
> *Whirring* venite; *and we held our ears.*
> *My mother's hollow sockets fill with tears.*

"Falling Asleep over the Aeneid" is as good—and as thoroughly and surprisingly organized—a poem about power and the self as any I can recall. Its subject matter and peculiar circumstances justify the harshness and violence, the barbarous immediacy, that often seem arbitrary in Mr. Lowell's poems; and these are set off by passages as tender and beautiful as this description of the dead Pallas:

> *Face of snow,*
> *You are the flower that country girls have caught,*
> *A wild bee-pillaged honey-suckle brought*
> *To the returning bridegroom—the design*
> *Has not yet left it, and the petals shine;*
> *The earth, its mother, has, at last, no help:*
> *It is itself.*

I have rarely had more of a sense of the terrible continuity of the world (and of the ego that learns neither from itself nor from the world what the dead face is made to tell Aeneas: "Brother, try,/O child of Aphrodite, try to die:/To die is life") than when I read the conclusion into which all the terms of the poem coalesce:

> *Church is over, and its bell*
> *Frightens the yellowhammers, as I wake*
> *And watch the whitecaps wrinkle up the lake.*
> *Mother's great-aunt, who died when I was eight,*
> *Stands by our parlor sabre. "Boy, it's late.*
> *Vergil must keep the Sabbath." Eighty years!*
> *It all comes back. My Uncle Charles appears,*
> *Blue-capped and bird-like. Phillips Brooks and Grant*
> *Are frowning at his coffin, and my aunt,*
> *Hearing his colored volunteers parade*
> *Through Concord, laughs, and tells her English maid*
> *To clip his yellow nostril hairs, and fold*
> *His colors on him. . . . It is I, I hold*
> *His sword to keep from falling, for the dust*
> *On the stuffed birds is breathless, for the bust*
> *Of young Augustus weighs on Vergil's shelf:*
> *It scowls into my glasses at itself.*

I am not sure how good this passage will seem in isolation; as the ending of this poem, an ending with every term prepared for, every symbol established, it is as magnificent as it is final.

"The Mills of the Kavanaughs," the long narrative poem that fills half the book, is an interesting and powerful poem; but in spite of having wonderful lines and sections—many of both—it does not seem to me successful as a unified work of art, a narrative poem that makes the same sort of sense a novel or story makes. It is too much a succession of nightmares and daydreams that are half-nightmare; one counts with amusement and disbelief the number of times the poem becomes a nightmare-vision or its equivalent. And these are only too successfully nightmarish, so that there is a sort of monotonous violence and extremity about the poem, as if it were a piece of music that consisted of nothing but climaxes. The people too often seem to be acting *in the manner of* Robert Lowell, rather than plausibly as real people act (or implausibly as real people act). I doubt that many readers will think them real; the husband of the heroine never seems so, and the heroine is first of all a sort of symbiotic state of the poet. (You feel, "Yes, Robert Lowell would act like this if he were a girl"; but whoever saw a girl like Robert Lowell?)

Occasionally, for a few lines, the poem becomes so academic and clumsy that one is astonished: "My husband was a fool/To run out from the Navy when disgrace/Still wanted zeal to look him in the face." I do not believe that even Cotton Mather ever managed to think in the style of that last line. If I quote a similar passage—"Soon enough we saw/Death like the Bourbon after Waterloo,/Who learning and forgetting nothing, knew/Nothing but ruin. Why must we mistrust/Ourselves with Death who takes the world on trust?/Although God's brother, and himself a god,/Death whipped his horses through the startled sod;/For neither conscience nor omniscience warned/Him from his folly, when the virgin scorned/His courtship, and the quaking earth revealed/Death's desperation to the Thracian field"—and then tell the reader that these rather labored and academic lines are three-fourths of the *last stanza* of the poem, I won't blame him for looking unbelieving.

The poem is hurt very much by being a sort of anthology of favorite Lowell effects—situations are repeated, there is even a passage adapted from an earlier poem; the reader gets confused and thinks, "Am I in 'Her Dead Brother' now? Here's the stove, but where's the suicide? Isn't this 'David and Bathsheba' now?" What Mr. Lowell is attempting to do in this poem is often beyond his powers and knowledge (where narrative verse is concerned everybody alive is an amateur, though Frost was a professional thirty years ago); usually the poet is having to try much too hard, so that one does not feel very often in this poem the spontaneity, the live half-accidental half-providential rightness, that some of the best poetry has or seems to have. Sometimes Mr. Lowell is having great difficulties, and sometimes he is seeking refuge from them in some of the effects that he has produced so well and so often before.

He is a poet of both Will and Imagination, but his Will is always seizing his Imagination by the shoulders and saying to it in a grating voice: "Don't sit there fooling around; *get to work!*"—and his poor Imagination gets tense all over and begins to revolve determinedly and familiarly, like a squirrel in a squirrel cage. Goethe talked about the half-somnambulistic state of the poet; but Mr. Lowell too often is either having a nightmare or else is wide awake gritting his teeth and working away at All The Things He Does Best. Cocteau said to poets: *Learn what you can do and then don't do it;* and this is so— we do it enough without trying. As a poet Mr. Lowell sometimes doesn't have enough trust in God and tries to do everything himself: he proposes and disposes—and this helps to give a certain monotony to his work. But probably the reader will want to say to me, by now, what Lincoln said about the drunkard Grant: "If I knew his brand I would order my other generals a barrel." And I have put my objections to his long poem rather too strongly; it is a powerful and impressive poem, with a good many beautiful or touching passages and a great many overwhelming ones, one of the better poems of one of the best of living poets.

In a Mood of Tragedy:
The Mills of the Kavanaughs

by William Carlos Williams

New York Times Book Review, 1951

In his new book Robert Lowell gives us six first-rate poems of which we may well be proud. As usual he has taken the rhyme-track for his effects. We shall now have rhyme again for a while, rhymes completely missing the incentive. The rhymes are necessary to Mr. Lowell. He must, to his mind, appear to surmount them.

An unwonted sense of tragedy coupled with a formal fixation of the line, together constitute the outstanding character of the title poem. It is as though, could he break through, he might surmount the disaster.

When he does, when he does under stress of emotion break through the monotony of the line, it never goes far, it is as though he had at last wakened to breathe freely again, you can feel the lines breathing, the poem rouses as though from a trance. Certainly Mr. Lowell gets his effects with admirable economy of means.

In this title poem, a dramatic narrative played out in a Maine village, Mr. Lowell appears to be restrained by the lines; he appears to *want* to break them. And when the break comes, tentatively, it is toward some happy recollection, the tragedy intervening when this is snatched away and the lines close in once more—as does the story: the woman playing solitaire in the garden by her husband's flag-draped grave. She dreams of the past, of the Abnaki Indians, the aborigines, and of how, lying prone in bed beside her husband, she was ravished in a dream.

Of the remaining five poems, "Her Dead Brother" is most succinct in the tragic mood that governs them all, while the lyric, "The Fat Man in the Mirror" (after Werfel) lifts the mood to what playfulness there is—as much as the mode permits: a tragic realization of time lost, peopled by "this pursey terror" that is "not I." The man is torn between a wish and a discipline. It is a violently sensual and innocent ego that without achievement (the poem) must end in nothing but despair.

Is the poet New England—or what otherwise is his heresy (of loves possessed only in dreams) that so bedevils him? At the precise moment of enjoyment she hears "My husband's Packard crunching up the drive." It is the poet's struggle to ride over the tragedy to a successful assertion—or is it his failure?—that gives the work its undoubted force.

Shall I say I prefer a poet of broader range of feeling? Is it when the restraints of the rhyme makes the man restless and he drives through, elbows the restrictions out of the way that he becomes distinguished or when he fails?

It is to assert love, not to win it that the poem exists. If the poet is defeated it is then that he most triumphs, love is most proclaimed! the Abnakis are justified, their land repossessed in dreams. Kavanaugh, waking his wife from her passionate embraces, attempts to strangle her, that she, like Persephone, may die to be queen. He doesn't kill her, the tragedy lying elsewhere.

The tragedy is that the loss is poignantly felt, come what may: dream, sisterhood, sainthood—the violence in "Falling Asleep Over the Aeneid"; "Mother Maria Theresa"; "David and Bathsheba in the Public Garden," excellent work. What can one wish more?

Review of *The Mills of the Kavanaughs*

by William Arrowsmith

The poetry of Robert Lowell has been saluted with much critical extravagance; but for good reason. For Lowell is a genuine poet of very great strength, and *Lord Weary's Castle* had the hardness of extraordinary achievement and hence the full promise. Its strength and its brilliance were, if anything, more than self-evident, and on these good grounds many critics—myself included—judged that Lowell's was the promise of the major poet. The promise remains; but *The Mills of the Kavanaughs* has done nothing to keep it and something to weaken it. *As yet* Lowell shows himself incapable of extending his strength—rather he concentrates even further what was already too concentrated; and he seems to be unaware of his weaknesses. Yet his performance within his habitual range is always exciting and sometimes perfect. By this I think I am saying that Lowell's verse is already assured minor poetry and that *The Mills of the Kavanaughs* is an unsuccessful attempt to extend his range—but without modulation—from minor to major.

Lowell's greatest virtue is his strength of line, rhythm, and language; this virtue, pushed to extremes or overextended, characteristically generates a vice. God knows, *Lord Weary's Castle* was nothing if not strong. That strength was achieved, like most strengths, at a necessary cost: a loss of delicacy, a forcing of effect, a monotony of violence in both language and subject. The cost was less apparent at the time, because *Lord Weary's Castle* was worth it; *The Mills of the Kavanaughs* raises the question. To understand why, we have to see that the sources of Lowell's strength are the beginnings of a characteristic weakness when the poet moves from a short lyric or ode to an extended narrative or revery.

His most obvious strength is one of diction, a harsh slamming language, heaped up by alliteration, assonance and blunt rhyming, by ruthless enjambing, and by substitutions for strength, particularly in the first foot. Liberal spondees form jagged, generally repulsive, com-

Review of *The Mills of the Kavanaughs* from "Five Poets" by William Arrowsmith. Reprinted by permission from *The Hudson Review*, Vol. IV, No. 4 (Winter, 1952). Copyright © 1952 by The Hudson Review, Inc.

pounds: *coke-barrel, fungus-eyeballs, nigger-brass, mud-flat, broom-pole butt, mole-tide,* etc. Add to this a breath-sweep so tasking it deserves comparison to Milton's; a bold disregard for logical or metrical pause; and, finally, a savageness of subject grafted to a savage language. These qualities are at least the more obvious sources of Lowell's strength; within the framework of a twenty- or thirty-line poem, they made a kind of explosion on the page, more consistently violent, it seems to me, than any "lyric" poetry of which I know. What Lowell had done was to take almost every device by which, normally, long poetry is protected from monotony—the enjambement, the substitutions, the breath-sweep, clause-piling and rhyme-roughening—and compress them within a shorter frame. It worked; magnificently so.

When he came to compose a long poem—*The Mills of the Kavanaughs* is over 600 lines—he seems never to have doubted that the same devices would work just as well. And they might have worked in any poetry less characteristically violent and effected. But in *The Mills of the Kavanaughs* one gets—no paradox—what can only be called a monotony of violence. Yet a different strategy would seem to be indicated. If you are going to compress the antimonotony devices of long poetry into a smaller frame, it stands to reason that you cannot merely expand your compressed lyric—*at the same compression.* The risk of doing so is that your devices may boomerang; my guess is that they have boomeranged in Lowell's long poem. *The Mills of the Kavanaughs* is, for all its extraordinary verse- or stanzaic brilliance, when taken at its length, a monotonous poem. Even explosions can become monotonous, after all. What I miss, technically, is the strophic and antistrophic balance which might have offset the characteristic slamming of his lines. For instance, in terms of line-groups: the basic pattern of the poem is heroic couplets; some rhyme-variation is clearly intended to irregularize the pattern; but his variations serve no other purpose. Yet economy and a sense of balance in big poetry might have suggested a tonal contrast between end-stopped couplets and enjambed verses. To my mind the four most nearly perfect lines of the poem— they are perfect—are the closing four. First, however, the run-ons:

> For neither conscience nor omniscience warned
> Him from his folly, when the virgin scorned
> His courtship, and the quaking earth revealed
> Death's desperation to the Thracian field.

And the end-stopped (I read a pause after "gave") lines which perfect their predecessors:

> And yet we think the virgin took no harm:
> She gave herself because her blood was warm—

> And for no other reason, Love, I gave
> Whatever brought me gladness to the grave.

This seems to me achievement of the real thing, and I am far from wanting to ascribe its success to a balancing device alone, however successful. It is meant to crown the whole poem, and not merely the preceding enjambement. But I think its contrast, even as a crown, with the rest of the poem is indicative of the extent to which something has been lost because too great attention has been paid to strength. Item: somewhere Lowell says "A beer can filled/With fishskins marks the dingle where they died." The *dingles* down Maine? Or the *dingles* in which you can alliteratively die, drown, diddle or dally? It is not a common kind of flaw, but indicative: *almost* anything for strength. But the strength of a narrative is not identical with the strength of the shorter poem, and no one but a lyricist could have thought that it was.

Emphatically, I should like to avoid giving the impression that Lowell's poetry is not one of the most remarkable poetries in America. It is at least that. Line by line, *The Mills of the Kavanaughs* would provide twenty poets with their best verses, their hardest hits, their surest whatevers. It is just that temptation that strength will make— a temptation to make more—that is the peril. It is easy to say, transform it, less easy to see how it would be done, where the mastery is so great that the merest misstep may mean the bog.

More important or less important than these technical points and their balancing flourish—I can't be sure—I wish I understood the poem. I don't, in any satisfactory, even early, way, understand it. And this might mean: wait till it works itself out, or, what six readings without success might suggest, speak up.

The Mills of the Kavanaughs looks like a narrative or an extended narrative revery. It is spoken by Anne Kavanaugh, the widow of a naval officer disgraced at Pearl Harbor and the impotent heir of an old Catholic logging fortune in Maine. The tenor of the narrative is a "revery of her childhood and marriage, addressed to her husband," and supported by the symbolism of the story of the rape of Persephone by Hades. Presumably supported, for it is just this symbolism that to me makes the narrative so difficult. In an ordinary way, it is of course all very clear, but the narrative seems to turn on it in a manner which finishes by blurring. I can see, with the intended force, I think, the resurrection carry-over into Red Kavanaugh's ring:

> *Cut down we flourish,* on his signet ring.

But what am I to make of "marriage by drowning," or is it even related? And yet it seems to be, for it is followed by some play upon Cinderella and then the analogue of Hades' offer to Persephone in the Hymn to Demeter: "Anne, my whole/House is your serf." And again, in some lines magnificent in themselves, but obscure in relation:

> This was Avernus. There, about this time,
> Demeter's daughter first reviewed the dead—
> Most doomed and pompous, while the maples shed
> Their martyr's rubric. . . .
>
> .   .   .   .
>
> There, hearing how she'd come to little good,
> She took a husband to dispirit hell.

Fall, yes. But "to little good"? Why should she come to little good? And since this is the motive offered for the marriage, isn't the question an important one for a narrative poem? But I can find no answer elsewhere, unless it is the point of her stressed poverty. In his preface to the poem, Lowell in a way gives a point to his symbols by a kind of phrasing: ". . . a marble statue of Persephone, the goddess who becomes a queen by becoming queen of the dead." And in the first stanza: "Harry, not a thing/Was missing: we were children of a king." In itself this is quite unobjectionable; but Persephone and Hades are rich enough symbols in themselves that they must be carefully controlled if they are not to become obscure, and it seems to me that *The Mills of the Kavanaughs* does not even attempt control. The danger of eschatologies is their very richness; they are so imbedded in language and thought that they tend to keep their own directions; Lowell ignores this, and proceeds, characteristically, to pack his symbols so that his simplicities assume a complexity which wrecks them. And in narrative, or dramatic, poetry, symbols have to be given a different kind of life than in lyric poetry; they have to bear the weight of motives, completions and pace. Lowell's poem does not have pace, and, I am afraid, in both technique and content long Lowell looks just like short Lowell. This is not to damn him; not by a long shot: *The Mills* is magnificent poetry, but not a narrative poem. Not yet, anyhow.

Robert Lowell's Family Album

by Stephen Spender

The great achievement of poets at the beginning of this century was their conquest of new areas of seemingly unpoetic experience in idiomatic language which, through their mastery of rhythm, became poetry. Pound and Eliot did not confine themselves to the themes which were "poetic" within the Georgian idiom; nor did they throw away everything except a kind of chaotic verbal subjectivism in the hope that the uninhibited subconscious touched at some points on poetry, as some free verse writers did then, and as the Beatniks do today. Robert Lowell is an outstanding pioneer extending the frontiers of language, making notable conquests of material which often seems too eccentric for poetry and consolidating it in very strong and compact form. Where even in Pound an anecdote remains poetically unresolved in the surface of the cantos, Lowell is able to make from the anecdotal a language like mosaic:

> "Anchors aweigh," Daddy boomed in his bathtub, ·
> "Anchors aweigh,"
> when Lever Brothers offered to pay
> him double what the Navy paid.
> I nagged him for his dress sword with gold braid,
> and cringed because Mother, new
> caps on all her teeth, was born anew
> at forty. With seamanlike celerity,
> Father left the Navy,
> and deeded Mother his property.

Most of these life studies are concerned with members of the Lowell family. Background material is supplied by a prose interlude called "91 Revere Street," which is an account of Robert Lowell's childhood among grownups whose portraits he draws in lines as strong as prison bars. The considerable hardness of his portrayals is not mitigated by the deep kind of charity which consists of being as honest about himself as about everyone else, and by a very great and idiosyncratic

"Robert Lowell's Family Album" by Stephen Spender, appeared first in *The New Republic* (140:17; June 8, 1959). Reprinted by permission of the author.

humor. His weakness is a judgment sure to the point of rigidity and lacking in a certain freedom: the freedom which allows that the judge might not be 100 percent right. He writes of his father:

> By the time he graduated from Annapolis, he had a high sense of abstract form, which he beclouded with his humor. He had reached, perhaps, his final mental possibilities. He was deep—not with profundity, but with the dumb depth of one who trusted in statistics and was dubious of personal experience. In his forties, Father's soul went underground. . . .

It is a brilliant characterization but perhaps a bit too final. This finality is the strength of the poetry, but also constitutes a danger for it. The poems are like beautifully made barrels, taut, tense and made of real wood with sprung hoops. The danger is that the essence of an invisible world which is poetry will be excluded. At present this danger lends drama to the poems. Taking pleasure in the workmanship, the idiosyncrasies, the solidity of anecdote tacked onto anecdote, one confidently awaits the moment of revelation. Sometimes, as in "Ford Madox Ford," one feels a bit deprived. The reward—in the form of a flat statement delivered as ironic anticlimax—seems of a kind that would only satisfy once:

> . . . Ford,
> you were a kind man and you died in want.

At other times, the writing is so effective that it is its own reward, especially when Lowell writes of his childhood:

> I picked with a clean fingernail at the blue anchor
> or my sailor blouse washed white as a spinnaker.
> What in the world was I wishing?
> . . . A sail-colored horse browsing in the bullrushes . . .
> A fluff of the west wind puffing
> my blouse, kiting me over our seven chimneys,
> troubling the waters. . . .

Sometimes most literal observation acquires a hallucinated intensity:

> Azure day
> makes my agonized blue window bleaker.
> Crows maunder on the petrified fairway.

What Lowell really does here is reverse the process whereby he has constructed an image of his soul from the most patient, humoristic, liberal studies of the behavior of friends and relations.

Doubtless some will say that he has created a "Lowell myth." But mythology is a slippery word, and perhaps it would be more to the point to say that he has shown a way out of the prisons of mythology

which most poets today feel they must construct as their habitats. He
has taken a lot of facts, observed or remembered (each of them strikingly separate as brittle shape or anecdote), and made from them his
own truth. This truth is obstinate, moving and sometimes even tragic,
for the way in which Mr. Lowell insists on treating all the truths that
strike him on the same level, as the same sort of truth. What these
poems point out is the possibility of a humanist kind of poetry, in
which disparate experiences are bound up within the sensibility of a
poet who has himself an immense compassion combined with clearness
and hardness. Tension is supplied by the reconciliation of very opposite
personal qualities of the poet within his poems.

The epigrammatic is, I suppose, the manner which binds together
these bundles of observation often as brazen as—this is what I have
been looking for!—Tolstoy!

> In the grandiloquent lettering on Mother's coffin,
> Lowell had been misspelled LOVEL.
> The corpse
> was wrapped like *panetone* in Italian tinfoil.

Is not that like something from *War and Peace*? And does not Lowell
often seem to be writing the poems of Pierre Bezukov?

Robert Lowell and the Poetry of Confession

by M. L. Rosenthal

A reluctance to destroy himself any more rapidly than he was already doing may have been one of the causes of Dylan Thomas's refusal to look steadily into the abyss in his poetry. But in the most powerful work of the modern period the great push is often precisely in that direction. Eliot's interest in the "inexpressibly horrible," Pound's violence, Crane's suicidal symbolism, and the psychological self-probings of younger poets all point the same way. "I get the feeling," one of them has written me, "that the madhouse is not far away from many poets writing now. I think there is something wrong in both my feeling that this should become accepted as part of the state of affairs and my feeling that this should be countered consciously and fiercely. . . . I think too that this kind of writing . . . will hurl poetry up a tree it can't descend from. . . . Where will it go? *Can* it make a 'return,' can it reaccept the culture that after all fed it and flung it on its way?"

No one can really answer these questions, although my correspondent supplied *his* answer to the last of them: "No." Emily Dickinson once called publication "the auction of the mind," but today many of our writers seem to regard it as soul's therapy. We are now far from the great Romantics who, it is true, spoke directly of their emotions but did not give the game away even to themselves. They found, instead, cosmic equations and symbols, transcendental reconciliations with "this lime-tree bower my prison," or titanic melancholia in the course of which, merging a sense of tragic fatality with the evocations of the nightingale's song, the poet lost his personal complaint in the music of universal forlornness. Later, Whitman took American poetry to the very edge of the confessional in his *Calamus* poems and in the quivering avowal of his helplessness before the seductions of "blind loving wrestling touch, sheath'd hooded sharp-tooth'd touch." More recently, under the influence of the Symbolists, Eliot and Pound

brought us into the forbidden realm itself, although a certain indirection in their work masks the poet's actual face and psyche from greedy
eyes.

Robert Lowell's poetry has been a long struggle to remove the
mask, to make his speaker unequivocally himself. As with Thomas,
whose style Lowell's sometimes (especially in a few earlier poems)
resembles, his chief mask has been that of the "crucified" man, over-
whelmed by compassion and at the same time a boisterous participant
in the human ordeal. He departs from Thomas in the specific meaning
of the mask: for him it is a mask of moral guilt, like Eliot's, for the
present decadence of values and the crash of a great tradition. He is
after all a *Lowell,* and he charges himself with all the meanness of
contemporary New England as he sees it—sunken in commercialist
degradation, the net result of the nastiness behind its long history
going back to the repressive Puritanism and to the heartless extermina-
tion of the Indians. A Catholic convert for a number of years, Lowell
worked this perspective into his poetry as Eliot has done with his
Anglicanism, but with a "jackhammer" passion (to use a figure from
his savagely depressed poem "Colloquy in Black Rock"). He is also a
social critic as uncompromising in his strictures as any Marxist. So
his mask is a composite one, as his "Children of Light" shows:

> Our fathers wrung their bread from stocks and stones
> And fenced their gardens with the Redman's bones;
> Embarking from the Nether Land of Holland,
> Pilgrims unhouseled by Geneva's night,
> They planted here the serpent's seed of light;
> And here the pivoting searchlight probe to shock
> The riotous glass houses built on rock,
> And candles gutter by an empty altar,
> And light is where the landless blood of Cain
> Is burning, burning the unburied gain.

The driving rhymes and indignant irony in this poem and such
others as "The Drunken Fisherman" and "As a Plane Tree by the
Water" demonstrate Lowell's power even while they induce certain
reservations. The feeling is genuine; it smashes home. And there is
no question of its moral bearing. But in these poems from *Lord
Weary's Castle* (1946), as in many of the pieces comprising Lowell's
first volume, *Land of Unlikeness* (1944), the emotion is stronger and
more immediate than the literal content. The level of *thought,* as
opposed to that of *feeling* and *statement,* is a bit stale—even juvenile.
He is shocked to realize what "our fathers" did to the Indians and
embittered by the unconscious hypocrisy of Puritanism and its historical results. While Lowell handles these set themes beautifully, we

have here an instance of the problem Eliot long ago raised of finding an objective correlative for an emotion not directly expressible, an emotion "in *excess* of the facts as they appear." Lines 4 and 5 of "Children of Light" will illustrate:

> Pilgrims unhoused by Geneva's night,
> They planted here the serpent's seeds of light . . .

As an intellectual proposition these lines are merely a hedging comment on a knotty point of doctrine of little interest to anyone now except theological apologists or historians. On the other hand, if we inquire into the emotional connotations of that paradoxical image "the serpent's seeds of light" we find that again and again in his writings Lowell uses snake and serpent images to suggest sly and furtive guilt, evil that *will* assert itself, and very often guilt or evil of a sexual character. The related meaning of "seeds" is obvious, and "light" suggests, if only ironically, that something not only desirable but valuable is associated with the guilt of the serpent's seeds. These implications are fully worked out in other poems. In "Between the Porch and the Altar," two guilty lovers, an unfaithful husband and his mistress, *become* snakes (in the husband's eyes) whenever they gratify themselves in the way that means "light" for them:

> . . . When we try to kiss,
> Our eyes are slits and cringing, and we hiss;
> Scales glitter on our bodies as we fall. . . .

If Lowell's lovers were not so oppressed by guilt, this would be exactly like the hissing end of Lawrence's "River Roses":

> . . . We whispered: "No one knows us.
> Let it be as the snake disposes
> Here in this simmering marsh."

"Between the Porch and the Altar" helped prepare the way for the maskless confessions of his most recent poems. Its adulterous, mother-dominated hero is first described in the third person, and its serpent imagery helps us see his pathological state:

> Meeting his mother makes him lose ten years,
> Or is it twenty? Time, no doubt, has ears
> That listen to the swallowed serpent, wound
> Into its bowels, but he thinks no sound
> Is possible before her, he thinks the past
> Is settled. . . .
>   Nothing shames
> Him more than this uncoiling, counterfeit
> Body presented as an idol. . . .

Throughout "Between the Porch and the Altar" the sense of sin, rather than sin itself, is clearly the protagonist's main problem. He is sick with the burden of his mother and of the crushing family traditions and "New England Conscience" associated with her, and he must throw the burden off even if it means, as his equally guilt-ridden sweetheart puts it, to "ruin" his two children and his wife. The Roman Catholic framework hardly solves the moral problems behind all this, but poetically it separates the protagonist's viewpoint sufficiently from that of the poem as a whole to enable us to see the difference. The speaker in Lowell's poems needs most of all the strength to "cast off remorse," as Yeats demanded. "Between the Porch and the Altar" begins to get at this need, and away from the half-relevant abstractions of other poems. Even "The Dead in Europe," with its picture of the bombed civilians who fell "hugger-mugger in the jellied fire," is marred by arbitrary and generalized religious rhetoric (whereas the later "A Mad Negro Soldier Confined at Munich" is not), and the magnificent elegy "The Quaker Graveyard in Nantucket" is almost betrayed by it. What saves the latter poem is the least pretentious thing about it, the crowded, sensuous concreteness of its description:

> A brackish reach of shoal off Madaket,—
> The sea was still breaking violently and night
> Had steamed into our North Atlantic Fleet,
> When the drowned sailor clutched the drag-net. Light
> Flashed from his matted head and marble feet,
> He grappled at the net
> With the coiled, hurdling muscles of his thighs. . . .

and

> . . . Sea-gulls blink their heavy lids
> Seaward. The winds' wings beat upon the stones,
> Cousin, and scream for you and the claws rush
> At the sea's throat and wring it in the slush
> Of this old Quaker Graveyard. . . .

or

> . . . a gaff
> Bobs on the untimely stroke
> Of the greased wash exploding on a shoal-bell
> In the old mouth of the Atlantic. It's well;
> Atlantic, you are fouled with the blue sailors. . . .

Lowell introduces into this elegy for his drowned cousin, Warren Winslow, motifs from *Moby Dick* and from Christian worship. (Section VI, entitled "Our Lady of Walsingham," is intended to suggest the ultimate calm confidence of true faith; the statue of Our Lady, "Expressionless, expresses God.") These motifs swell the organ music of the poem, enabling the poet to identify the death of young Winslow with that of Ahab and the *Pequod*'s crew and providing a specific religious and literary context for his contemplation of the ironies and the intransigence of existence, of "is, the whited monster." Though Lowell relates them skillfully to his theme of one specific death and to his sea music, they are nevertheless extraneous to the essential elegy. For this reason the poem lacks the piercing emotional authority of "Between the Porch and the Altar" and of some less elaborate poems (for instance, "The Slough of Despond," "The Death of the Sheriff," and "Rebellion"). Nor does it convey the terror of "is" as effectively as the less expansive "After the Surprising Conversions," "Mr. Edwards and the Spider," "Colloquy in Black Rock," and "The Ghost" (adapted from Propertius).

Lowell's 1951 volume, *The Mills of the Kavanaughs,* moves into the foreground themes more or less suppressed previously. In these poems, Lowell gives freer play to his driving motives of distorted and blocked love, mental exacerbation verging into insanity, and symbolic and actual homicide and suicide. The title sequence takes us into the mind of an elderly woman remembering her impoverished and loveless childhood and compensatory self-love, her unsatisfactory marriage and the later breakdown of her husband, a wartime naval officer, his homicidal jealousy after his return, and her own burning but unsatisfied sexual need. She thinks of herself in terms of the myth of Persephone, as one who has given "whatever brought me gladness" to death and the grave. "Her Dead Brother," with its theme of incest, and "Thanksgiving's Over," with its sexual cruelty, would-be suicide, and madness, and other poems in this volume show how Lowell is approaching the revolutionary breakthrough of *Life Studies.*

In this book he rips off the mask entirely. *The Mills of the Kavanaughs* had one ludicrous aspect, the circumstances of the protagonists cumbersomely devised to account for their pressing psychological despair. In most of *Life Studies* there is one protagonist only—Robert Lowell. Through what he has to say about himself we discover the real, essential bearing of most of the earlier work. As a result, it is hard not to think of *Life Studies* as a series of personal confidences, rather shameful, that one is honor-bound not to reveal. About half the book, the prose section called "91 Revere Street," is essentially a public discrediting of his father's manliness and character, as well as of the family and social milieu of his childhood. Another section, the concluding sequence of poems grouped under the heading "Life Studies," reinforces and even repeats these motifs, bringing them to bear on the poet's psychological problems as an adult. The father, naval officer *manqué* and then businessman and speculator *manqué*, becomes a humiliating symbol of the failure of a class and of a kind of personality. Lowell's contempt for him is at last mitigated by adult compassion, though I wonder if a man can allow himself this kind of operation on his father without doing his own spirit incalculable damage. But the damage has clearly been in the making a long time, and Lowell knows very well that he is doing violence to himself most of all:

> . . . I hear
> my ill-spirit sob in each blood cell,
> as if my hand were at its throat. . . .
>
> ("Skunk Hour")

He does not spare himself in these poems, at least two of which have to do with sojourns in mental hospitals and his return home from them. We have grotesque glimpses into his marital life. "Man and Wife," for instance, begins: "Tamed by *Milton,* we lie on Mother's bed." It later tells how

> All night I've held your hand,
> as if you had
> a fourth time faced the kingdom of the mad—
> its hackneyed speech, its homicidal eye—

"My mind's not right," says the speaker in "Skunk Hour," the poem which ends the book. It is partly Lowell's apology for what he has been saying in these pieces, like Gerontion's mumbling that he is only "an old man, a dull head among windy spaces." And it is partly his assertion that he cannot breathe without these confessions, however rank they may be, and that the things he has been talking about are too stubbornly alive to be ignored:

> I stand on top
> of our back steps and breathe the rich air—
> a mother skunk with her column of kittens swills the
>   garbage pail.
> She jabs her wedge-head in a cup
> of sour cream, drops her ostrich tail,
> and will not scare.

It will be clear that the first impression given by *Life Studies* is that it is impure art, magnificently stated but unpleasantly egocentric, somehow resembling the triumph of the skunks over the garbage cans. Since its self-therapeutic motive is so obvious and persistent, something of this impression sticks all the way. But as the whole work floods into view the balance shifts decisively. Lowell is still the wonderful poet of "The Quaker Graveyard in Nantucket," the poet of power and passion whose driving aesthetic of anguish belies the "frizzled, stale and small" condition he attributes to himself. He may be wrong in believing that what has happened to New England's elite is necessarily an embodiment of the state of American culture, the whole maggoty character of which he feels he carries about in his own person. But he is not wrong in looking at the culture through the window of psychological breakdown. Too many other American poets, no matter what their social class and family history, have reached the same point in recent years. Lowell is foremost among them in the energy of his uncompromising honesty.

Furthermore, *Life Studies* is not merely a collection of small moment-by-moment victories over hysteria and self-concealment. It is also a beautifully articulated sequence. I say "articulated," but the impact of the sequence is of four intensifying waves of movement that smash at the reader's feelings and break repeatedly over his mind. The poems that make up the opening movement are not personal in the sense of the rest of the book. They are poems of violent contradiction, a historical overture to define the disintegration of a world. In the first a train journeys from Rome to Paris at mid-century. The "querulous hush-hush" of its wheels passes over the Alps and beyond them, but nowhere in the altitudes to which it rises does it touch the sanely brilliant heights of ancient myth and thought. For its riders there are, at one terminal, the hysteria of *bella Roma,* where "the crowds at San Pietro screamed *Papa*" at the pronouncement of the dogma of Mary's assumption and where "the Duce's lynched, bare, booted skull still spoke"; and at the other terminal, the self-destructive freedom of "Paris, our black classic." The next poem reaches far enough back in time to reveal the welter of grossly sensual, mindlessly grasping egotism that attended the birth of the modern age. Marie de Medici, "the banker's daughter," soliloquizes about "blood and pastime," the struggle between monarchy and the "pilfering, pillaging democracies," the assassination of her husband. The third poem returns from modern Europe and its bloody beginnings to our own American moment. All that turbulence of recent centuries now seems frozen into intellectual and moral death:

> Ice, ice. Our wheels no longer move.
> Look, the fixed stars, all just alike
> as lack-land atoms, split apart,
> and the Republic summons Ike,
> the mausoleum in her heart.

But then the fourth poem hurls at us the monologue of a mad Negro soldier confined at Munich. Here the wit, the audacious inti-

macy, the acutely bizarre tragic sense of Lowell's language take on
jet speed. In this monologue the collapse of traditional meaning and
cultural distinctions is dramatized in the frenzy of one contemporary
figure. Thus Lowell begins to zero in on his main target, himself as
the damned speaking-sensibility of his world. The humiliated, homicidal fury of the Negro soldier throws its premonitory shadow over the
disturbed "comedy" of "91 Revere Street" which follows. It helps us
to see, beneath the "Jamesian" nuances of relationship in a society
of ritual pretensions but no center of gravity, how anguished is this
prose section's murderous dissection of the poet's parents and its
complaint against a childhood gone awry. In this way it prepares us
for the personal horrors with which the book closes.

But before that long, devastating final wave of poems, there is
a smaller one, corresponding in gathering force with the first group.
This third wave is again made up of four poems, each of them about a
modern writer with whom Lowell feels kinship as an embattled and
alienated spirit. Following hard upon the prose, these poems clearly
say: "This is what the predatory centuries, and the soul-devouring
world in which I walked the maze of my childhood, have done to
man's creativity." Lowell first portrays Ford Madox Ford, the "mam-
moth mumbler" cheated out of his earned rewards, scratching along
in America, sick and "gagged for air." Then, dear to Lowell's heart,
the self-exiled Santayana looms before us, "free-thinking Catholic
infidel." The third poem recreates with sentimental bitterness a
winter Lowell and Delmore Schwartz spent at Harvard in 1946.
Nothing could be more pathetically open about Lowell's state of mind
concerning himself and his art than the parts of their conversation
he chooses to record and even to italicize:

> . . . "Let Joyce and Freud,
> the Masters of Joy,
> be our guests here," you said. The room was filled
> with cigarette smoke circling the paranoid,
> inert gaze of Coleridge, back
> from Malta—his eyes lost in flesh, lips baked and black. . . .
> You said:
> *"We poets in our youth begin in sadness;*
> *thereof in the end come despondency and madness;*
> Stalin has had two cerebral hemorrhages!"

The ironic facetiousness that so often marks Schwartz's writing and
conversation is here absorbed by Lowell into a vision of unrelieved
breakdown centered on the image of Coleridge's "paranoid gaze" in
the picture. That image, together with the mocking allusion to Stalin

as one of "we poets" who came at last to madness, brings past and
present, and all political and psychological realities, into a single
focus of defeat. Then in the fourth poem, "Words for Hart Crane,"
the group comes to a climax paralleling that of "A Mad Negro Soldier"
in the first group. Crane's brief, self-destructive career is seen as the
demand of the creative spirit, deliberately wearing the most loathsome
mask it can find, for unquestioning love from the culture that has
rejected it. Here, just before he plunges back into his major theme,
the "life studies" of himself and his family, Lowell again, at the most
savagely committed pitch he can command, presents the monologue of
a dramatically suffering figure whose predicament has crucial bearing
on his own situation.

In large part, the fourteen poems of the final section echo the prose
of "91 Revere Street." But they echo it as a storm echoes the fore-
boding sultriness of a threatening spell of weather before it. Apart
from the obvious differences that verse makes, they break out of the
cocoon of childhood mentality that somehow envelops "91 Revere
Street" despite its more sophisticated aspects. Lowell, like Yeats and
Thomas, casts over his autobiographical prose a certain whimsey
(though often morbid) and childlike half-awareness. But the poems
are overborne by sadness first and then by the crash of disaster. Side
by side Lowell places memories of his confinement in mental hospitals
and a denigration of his great act of defiance as a conscientious
objector in World War II which led to his imprisonment for a year:

> I was a fire-breathing Catholic C.O.,
> and made my manic statement,
> telling off the state and president. . . .

The only poem of this group in which he does not talk in his own
person, " 'To Speak of Woe That Is in Marriage,' " is a monologue by
the wife of a lecherous, "hopped-up" drunkard. It is placed strategically
just before the last poem "Skunk Hour," and after "Man and Wife,"
in which Lowell makes certain we know he is discussing his own
marriage, and it is a deliberate plunge into the depths of the theme of
degradation at all but the last moment. Finally, "Skunk Hour," full
of indirections and nuances that bring the sickness of our world as a
whole back into the scene to restore a more universal vision, reaches
a climax of self-contempt and of pure symbol-making. This is Lowell's
fantastic, terrifying skunk image for the secret self's inescapable drive
to assure itself of continued life:

> I myself am hell;
> nobody's here—

only skunks, that search
in the moonlight for a bite to eat.
They march on their soles up Main Street:
white stripes, moonstuck eyes' red fire
under the chalk-dry and spar spire
of the Trinitarian Church

Life Studies brings to culmination one line of development in our poetry of the utmost importance. Technically, it is an experiment in the form of the poetic sequence looser than but comparable to *Mauberley* and *The Bridge*. To build a great poem out of the predicament and horror of the lost Self has been the recurrent effort of the most ambitious poetry of the last century. Lowell's effort is a natural outgrowth of the modern emphasis on the "I" as the crucial poetic symbol, and of the self-analytical monologues of the sensibility which have helped define that emphasis from "The Love Song of J. Alfred Prufrock" to Miss Rukeyser's *Elegies*. It is also an outgrowth of the social criticism that has marked almost the whole sweep of poetry in this century. Thus, Lowell's poems carry the burden of the age within them. From this fact they derive (given Lowell's abilities) an authority not quite present in the post-Byronics of *The True Confession of George Barker*,* or in other works in which the speaker thrusts himself to the fore mainly as an *interesting* person.

It is important, I think, to remember one implication of what writers like Robert Lowell are doing: that their individual lives have profound meaning and worth, and that therapeutic confession will lead to the realization of these values. In this respect their explorations are very different from the sense of bleakness in some of Hart Crane, or in a poem like Kenneth Fearing's "Green Light" whose predicate sentences (in which the subject is omitted) and half-images suggest a universal irrelevance of experience:

Bought at the drug store, very cheap; and later pawned.
After a while, heard on the street; seen in the park.
Familiar, but not quite recognized.
Followed and taken home and slept with.
Traded or sold. Or lost.

To what subject do these predicates belong? Certainly the images are of the commercial world, yet they refer also to love and memory. Later, other images, absurd or fantastic or commonplace, are added: the predicates of human existence. The poet makes the point that all the impressions of daily life and of fantasy, inseparable from the self-

* George Barker, *The True Confession of George Barker*, Alan Swallow, Denver, 1950.

centered and brooding mind, are "strange, and yet not extraordinary."
A tragic pointlessness of truth is suggested, simultaneously defining
the universe as zero and raising the pettiest details, such as the green
light of the busy corner, to a level of universal signifiance. If truth
is pointless, then so are the facts of wisdom, morality, desire, and
death. They are facts

> Bought at the drug store down the street
> Where the wind blows and the motors go by and it is always
> > night, or day;
> Bought to use as a last resort,
> Bought to impress the statuary in the park.

Fearing's poem represents a letting go, while the work of poets with
a perspective like Lowell's is an attempt to hold fast to a moral perspective. Such poets, in their way, are carrying on where Yeats left off
when he proposed that the time had come to make the literal Self
poetry's central redeeming symbol:

> I must lie down where all the ladders start,
> In the foul rag-and-bone shop of the heart.

Despondency and Madness

by John Berryman

A title opaque and violent. Since it throws, at once, little or no light on the poem, we inquire whether the poem throws any light on it, and are under way. Our occasion is the approach of a crisis of mental disorder for the "I" of the poem—presumably one leading to the hospitalization, or hospitalizations, spoken of elsewhere in the volume, *Life Studies,* where it stands last. Mr. Lowell's recent poems, many of them, are as personal, autobiographical, as his earlier poems were hieratic; and it is certain that we are not dealing here purely with invention and symbol. One thing critics not themselves writers of poetry occasionally forget is that poetry is composed by actual human beings, and tracts of it are very closely about them. When Shakespeare wrote "Two loves I have," reader, he was *not kidding.*

Back to the title then. The Hour of the Skunk, I suppose, would be one of the most unprepossessing times of the day, far less livable than the Hour of the Bear, say, or the (Chinese) Month of the Dog. Noon is held a luckless time for Sikhs. Up and down India, when anything goes wrong for a Sikh near midday, all nearby Hindus and Moslems have a ball. Skunk hour: the poet's Sikh noon. The skunk is a small, attractive black-and-white creature, affectionate and loyal when tamed I believe, but it suffers (or rather it does *not* suffer, being an animal) from a bad reputation, owing to its capacity for stinking. (The poet, in the identification, knows; and suffers.) Cornered, it makes the cornerer wish he hadn't. Painful, in symbolization, is the fact that its sting, so to speak, can be drawn, its power of defending itself re-moved—as the poet can be made helpless by what is part of his strength: his strangeness, mental and emotional; the helplessness of a man afraid of going mad is the analogue. The skunk is an outcast; this is the basis of the metaphor, and how a mental patient feels. I hate to call the associations complex, but they are, and with a poet so daring or offhand that he once arranged a masterly elegy around his literal translation of the gambling expression *"Rien ne va plus,"* we must take it. The skunk, its little weakness or weapon apart, is charming; cheer-up. But nobody likes; paranoia. It is not what it seems: the reality belies the benign appearance—as with the statesman Forrestal who supervises American industry's brawl-for-contracts with scrupulous honor and kills himself, or the poet, brilliant, famous, appearing, who goes off his rocker. We like, in mature professional life, to know who we are; which may be on the point of becoming out of the question for the "I" of the poem.

If the topic seems to anyone theatrical, may I mention suicides: two of the three or four most important early Soviet poets, Essenin and Mayakovsky; while Hart Crane and Vachel Lindsay (and for that matter Sara Teasdale—writing really well toward the end) who destroyed themselves here were not our worst poets. Poets in odd ages have killed themselves or gone mad, Poe and Dylan Thomas as clearly as Swift, Chatterton, Smart, Beddoes, and many have written about it from inside and outside, from Cowper's postumous "The Castaway" to Miss Bishop's wonderful "Visits to St. Elizabeth's" and Rilke's *"Das Lied des Idioten."* It is better not to feel so strongly:

> We poets in our youth begin in gladness,
> But thereof comes in the end despondency and madness.

Wordsworth once said that if he had written what he most deeply felt no reader could have borne it, Coleridge that he gave up original poetical composition (but the fine, bleak "Work Without Hope" is late) because he was unable to bear it. One poem does not edge into the terror but starts there and stays there: Jon Silkin's "Death of a Son." This you will find in the Hall-Simpson paperback anthology of recent verse, and it is as brave, and harrowing, as one might think a piece could be. But Lowell's subject is different from all these others'.

His target is the dreadful aura—in epileptic analogy—the coming-on, handled by Hölderlin in *"Hälfte des Lebens,"* which may be the deepest European poem on this unusual theme. You feel you're going too fast, spinning out of control; or too slow; there appears a rift, which will widen. You feel *too* good, or too bad. Difficult subject. Perhaps there is a quarter-inch of mordant humor, by the way, very like this author, in the title: dogs have their day, even the skunk has an hour, characteristic. An inverted celebration. Take the poet's arrangements in three parts, and one critical problem will be to determine how they culminate in the hallucinatory intensity of the seventh stanza. We have the opening stanzas (*praeparatio*), then statement— understatement ("My mind's not right"), then the skunks. One of the poem's desperate points is their *cyclical* approach, each night; as episodes of mental illness are feared to recur. The skunks too, can we wonder, replace him (they will survive as he goes or is taken off) as well as figure him. But we're getting too far ahead.

Very good poem, incidentally, and gets better, explored. Perhaps one of his absolutely best; early to say. Maybe the Faustus allusion is overdrawn. Who cares to hand grades to a writer who could first *make* the Ovid stanza in "Beyond the Alps" (I believe it appeared in the *Kenyon* version) and then delete it? The reader may not have come on this, so I put it in evidence.

> I thought of Ovid, for in Caesar's eyes,
> That Tomcat had the number of the Beast.
> Where the young Turks are facing the red east
> And the twice-stormed Crimean spit, he cries:
> "Rome asked for poets. At her beck and call,
> Came Lucan, Tacitus and Juvenal,
> The black republicans who tore the teats
> And bowels of the mother wolf to bits.
> Beneath a psychopath's divining rod,
> Deserts interred the Caesar-salvaged bog.
> Imperial Tiber, O my yellow Dog,
> Black earth by the Black Roman Sea, I lie
> With the boy-crazy daughter of the God,
> Il duce Augusto. I shall never die."

Mr. Lowell once told the present writer that the stanza took him a hundred hours; it is worth every second of the time, and may be read, despite its author, for as long as things not formular are read.

I hear the first four stanzas of "Skunk Hour" as a unit. Grandiose figures—the senile aristocrat, the summer millionaire—from the past, outworn, gone, or not gone: the theme of the first stanza is Survival— but survival how?—doting; anti-gainfully employed (second stanza, and the "eyesores" "let fall" are the first prefigurings of the paranoid aspect of the skunk-symbol), living in the past. Relevance?—for re-reading (all poems are built of course for re-reading, but this more than most): the poet is afraid of outliving himself, going away, like Hölderlin, Swift, Maupassant. Destructive second stanza, but queerly abstract and arbitrary, anachronistic; as for "privacy," in the modern world (so the underground thought goes) unattainable, hospital life is unspeakably public—one is available without will to doctors, nurses, even (usually) other patients. The sheep have things easy, so to speak, and the radio "bleats" to the untense satisfied lovers in stanza VI; no human responsibilities, any more than the skunks are to have. The poem makes use of the animal-morality tradition without quite belonging to it. "Spartan" I reserve. "Hermit" and "winter" make nearly standard associations with madness.

Note that we have first a true aristocrat, irresponsible ("heiress"—mental illness can be inherited), then a pure money-figure; an ominous declension. (L. L. Bean: I haven't seen a catalogue for years, some boys at my school in Connecticut had them; they were beyond Sears Roebuck and even Alex Taylor for fascination—compare Abercrombie & Fitch, if they put out a catalogue.) Somebody rooted, but off; somebody rootless, gone. Blue Hill I take to be Blue Hill, Maine, where I never saw foxes but don't doubt that they flourish. Thus is the poem's hard line. "A red fox stain covers Blue Hill." Even the syntax is ambiguous—the stain may be red, or it may merely be that red foxes stain with their numbers (a plague to farmers) Blue Hill. Is the sportsman accused of having shot foxes?—but this seems sentimental and improbable; or is the fox population said to have increased since he quit shooting foxes?—but this seems even more implausible. I can't feel the implied narrative is clear. Perhaps there is no implied narrative (but shouldn't there be, tied to the millionaire as the line is?) and we have a straight dream item: for the meaning is certainly to be found in the association backward to "Spartan." This is the boy who stole a fox which, hugged to him in public, ate his vitals, the stain spreading, until stoical he fell dead; clearly a figure for the poet, still unheard of, with his growing hidden wound. At this point "Blue Hill" becomes extra-geographical and macabre: the dying Spartan boy turning blue, the tall poet sad, "blue" (the use of a popular song presently makes this likely).

Now in a succinct modulation from blood (and courage) to pale "orange," appropriate to the "fairy," comes the decorator, to fix things up inside (as psychiatrists will try to do for the poet); miserable, though, things not going well. "Marry" is callous and fraudulent, a last resort. The three figures, on their descending scale, are fruitless. The useful put just to decoration (fishnet), deprived of function, looks on to the poet's fear. One will get, in the poem, no sense of his *doing* anything, only waiting, driving about, skunk-watching, sleepless. (In the opposite conversion, just before, the sporting being put to work, the yawl, I hear as the dominant affect: longing.) This is a late-summer poem, idle, apprehensive.

It's half over. Outworn, gone, queer; analogous figures, tangential all—the first *having been* central, the second having mattered to local revenue. The four stanzas are unemphatic, muted. But their quiet, insistent mustering of the *facts* of an extant world opens toward the danger of its being swept away, into delirium. I have seldom seen stanzas (and by this poet, composer of the Ovid stanza) so un-self-evident. He's holding his fire, let's say. Down-rhyme, casual, unlike earlier

Lowell, suggests Miss Bishop's practice; to whom the poem is dedicated; though the heavy, fierce rhyming of "The Quaker Graveyard" will be admitted in the final stanzas. Money-wellness, however misused (compare Eliot's ruined millionaire, Adam, in the *Quartets*—the auctioning off of the boat does not suggest that this one is doing very well), seems important all through the three figures and winds up in a "rich" air, freedom, the poet's to lose. The "fairy," poor, is already sick with perversion.

Since, on the entrance of "I" in stanza V, he climbs a sort of Golgotha (Place of the Skull), I will observe that there is more Christian detail in the poem than might have been expected. There's the bishop (I see no assimilation here to Chekhov's overwhelming story, which however I haven't read for years), the Marlovian hell of stanza VI ("where we are in hell," as Mephistophilis says at line 554 of Tucker Brooke's criminal edition, and compare other texts in that corrupt play, which even Greg was unsatisfactory with), the Trinitarian Church, and even the interior decorator goes in for suspicious properties: a fishnet (Peter, but Peter was married), cobbling (but Christ is said—on the Synoptic evidence, see Guignebert's *Jesus*, p. 106 —to have been a carpenter). The detail is not, I think, systematic, and serves the purpose of a kind of hopeless casting about for aid;— unavailable, as in Hemingway's "A Clean, Well-lighted Place," in *The Trial,* in *Waiting for Godot,* you name it. I should say that Lowell works rather in parable-form than in forms of allegory. There is no point-to-point correspondence, the details are free. The (hoped for?) rescue-figures are simply sinister and pathetic, the senile old lady who lets houses decay, the unhappy homosexual who would like to fix up their interiors. Who knows where the bishop is?

In stanza V there is much more than: furtive love, furtive madness. But both come out loud and open in stanza VI, and the loss of the person, in its last line, leads to the oneiric vision of the skunks.

Their ceremonial line, for (their kind of) nourishment, may belong with the religious traces. They have taken over the world; the poet has a final instant of freedom at the start of the last stanza. "Moonstruck" and "ostrich" (I am lunatic, hidden—hidden?) then take over. We began with one mother (of a bishop) and wind up with another (of a column of little skunks) in a sort of greedy parody of the Eucharist; the ultimate help. Some of Lowell's early poems were savagely Marian. I would not call this poem at all friendly to Christianity, which appears to have failed the shelving (and to be shelved) man. We feed instead on garbage. The "cream" is sour. The last line equals: "I will, I *do* 'scare.'" It is man's right, foreseeing, to be frightened. But the stubbornness of the mother skunk, like that (merely in association) of the Spartan boy, make up a small counterpoise to the poem's terror.

We attend, so, to a sense of having been failed by the biological and mental and emotional (and religious) probabilities: not all, or most, have to feel this way; many can believe. There is a staving-off, with dramatization, of self-pity; an implied (at the end) confession of fear. I have a feeling that the poem may look better fifty years from now, even better. Snatching at war-terms irritates one, as of writers; Baudelaire hated "avant-garde"; but it takes moral courage, at least, to write in this poem's direction.

I must pause, briefly, to admire its administration of Time. In general for it Time narrows: a vista of decades, "The season's ill," *one* night, and so down to the skunk hour. But I notice two substantial exceptions to the method. The second stanza opens a longer vista still than the first, with "century." And the "Hour" is *nightly,* expanding again into a dreaded recurrence. Most real poets work in this way, but Lowell decidedly rather more than most. I will now admit that I cannot like "my ill-spirit sob in each blood cell"; the expression is just what it should not be, rhetorical, exterior, especially with "hear."

For convenience in exposition, with a poem so personal, I have been pretending that "I" is the poet, but of course the speaker can never be the actual writer, who is a person with an address, a Social Security number, debts, tastes, memories, expectations. Shakespeare says "Two loves I have": he does not say *only* two loves, and indeed he must have loved also his children, various friends, presumably his wife, his parents. The necessity for the artist of selection opens inevitably an abyss between his person and his persona. I only said that much poetry is "very closely about" the person. The persona looks across at the person and then sets about its own work. Lowell's careful avoidance, in "Skunk Hour," of the grand style he was still wielding in the Ovid stanza, for instance, makes the distinction material here. This mysterious "I" that poets deploy can certainly never be defined, but a good recent stab at characterization was Mr. Ransom's in an earlier one of these symposia, about Roethke: "The true self or soul or mind of the highly compounded authorial I . . ." I would call it virtually certain that Lowell had in mind and at heart during this poem not only his own difficulties whatever they may be or have been but the personal disorders to which other poets of his age and place have been furiously subject.

Another question raised with acuteness by the poem is how far it is fair to take associations. A characteristic vice of modern criticism is taking them too far. One of Randall Jarrell's remarks sticks in my head: "as people ought to know, very complicated organizations are excessively rare in poetry." I am in ringing agreement. Hurrah. But whether the dictum applies to Lowell's poems, or to an onslaught against the Old Testament and the New Testament like Thomas's "A

Refusal to Mourn . . . ," seems to me very doubtful; as I think Jarrell concedes in his handsome, better than handsome, studies of Lowell. No rules will help, naturally, but can we seek guideposts? Suppose we try two: (1) When there is something imperfectly narrative, imperfectly dramatic, which obstinately *needs accounting for,* we allow ourselves, as readers, more liberty of interpreting than otherwise; (2) Where accident and coincidence seem implausible, we stick by the textual and psychological (even depth-psychological) probabilities. Both signs point to a connection of "Spartan" and "fox stain," though fifteen lines separate them. I have several times gone too far here, deliberately, in order to repudiate my (non-) findings. But I think we must allow, with some poets, for broad and complex areas of suggestion; and I would propose a third guidepost: (3) Whatever relates, however uncertainly, to the *ruling theme* of the poem deserves the reader's intimate attention. Thus, in the fifth stanza, the fact of its being a *dark* night may suggest in our tradition spiritual despair (St. John of the Cross), and the desolate "hull to hull" may look back to the "Nautilus," adventurous, submerged; or they may not. I have made no attempt to exhaust the poem. If we were a little longer civilized here, the poet would plainly be declared, in Japanese fashion, a National Cultural Asset, and exempted from coarse analyses of his subtle, strong, terrible poems.

On "Skunk Hour"

by Robert Lowell

I. The Meaning

The author of a poem is not necessarily the ideal person to explain its meaning. He is as liable as anyone else to muddle, dishonesty and reticence. Nor is it his purpose to provide a peg for a prose essay. Meaning varies in importance from poem to poem, and from style to style, but always it is only a strand and an element in the brute flow of composition. Other elements are pictures that please or thrill for themselves, phrases that ring for their music or carry some buried suggestion. For all this the author is an opportunist, throwing whatever comes to hand into his feeling for start, continuity, contrast, climax, and completion. It is imbecile for him not to know his intentions, and unsophisticated for him to know too explicitly and fully.

Three papers by three poets on another's poem! Perhaps they should be considered as short stories and variants on my original. I shall comment on them later; here, I only want to say that I learned much from them. Very little of what I had in mind is untouched on; much that never occurred to me has been granted me. What I didn't intend often seems now at least as valid as what I did. My complaint is not that I am misunderstood, but that I am overunderstood. I am seen through.

I am not sure whether I can distinguish between intention and interpretation. I think this is what I more or less intended. The first four stanzas are meant to give a dawdling more or less amiable picture of a declining Maine sea town. I move from the ocean inland. Sterility howls through the scenery, but I try to give a tone of tolerance, humor, and randomness to the sad prospect. The composition drifts, its direction sinks out of sight into the casual, chancy arrangements of nature and decay. Then all comes alive in stanzas V and VI. This is the dark night. I hoped my readers would remember John of the Cross's poem. My night is not gracious, but secular, puritan, and agnostical. An

Existentialist night. Somewhere in my mind was a passage from Sartre or Camus about reaching some point of final darkness where the one free act is suicide. Out of this comes the march and affirmation, an ambiguous one, of my skunks in the last two stanzas. The skunks are both quixotic and barbarously absurd, hence the tone of amusement and defiance. "Skunk Hour" is not entirely independent, but the anchor poem in its sequence.

II. How the Poem Was Written

What I can describe and what no one else can describe are the circumstances of my poem's composition. I shan't reveal private secrets. John Berryman's pathological chart comes frighteningly close to the actual event. When I first read his paper, I kept saying to myself, "Why he is naming the very things I wanted to keep out of my poem." In the end, I had to admit that Berryman had hit a bull's-eye, and often illuminated matters more searchingly and boldly than I could have wished. Is his account true? I cannot decide, the truth here depends on what psychologists and philosophers one accepts. Berryman comes too close for comfort.

"Skunk Hour" was begun in mid-August, 1957, and finished about a month later. In March of the same year, I had been giving readings on the West Coast, often reading six days a week and sometimes twice on a single day. I was in San Francisco, the era and setting of Allen Ginsberg, and all about very modest poets were waking up prophets. I became sorely aware of how few poems I had written, and that these few had been finished at the latest three or four years earlier. Their style seemed distant, symbol-ridden and willfully difficult. I began to paraphrase my Latin quotations, and to add extra syllables to a line to make it clearer and more colloquial. I felt my old poems hid what they were really about, and many times offered a stiff, humorless and even impenetrable surface. I am no convert to the "beats." I know well too that the best poems are not necessarily poems that read aloud. Many of the greatest poems can only be read to one's self, for inspiration is no substitute for humor, shock, narrative and a hypnotic voice, the four musts for oral performance. Still, my own poems seemed like prehistoric monsters dragged down into the bog and death by their ponderous armor. I was reciting what I no longer felt. What influenced me more than San Francisco and reading aloud was that for some time I had been writing prose. I felt that the best style for poetry was none of the many poetic styles in English, but something like the prose of Chekhov or Flaubert.

When I returned to my home, I began writing lines in a new style.

No poem, however, got finished and soon I left off and tried to forget the whole headache. Suddenly, in August, I was struck by the sadness of writing nothing, and having nothing to write, of having, at least, no language. When I began writing "Skunk Hour," I felt that most of what I knew about writing was a hindrance.

The dedication is to Elizabeth Bishop, because re-reading her suggested a way of breaking through the shell of my old manner. Her rhythms, idiom, images, and stanza structure seemed to belong to a later century. "Skunk Hour" is modeled on Miss Bishop's "The Armadillo," a much better poem and one I had heard her read and had later carried around with me. Both "Skunk Hour" and "The Armadillo" use short line stanzas, start with drifting description and end with a single animal.

This was the main source. My others were Hölderlin's *"Brod und Wein,"* particularly the moon lines:

> *Sich! und das Schattenbild unserer Erde, der Mond,*
> *kommet geheim nun auch; die Schwärmerische, die Nacht kommt*
> *"vohl" mit Sternen und "wohl" wenig bekummert um uns,*

and so forth. I put this in long straggling lines and then added touches of Maine scenery, till I saw I was getting nowhere. Another source, probably undetectable now, was Annette von Droste-Hülshoff's *"Am letzten Tage des Jahres."* She too uses a six-line stanza with short lines. Her second stanza is as follows:

> *'s ist tiefe Nacht!*
> *Ob wohl ein Auge offen noch?*
> *In diesen Mauern ruttelt dein*
> *Verrinnen, Zeit! Mir schaudert; doch*
> *Es will die letzte Stunde sein*
> *Einsam durchwacht.*
>
> *Geschehen all*

Here and elsewhere, my poem and the German poem have the same shudders and situation.

"Skunk Hour" was written backwards, first the last two stanzas, I think, and then the next to last two. Anyway, there was a time when I had the last four stanzas much as they now are and nothing before them. I found the bleak personal violence repellent. All was too close, though watching the lovers was not mine, but from an anecdote about Walt Whitman in his old age. I began to feel that real poetry came, not from fierce confessions, but from something almost meaningless but imagined. I was haunted by an image of a blue china doorknob. I never used the doorknob, or knew what it meant, yet somehow it started the current of images in my opening stanzas. They were written in reverse order, and at last gave my poem an earth to stand on, and space to breathe.

III. The Critics

I don't think I intended either the Spartan boy holding the fox or Satan's feeling of sexual deprivation, while he watched Adam and Eve in the Garden. I may have, but I don't remember. The red fox stain was merely meant to describe the rusty reddish color of autumn on Blue Hill, a Maine mountain near where we were living. I had seen foxes playing on the road one night, and I think the words have sinister and askew suggestions.

I can't imagine anything more thorough than Nims's stanza-by-stanza exposition. Almost all of it is to the point. I get a feeling of going on a familiar journey, but with another author and another sensibility. This feeling is still stronger when I read Wilbur's essay.* Sometimes he and I are named as belonging to the same school, what *Time* Magazine calls "the couth poets." Sometimes we are set in battle against one another. I have no idea which, if either, is true. Certainly, we both in different ways owe much to the teaching and practice of John Crowe Ransom. Certainly, his essay embodies and enhances my poem. With Berryman too, I go on a strange journey! Thank God, we both come out clinging to spars, enough floating matter to save us, though faithless.

* [The essays by Richard Wilbur and John Frederick Nims are included in *The Contemporary Poet as Artist and Critic,* ed. Anthony Ostroff (Boston: Little, Brown and Company, Inc., 1964)—ED.]

Benito Cereno from Melville to Lowell

by Robert Ilson

Benito Cereno is the name of a novella by Herman Melville. It is also the name of a verse play by Robert Lowell, who won an "Obie" for it.[1] Not only did Lowell's play enjoy an unexpectedly long off-Broadway run, but it was greeted by some critics as the beginning of a new interest in poetic drama in the United States.

I went to see the play with a good deal of eager anticipation. It was not just that Lowell is a fine writer and Melville's story an authentic masterpiece; it was that Lowell had chosen to dramatize a work of great complexity and indirection, one that presents very difficult problems for anyone who wants to re-create it on the stage.

For one thing, there is the structure of the story. In 1799 (1800 in Lowell's version) the American captain Amasa Delano sees a Spanish ship behaving curiously in South American waters and forms four successive hypotheses about it. First: it is a shipload of "Black Friars." Second: the "monks" are really slaves under the command of Don Benito Cereno. Third: Benito Cereno is really a pirate bent on killing Delano and capturing his ship. Fourth: not Cereno but the slaves are really pirates. They have forced Cereno to pretend he is still in command, but in fact have seized control of his ship in a "ferocious piratical revolt." Now Delano sees the Negroes "with mask torn away."

Delano believes this fourth hypothesis to be the correct one. He acts on it and has his men capture the *San Dominick* and take the Negroes back to Lima "in irons." The Peruvian court that hears the case agrees with him and calls him "noble" and "generous." After being deceived three times in succession, Delano has concluded that the Negroes are "ferocious" pirates. He is at last undeceived.

But is he? In Melville's story we are left to decide this question for ourselves. But we are not without some hints of Melville's own views. After the whole episode is over, Benito Cereno reminds Delano that

"*Benito Cereno* from Melville to Lowell" by Robert Ilson. From *Salmagundi*, Vol. 1, No. 4. Reprinted by permission of *Salmagundi*.

[1] The play, which had its premiere on November 1, 1964, has been published as part of a trilogy of plays under the title *The Old Glory* (Farrar, Straus and Giroux, New York, 1965). Page references in this article are to that edition.

Delano once believed him to be "a villain," when in fact he was only a pawn. "So far may even the best men err," says Don Benito, "in judging the conduct of one with the recesses of whose condition he (sic) is not acquainted." Delano judged Cereno falsely because he was not acquainted with Cereno's true condition. But when Delano judged the Negroes to be ferocious pirates, one is entitled to wonder whether he was acquainted with the recesses of *their* condition.

We have another hint on a symbolic level. As Captain Delano boards the *San Dominick* one of the first things he sees is a scene carved on the ship's stern representing "a dark satyr in a mask, holding his foot on the prostrate neck of a writhing figure, also masked." In light of what we learn later on, it is easy to assume that the masked satyr is a Negro and that the masked writhing figure is white. A reader who is linguistically oriented, however, will notice not only that the writhing figure is not described as white, but that *nowhere in the text* are the Negroes called "dark." "Black," yes, but not "dark." Indeed the only character described as "dark" in the story is—Benito Cereno, called at one point "the dark Spaniard . . . the central hobgoblin of all." [2] Moreover, it is difficult not to be struck by the curious fact that there is only one person in the story who actually puts his foot on someone else: it is Captain Delano, under whose "right foot" the "prostrate" Babo, leader of the Negroes, is "ground."

So it is at least possible that Captain Delano was most deceived just when he thought he was at last undeceived. But Melville nowhere says this directly; we are left to judge for ourselves, and many readers seem to have judged otherwise.

Lowell changes the satyr symbol in his play. The writhing figure in *his* carving has no mask, and has become explicitly a "big white goddess" (p. 125)—and with "quite a figure." And nowhere else in the text of the play or in the production of it that I saw does anybody's foot go onto anybody's neck.

This illustrates the first major difference between Melville and Lowell, for in Lowell's play we are not left to judge for ourselves. Things are explicit. At the end Babo (called Babu in the play) even steps right up and tells us what he has done, and why (p. 193):

[2] The confirmation of this point required a comparison of several editions of Melville's novella, for the one originally consulted, the well-known *Shorter Novels of Herman Melville* (Horace Liveright, New York, 1928), contains the following embarrassing counter-example on pages 36 and 37: "There was a difference between the idea of Don Benito's *darky* pre-ordaining Captain Delano's fate, and Captain Delano's lightly arranging Don Benito's." (my emphasis) But three other editions all concur on a reading of *darkly* for *darky* in this passage (see, for example, Herman Melville, *4 Short Novels*, Bantam Classics FC16, New York, 1959, p. 135), thus making the disputed word refer not to a Negro, but to Benito Cereno himself.

> I . . .
> . . . planned, dared and carried out
> the seizure of this ship, the *San Domingo*.
> Untouched by blood myself, I had all
> the most dangerous and useless Spaniards killed.
> I freed my people from their Egyptian bondage.
> The heartless Spaniards slaved for me like slaves.

This final speech is very different from what happens in the original, at the end of which Babo, "seeing all was over . . . uttered no sound, nor could he be forced to," and, remaining silent throughout his trial and sentence of execution, "met his voiceless end." It is only from the records of the court at Lima that we learn the details of the slave insurrection and its goal: the return of the Negroes to Africa on board the *San Dominick* (a type of project, one might add, by no means unknown during slavery, and sometimes successful). Melville goes to great lengths to arrange things so that Babo never speaks directly to Delano about his past deeds or his intentions, and reveals almost nothing of his true self. He is there for Delano to interpret rather than the dramatic character that Lowell makes him. Anyone who thinks that this change was forced upon Lowell by the nature of the drama-form should ponder Iago's last lines (*Othello*, Act 5, Scene 2), so strikingly reminiscent of the way Melville's Babo behaves: "Demand me nothing: what you know, you know:/From this time forth I never will speak word."

This difference in style between Melville and Lowell is not confined to the difference between Melville's silence and Lowell's elaborate explanations, however. There are times when they both speak, but with a different voice. Reference has previously been made to Benito Cereno's observation "So far may even the best men err in judging the conduct of one with the recesses of whose condition he is not acquainted." This observation does not appear in Lowell's play. Instead, on page 177 of the published version Don Benito says: "Only the unfortunate can understand misfortune." Both of these statements seem to serve equivalent and important functions in the two works under discussion. Both seem to be critical of Delano. (At the end of the play, on page 193, Cereno even exclaims: "My God how little these people understand!") But Lowell has reduced Melville's statement about the obligations of consciousness to a crude and by no means self-evidently true observation about material circumstances.

Nonetheless, Lowell's language has its own rewards, as one might expect in any work by so eminent a poet. For example, on page 166 Benito says to Babu: "You belong to me. I belong to you forever."

This line has not only an obvious ironic reference to their real and dissembled relationship at this point in the play, but reinforces this irony by echoing a great line addressed under interestingly analogous circumstances by Iago to Othello (Act 3, Scene 2): "I am your own forever." This hint of a parallel with *Othello* is, however, not without foreshadowings in Melville, as we have seen.

The second major difference between Melville and Lowell is the character of Amasa Delano. In Lowell's play Babu is moved to reveal the slave revolt by the increasingly aggressive behavior of Captain Delano, who begins to order everyone about as if *he* were master of the Spanish ship. On page 185 Babu exclaims: "I can't stand any more of their insolence;/the Americans treat us like their slaves!" But in Melville's story Delano behaves throughout his stay on the *San Dominick* in the mildest manner imaginable.

In Melville, Delano is "a person of a singularly undistrustful good nature," capable of compassion for individual slaves while unable to understand the monstrosity of the system of slavery.

Another characteristic of this Delano, which is omitted by Lowell, is his general inability to imagine the Negroes as fully human. He sees a Negro child trying to nurse at his sleeping mother's breast, but perceives the situation thus:

> Sprawling at her lapped breasts was her wide-awake fawn . . . its hands, like two paws . . . its mouth and nose ineffectually rooting to get at the mark . . .

This language may make it seem that Delano was disgusted by the scene. Not at all: as soon as the mother, wakened by all this activity, covers her child with kisses, Delano, "well pleased," thinks: "There's naked nature now, pure tenderness and love . . ." And he praises the "negresses" as highly as one can praise creatures not quite of one's own species: "Unsophisticated as leopardesses; loving as doves."

In Lowell's play Delano's character has almost completely changed: he has become a worldly cynic. This new Delano is neatly described in Robert Brustein's introduction to the version of Lowell's play published in *The Old Glory*. Brustein says (p. xiii) that Lester Rawlins played Delano as "suave, smug and self-satisfied." Lowell's Delano has travelled more widely than Benito Cerento; he makes jokes about French women and—he talks extensively about politics. In a lengthy conversation that Lowell puts at the beginning of the play (pp. 121–122) Delano says he thinks that at bottom, for all their apparent differences, Adams and Jefferson are both "gentlemen," which means, to Delano, moderates and ultimately upholders of the *status quo*. This conversation does not appear in Melville. It was entirely invented by Lowell. And indeed it was probably in order to introduce this discussion that Lowell changed the date of the story from 1799 to 1800, since 1800 was the year of the Presidential election in which Jefferson defeated Adams. In this connection, one of the most interesting changes of detail in the play is the name of Captain Delano's ship. Melville's naive Captain Delano has a ship called *Bachelor's Delight,* while Lowell's Delano, the political commentator, has a ship called the *President Adams.* In a word, Lowell's Delano is no longer *innocent.*

There is no better way to summarize the two differences between Melville and Lowell that have been discussed so far—the difference in style and the difference in their chief character—than by considering the Atufal episode, which occurs in both novella and play. In an effort to make Delano believe that Benito Cereno is still in command of his ship, Atufal, subsequently revealed as Babo's "lieutenant in all" in the slave revolt, is led to Benito Cereno in chains that appear to be (but only appear to be) locked. In order to be set free, Atufal must ask Don Benito to pardon him. This Atufal refuses to do, and he is dismissed, seemingly still in chains. In Melville, Delano is impressed by Atufal's adamant refusal to beg Benito Cereno's pardon. Atufal's undaunted pride makes Delano exclaim: "Upon my conscience then . . . he has a royal spirit in him, this fellow." And Delano intercedes on Atufal's behalf: ". . . take a fool's advice, and, in view of his general docility, as well as in some natural respect for his spirit, remit his penalty." This advocate of mercy for the individual slave is the same Delano who will shortly destroy the slave rebellion and bring the slaves back into custody. As Melville draws him, Captain Amasa Delano is a classical and even a definitive portrait of a social type which in the language of our contemporary controversialists has come to be called the "white liberal."

In the Atufal episode as it appears in Lowell's play, Delano does not show any admiration for Atufal's spirit, nor does he intercede on his behalf. Indeed, he says (p. 148): "I never interfere with another man's ship./Don Benito is your lord and dictator." A result of this change is a sacrifice of Melville's exquisite contrast between Delano's perception of the individual case and his inability to comprehend the general situation which it illustrates. One may even say that hardly a trace of Melville's original drama of cognition survives in Lowell's play. But the categories by means of which Lowell's Delano perceives the world are essentially political, and his language is an appropriately ironic comment on non-intervention when it is remembered that the same Delano who is not willing to intervene on behalf of a slave will shortly be willing to intervene against the whole slave revolt.

From a stylistic point of view, it is interesting to note that the "crime" for which Atufal is supposedly being "punished" is never revealed in Melville. But in Lowell it is, in the next scene: according to

Babu (p. 148): "He used the Spanish flag for toilet paper." This addition in Lowell's play may be extenuated on the grounds that his *Benito Cereno* is part of a trilogy of plays under the collective title *The Old Glory*—a trilogy in which one of the unifying elements is flag symbolism. A further justification may be provided by Delano's subsequent comment (p. 148): "Perhaps the flag was left somewhere it shouldn't have been," which may be taken as a symbolic statement that Spain had no right to acquire slaves in Africa. But in spite of these justifications it is difficult to suppress a shudder at the obvious crudity of the image that Lowell has provided where Melville chose to be silent.

And yet this very crudity contributes to what is perhaps the high point of Lowell's play (pp. 189–190). It is very near the end. The pretense that Benito Cereno is still in command of his ship has been abandoned, and now it becomes *his* turn to be loaded with chains and forced to ask pardon. But with a difference:

Babu
Former Captain Benito Cereno, kneel!
Ask pardon of man!

Benito
(Kneeling)
I ask pardon for having been born a Spaniard
I ask pardon for having enslaved my fellow man

Here, in addition to all the obvious similarities and contrasts with the Atufal episode there is another contrast that is implicit. Atufal's supposed crime was using the Spanish flag for toilet paper—the sort of lurid offense that makes headlines in the press. Benito Cereno's crime was having enslaved his fellow man.

As the character of Amasa Delano changes, so the focus of the play changes from the focus of the novella, in a way that could be described as a difference of emphasis if such a phrase did not imply a certain triviality. This is the third major difference between Melville and Lowell. What Melville's story means can be and has been a subject for argument. But there seems little room to doubt that it is *about* slavery, even if only in some simple denotative sense. On the other hand Lowell's play, although representing the same general situation, leads us very quickly to an enlarged frame of reference. The process begins even before the *San Domingo* is clearly visible. Delano trains his telescope on the sea and observes (p. 123): ". . . an ocean undulating in long scoops of swells;/it's set like the beheaded French Queen's high wig." The first line is essentially taken from Melville (who describes the sea as "undulated into long roods of swells"). But the second line is Lowell's own. Similarly, a little later, when the ship itself is closer, Lowell's Delano remarks (p. 125): "The battered forecastle looks like a raped Versailles." References to the French Revolution recur in the play (though not, apparently, in the novella), but also comments of a more contemporary nature. On page 178 Delano says: ". . . This old world needs new blood/and Yankee gunnery to hold it up," and on page 184 his boatswain Perkins says: "They think America is Santa Claus." [3] And indeed, one of the most striking lines in the play occurs in a scene where an episode from "classical" American history is referred to against the background of a more recent reference. Near the end of the play the Negroes force Bosun Perkins to walk over the Spanish flag and kiss the mouth of a white man's skull. Captain Delano cries out (p. 191):

> You are dishonoring your nation, Perkins!
> Don't you stand for anything?

To which Perkins replies:

> I only have one life, Sir.

The one life that Nathan Hale had to give for his country becomes the "one life" that Bosun Perkins has to save. But the whole scene, which has no counterpart in Melville, reminded me quite strongly of one of the more lurid rumors about the Congo in circulation at about the time the play was written: the rumor that various members of the American diplomatic corps there had been forced to eat the American flag.

In other words, we have been transported, as it were, from the world of domestic policy in Melville to the world of foreign policy in Lowell, and, in particular, to the world of revolutions.[4] The revolt of the slaves in Lowell has much more clearly the international appearance of a colonial revolt than its counterpart in Melville. It is as if we had moved from the era of the Dred Scott decision (when Melville wrote, according to Alexander Laing in *The Nation* of 24 January 1966) to the era of the war in Viet Nam,[5] and the question is not so much how Lowell's Delano is going to react to slaves attempting to free themselves as how he is going to react to whole nations in revolt.

This change in emphasis lends special poignancy to that moment at the very end of the play when Babu, who had earlier (p. 147) expressed the sentiment that "the United States must be a paradise for people like Babu," confronts Captain Delano with the appeal (p. 194):

[3] An international flavor is also, though perhaps unintentionally, given to the play by its use of phrases in French and Italian as well as Spanish.

[4] I would like to thank Dr. Sava Klickovic for pointing out the emphasis on foreign policy in Lowell's play.

[5] Interestingly enough the play was produced *before* the recent events in *Santo Domingo*.

"Yankee Master understands me. The future is with us." But the proffered alliance is rejected.

These differences between Melville and Lowell—the change in Amasa Delano's character and the change in focus from the domestic problem of slavery in Melville to the problem of America's foreign policy in Lowell—prepare us for, and perhaps are necessary for, the last difference between the two writers: the way their stories end. In the final scene of the Lowell play Captain Delano kills Babu. Delano's crew suddenly appear and shoot down all the slaves, leaving only a Negro woman to wail over the destruction, and Delano himself shoots Babu in spite of Bosun Perkins' cry (p. 194): "Let him surrender. Let him surrender./We want to save someone." But in Melville the ending is different. Captain Delano, who has returned to his own ship, prudently stays behind while his men row out to capture the *San Dominick*. As we know, the slaves are taken alive and brought to Lima. "To kill or maim the negroes was not the object. To take them, with the ship, was the object." [6] Thus Melville's Delano instigates the final events of the story but at the same time tries to avoid personal involvement in them. And in this way Melville produces a remarkable comparison between his Delano and his Babo. For it turns out in the court records that although Babo was "the plotter from first to last" who "ordered every murder" during the revolt, he "committed no murder" himself. So Babo's hands, as well as Delano's, are clean. Yet Babo is officially judged guilty and executed; Delano officially judged innocent, and indeed praised.

The difference between Melville's Delano and Lowell's reflects the century that separates the two writers. Violence has increased during that century, and so has America's conscious participation in that violence. The naive *bonhommie* and self-deception of Melville's Delano have made way for the hardheaded cynicism of Lowell's Delano, a man who has no small-scale illusions and is willing to dip his own hands in blood. The white liberal has become a fascist.

And as the consciousness of violence has increased, so the rationale of violence has changed. In Melville's story, Delano's sailors are encouraged to capture the *San Dominick* by the promise of a share in her and her cargo, which they are told are together "worth upwards of ten thousand doubloons." But the crewmen of Lowell's Delano need no special incentive to exterminate the whole slave population. Mere profit has been transcended, and pacification is the order of the day.

[6] Though it should be pointed out that in the fight to recapture the ship "nearly a score of the negroes were killed," and some more were killed by Delano's sailors while in chains on route to Lima—out of a total which may have gone as high as 160 slaves.

For the Union Dead

by Thomas Parkinson

It is no longer possible for any member of my generation to approach a book like *For the Union Dead* with genuine freshness or innocence, as we could *Land of Unlikeness* or *Lord Weary's Castle* when they first struck our attention. It would take a more elaborate artifact than seems to me worthwhile to give the impression that Lowell—whatever "Lowell" is—had not been central to my awareness for a long time. There are, however, certain growing platitudes that I should like to squelch from the outset. Lowell, for people who came to maturity during the second World War, was not *our* poet in the way that Eliot and Auden and Thomas and even Archibald Macleish was "our poet" for a large body of people. It makes me uneasy to hear the period from c. 1945 to the present referred to as "The Age of Lowell"—the phrase has a tinny fabricated sound. Lowell was something we reacted to and against, but there was never a sense of coziness about the whole thing, especially if one met it, except briefly, in cool print. He was, rather, an other and representative reality. One reacted to what he represented, religiously and aesthetically, as much as to whatever it was that he was. And finally he sent us back to his constituents, so that he hardly seemed an individual force but a literary figure, that is, a complex type. He embodied various elements and gave them a special uneasy bond. There was a basic instability in his work precisely because of the incompatibility of the orders it accepted.

Taking only one example: that generation, and it is really a generation now with children and defined intellectual contours and tastes and powers, held a vision of itself as politically radical while practicing and admiring art that is culturally conservative. Wisdom should have warned us that confusion lay in that direction, and *The Mills of the Kavanaughs* is a monument to that confusion. Those of us who have remained alive to pressures of being, learned painfully and fully the results of such confusions. Lowell was a reminder of pain. He dramatized, not knowing it himself any more than the rest of us, that pain was normal for our generation because of the irrecon-

"For the Union Dead" by Thomas Parkinson. From *Salmagundi*, Vol. 1, No. 4. Reprinted by permission of *Salmagundi*.

cilabilities we had chosen as our substance, and then the ultimate numbness that great pain imposes. It always surprises me to contemplate how many of my contemporaries carry lead or the weight of prison sentences or the shock of the violence of the state in its many forms as part of their physiology. The experience of depression, war, and cold war was violent and constricting, so that when Lowell writes of

> . . . pain
> suffering without purgation,
> the back-track of the screw. . . .

he says cogently what was at the base of the matter. Pain was what we expected society to impose, and all our cultural conditioning had led us to associate purgation and genuine suffering with that pain.

Hence Lowell's painful poetry was accepted for the moral and emotional orders it sanctioned. Now with *For the Union Dead* he has written a book that carries this painfulness one step further, and he has written a genuinely popular book—people who wouldn't otherwise read poetry read it. At the same time I find it very hard to defend *For the Union Dead* on poetic terms. It is possible to say all sorts of nice things about it as part of an œuvre and on, once again, representative terms. We can assert its equivalence to the freedom that Lowell has earned in his theater pieces, and we can place it in relation to *Life Studies* as a continuation of the relaxed tone and feeling for a tradition of the self started in that book. We can move out into comments on confessional poetry and the sentiment of release engendered by Sylvia Plath and Ann Sexton. In the larger history of American poetic idiom it extends the poetic world of Williams and others so that our tradition can be defined more clearly. Only folly or malice could deny the biographical and historical function of the book.

Beyond these generalities, other qualities in the poems are compelling as subject matter and inescapable images, especially the crucial metaphor of the animal. The poetry does in the movement of its imagery do more than make a sentimental claim on the audience by referring to other poems in the Lowell canon and the contours of his life. Domesticated animals are monsters. Beasts associated with men become more or less than beasts—dogs, rats, chickens, pigs are all revolting as ideas, however charming any single specimen may be. They are parodies and realizations of our natures. *For the Union Dead* is full of animals that have been made monstrous by human tones and cagings. The muskrat that slices the poet's thumb and smashes a wooden crate to pieces in its furious frustration is not an animal but a being made monstrous by human impositions. When

Lowell urges us to pity the monsters, he is in effect asserting that we are in some sense responsible for their monstrosity, our perception has made them extra-natural, even though our perception is not natural. In this book there are no innocent animals because there are no innocent human relations to animals. The animals in themselves do not represent human traits; they evoke them, become the occasions for self-degradation and disgust. Men may be sovereign but they have abused their power to the point of lessening themselves and all in their custody.

Thematically the animals relate to the fallen, even collapsed, state of the protagonist, who lives again through paradise lost. Heaven, paradise, nature, youth, the past which has real youth that no present can ever have had—these are all losses in this book, so that the personal life effectively goes through the processes of the racial. Animals in our world have been monstered by human action as much as the free beasts of the pre-lapsarian state were monstered by the primal crime. That crime has, in the background of the poetry, been re-enacted. The poems are post-Christian; even more than that: they are poems of a world that has denied its second and would deny a third chance by taking the whole matter out of the hands of any god at all. Men really are as gods; they really can control their environment at all levels, tidal, meteorologic, cosmic; they can destroy it, this being the ultimate control, just as violence is the ultimate ratio. Reason and measure are simply not relevant terms.

The poetry shapes most powerfully a world of feeding and devouring in which life can be resolved to the purest of force, no more, no less than force. Submarine or strangling in a false element, lives become archaic like paleontological reminders of witless disaster, immobilized in gestures that have fragile lost meanings like those of statues whose social motive is exhausted now or was false from the start. The animals complement the statues, and the architecture has as much and as little meaning as beast and human imitation.

"This might be nature," he says wistfully—two water-towers in New York? The claims of tenderness that the poem makes won't stand up under the data, so the poem is not finished. There is a kind of savagery operative, not the famous savagery or vindictiveness of tone that is the physical voice of a Lowell poem, but the sophistical savagery that denies the art that it practices. It won't do, the kind of evasion that says this or that poem is about poetry or about the impossibility of finishing even the poem that one is working on at the very moment. We should ask what it is that the poetry refers to that *makes* it poetry or impossible to be poetry.

With this book it seems to me that Lowell has moved past the pain and disgust of his earlier work toward impatience. This may be our great collective psychosis right now, and once again Lowell has taken on himself a representative role. But with impatience, which won't do in art or science, comes the more specifically poetry-destroying force of futility and guilt. Whatever the personal position of the man writing poetry, poetry is not guilty; the author may hold what attitude he will, the poem has to be free, innocent. The poet may, as Wordsworth did, as Yeats did, doubt the efficacy of his enterprise; the poem cannot. Guilt and futility are bound together, and if they had been present to any degree in *The Divine Comedy,* then it would have been neither divine nor a comedy; and their presence in the structure of "Among School Children" is enough to cloud even so brilliant a poem. What happens in *For the Union Dead* is that so long as guilt and futility remain subjects, even attitudes, the poem can take care of itself; when they become the poem, the entire process breaks down. Then the poem is warranted by the momentum of the book, and since the linear movement has pace and direction, the book doesn't suffer.

The poem does. The kind of operation involved in taking, as I am arbitrarily doing, a book separated from an œuvre is drastic (e.g., there are lots of animals in other books by Lowell), and excising a poem from a book is even more radical surgery. Books of poetry, let me plead, are books of poems, and if this common sense judgment can be kept free from academic notions of form, it has legitimacy. There is a danger that in reacting against the doctrine of the autonomous poem, current poetics is putting in its place the autonomous book and eventually the autonomous man. And, looking at the books so engendered and encouraged, one sees a facile vindication of the lax and shoddy. Poets should and do compose books—only lunacy could suggest that mature writers should not know what they are doing or have any notion of larger design. The books should be books of poems.

Even granting the power of the dramatic spectacle of *For the Union Dead,* its least ingratiating qualities are evident in the structures of individual poems. The general architecture seems grand, but the main difficulty is within each poem, structural. The temptation of the poems is to make violent resolutions by language that is not accurate because literary or excessive: ". . . my child exploding into dynamite" doesn't make sense, and the poems often make such resolutions that sound proper only because of their rhetorical violence. This extreme of tension is matched by another extreme of passive laxness: ". . . beginning in wisdom, dying in doubt." As an ending of a poem, this is unforgivable as measure even if right in judgment, and it is the ends of poems, their conclusions, that do not conclude but stop, run down. Frost said once that any damn fool can get into a poem but it takes a poet to get out of one. These poems just end. Hence the deliberate flatness, the rhetorical questions, the return at the close to the phrasing of the opening. Wherever the poem would take the poet, he won't go. At these points, in the texture and structure of the verse, imaginative control wavers or cannot maintain itself, and they account for the sense of many earnest sympathetic readers that the poems don't live up to their promises, their subjects and feelings. Interjections of irrelevances, however powerful, don't let the poems follow out their limits. The subject of "The Severed Head," from Hawthorne's butterfly on, is the imagination, and the alter ego of the poem is the poet objectified to his terror and disgust, so that when it says "Sometimes I ask myself, if I exist," the result is genuine terror since the narrator's existence is entirely dependent on that of the alter ego. Yet when the basic subject of the poem is ready to be seen freshly, the poem in effect takes back its full vision and substitutes for it domestic trouble: "Her folded dress lay underneath my head" asks us to consider all that we have found in the poem of the claustrophobic imagination and the self-feeding animal world and effectively explain it away. Ernest Jones on Hamlet is hardly more devastating than that concluding line. And the poem's data are inexplicable by this intervention.

I have deliberately chosen one of the most powerful and attractive poems to make this point. Any commentator on this book finds it hard to be particular without ending with an argument ad hominem. It's hard to imagine, for instance, that a line like ". . . where the fish for bait were trapped" is really justifiable, and equally hard to say that the poet who wrote "Those Before" or "Eye and Tooth" could write this line without full intent. One comments on Lowell rather than on the book, and one resents this imposition, not for fear of offending poet or fashion but because one is judging (is driven to judge rather than explore) twenty years at hard labor and asking if this is all. There are few poets among Lowell's contemporaries who require such severe questioning, and even fewer who survive it.

Such questioning is then a form of praise. To return more positively to the large dramaturgic question, the person in history is the main subject, and it is good to see poetry treating the moment where person and history meet even without maximum continuous concentration. Retrieving from the novel this subject matter has been a steady obsession of poets for over half a century now. The local data of Lowell's poems, even when irritating, remind us of what those historical problems are, as do his themes and images. Closely related to the book's larger problems are the details of language.

Poets may begin emotionally and thematically anywhere, but they really end in language. Lowell's language in this book offers invitations to corruption that are quite serious. "My old flame, my wife!" Well, yes, every one feels this as being in some depreciatory sense right, exact, and still false. Old flames are jokes, and sure, there are no old flames, not even that for le soldat inconnu or John Fitzgerald Kennedy. So we know from the start that we are being jollied, as is the apostrophized woman. The tone is that of indolent play, fun and games, but fun with questionable rules and premises. "Reading how even the Swiss had thrown the sponge/in once again . . ." They hadn't; scaling the Himalayas is not, has nothing to do with, a boxing match, and the poem makes nothing of the metaphor; we are presented with limited cleverness. And so with "long-haired Victorian sages accepted the universe"—not really, what is involved is a joke by one of the sages against a silly woman, and the depreciation of even that common currency is redundant. Why write a poem on the cliché expression "killing time" and prove it impossible? Are we to take seriously this language as we might the experience rendered? And if the experience is limited to this language, what are we to make of it, what *can* be made of it?

Nobility, tranquillity. These are not proper to these poems and would destroy them. Surely the world of their reference, I concede at once, neither possesses nor admires those qualities, and denying the conditions of life is a form of moral suicide. The language Lowell uses as his base, like the syntax of Berryman's *Dream Songs,* has lost the capacity for resisting, probing against, the world it posits. It is not a language that permits genuine tension, and tension is a basic aesthetic premise that the poetry nowhere else questions. If a poet like Gary Snyder uses such language, we know where we are because his poetry denies the aesthetic and psychological primacy of tension as ordering force. But with Lowell we are asked to accept dramatic but not linguistic tension, at least until the language reaches the level of metaphor. This accounts for, even promotes, the appearance of impotence, especially since the poetics, unlike that of Snyder, is not sequential and processive. With Lowell it is not a matter of fine indifference or recklessness; the poetry takes no pleasure in its processes, meaning the continuities break down. Many of the poems are narrative and dogged in tone, anecdotal, reminiscent, as if only that procedure could be trusted to move from point to point. Hence the very bald repetitions, so evident that they are taken to be the result of conscious will rather than imposed by the chosen idiom—the poetry loses its freedom.

This is important not only for Lowell's poetry and its heavy influence by example on all our poetry but as index to the state of the arts. Behind the grander modern authors, who are now our classics, was a nineteenth century knowledge, and it was knowledge felt along the bone, of design that transcended the human. Lowell's mentor Allen Tate still participated in that knowledge, and it was the reason for his otherwise incomprehensible railing against solipsism (it would be interesting to read his comments on *Being and Nothingness*). Orders and laws and permissions that grew from a paramount structure that human will or perception could propitiate but not substantially change —these were accepted as possible by Eliot, Lawrence, Yeats, and their work was to realize them in structured language. It is Pound's ambivalence and Williams' deep philosophical indifference that makes them seem more likely models for the young. Indeed for our young, the only agreed transcendent paramount structure seems to be the United States Constitution, an admirable document but still premised on an order of transcendent natural force. Without such sanction it becomes a matter of opinion expressing a taste and style. The principle of prior order means that the medium of art is not its essence but an inescapable material, and the art of the past twenty years represents first a surrender before media and second a surrender before a man-made order.

The abortive Catholicism of both Lowell and Tate was an effort toward evading or solving or protecting themselves against this very problem. The frantic anti-humanism of many of our best and most admired classics comes from this struggle to transcend a society controlled by the very worst of the merely human motives, the principal one being greed. Moral resistance against this is very fine, and Lowell holds the hard-earned position of being one of our primary moral consciousnesses. It may be that we respond excessively to his earnestness, his moral charm, his personal integrity, and not enough to the aesthetic surface of these poems. After all, a distinguished writer who can publicly and quietly rebuke Lyndon Johnson, without fury, rudeness, or bad taste, has something working for him. The question is whether the poems are equal rebukes to the order, if we can call it that, of a society that makes even Johnson seem sometimes adequate.

The language of *For the Union Dead* often brings to my awareness the surface of pop art. Admirers of pop art stress its reference to an objective world and contrast it with the inner reference of abstract expressionism; and we are already reading fairly laborious accounts of poetry as confessional with Plath, Sexton, Snodgrass, and Lowell adduced as exemplars, the point being that here is a poetry that frankly takes its position as referring to something outside its language. Yes, how could poetry do otherwise? What is impressive, though, in both the poetry and the visual art, is the fact that the quality of the humanity is not queried, as it must be by the premises of the art. Poets accepting the confessional burden as their subject are also asking for the confessional judgment, willy-nilly, and criticism doesn't seem equipped for the priestly role thus forced on it. Painful, honest, naked, and parallel terms are used as implied honors. Are they necessarily so?

The quality of realized experience is surely much more at stake, and the audience defined by this quality. Taking mock-comic strip art as a norm, what it asks its audience to be is at once superior to and willing to relax into a world that it knows to be less than their best beings can entertain. Art can be judged, perhaps must finally be so judged, by what it asks its audience to become, and pop art and confessional poetry coerce their audience into postures that I find not at all edifying. Poets that we take to be confessional—Whitman, Baudelaire, Yeats—are often not at all confessional but artists freely constructive in intent and effect. They require something more than relaxation from their audience. They present a being more or less invented.

If we meditate on human nature, what we are composed of, most of us will agree that our nature hardly exhausts itself by what happens to it and that what is called confession is not that at all but a more or less systematic evasion and fraud. Being honest is artificial; being sincere is an invention—the skills required for art are not moral except in a final sense. Whatever is confessed in Donne or Herbert resolves itself to a complex type of humanity and is hardly individual. The drag toward individuality in confession is out of place in poetry as in religion. Carpaccio is more sincere and honest than Warhol. Passivity before events means a lack of involvement in the process that creates the ground for events, in art as in life.

In pop art and in *For the Union Dead* (insofar as it participates in the merely confessional mode), the age of anxiety evolves into an age of panic and ultimate helplessness. Action in Lowell's book becomes possible only in memory personal and historical; elegiac separation from experience, from doing anything about it, is the norm. The frequent topographical poems are related to the sense of helpless personal aging. Literary and historical analogues are muted commentaries that vindicate an air of wastefulness in the entire book. The visionary poems leave the seer perplexed, isolated, unchanged by the vision, unfit for the life that the vision presents as he is unfit for the life it takes him out of. Helpless panic—it seems to suit the tone of these very bad years where explosive action creates hopeless apathy and social action of the most dangerous and often pointless sort is followed hard upon by artificial paradises and communities "created" by lapsed papists in their sad role of spoiled priests. Collapsed morale, lost heart, gone mind—how much of our art has its only validation in a world where those qualities prevail.

So once again we are back with Lowell as representative figure. It is hard to deny or even question his expressive integrity. It would be silly to thrust aside the moral and personal charm of the poems. Only a large talent like Lowell's urges that we ask whether expressiveness and integrity are quite enough. The book has as its continuous subject the poetic sensibility in a world that is over-humanized, bleared and smeared with pointless and devastating toil, the legacy of wasted power and emotions, the corruption of meaning with false and irrelevant symbols. "Were it in my hands," Diane di Prima once wrote, "The atomic war would be past history." Lowell himself, in his incidental comments in interviews, has remarked on the danger that lies in the American sensibility, and in his own, in wanting total drastic solutions to the human condition. These poems, however, present a human condition to which there is no solution. All literature does. It may be wisdom on our part to admit that there are in experience as well as art insoluble problems, even that we are freshly creating problems that have as their chief characteristic built-in insolubility. Where this leaves us, *For the Union Dead* suggests. Artistically, even if this is so, it seems necessary to assert that expression, integrity, and representativeness are not in themselves valid. Art is a shaping spirit.

The Two Voices of Translation

by Donald Carne-Ross

The strong personal accent in Lowell's translations has led some readers to wonder whether he can be said to translate at all. He takes a foreign text, it sometimes seems, and uses it to make a new poem of his own. "*Not* a book of translations," A. Alvarez wrote in a review of *Imitations;* "it is a magnificent collection of new poems by Robert Lowell, based on the work of eighteen European poets." This provides a short way of dealing with critics of the Where-is-this-in-the-original? school; and it takes care of the fact that Lowell's renderings of other men's poetry constitute a part of his own poetic œuvre. (This is specially clear in his latest book, *Near the Ocean,* in which the original poems of the first section are balanced—Lowell claims not to know exactly how—by the translations of the second section.) But it adopts far too limited a view of translation and virtually hands it over to the literalists. On this view, a translation is primarily a means of access to texts we could not otherwise read; the translator's task is to write literate English and observe the house rules of contemporary style (thus he will normally shun archaisms and the more elaborate verse-forms), but his first obligation is to the (unknown) letter of the original.

Richmond Lattimore's well-known version of the *Iliad* was carried out in this selfless spirit. "I must try to avoid mistranslations," Professor Lattimore told himself, "which would be caused by rating the word of my choice ahead of the word which translates the Greek."

There is however an older view of translation which, thanks in large part to Ezra Pound, we have recovered. A paragraph in Johnson's essay on Sir John Denham puts the matter very clearly:

[Denham] appears to have been one of the first that understood the necessity of emancipating translation from the drudgery of counting lines and interpreting single words. How much this servile practice obscured the clearest and deformed the most beautiful parts of the ancient authors, may be discovered by a perusal of our earlier versions, some of them the works of men well qualified, not only by critical knowledge, but by poetical genius, who yet, by a mistaken ambition of exactness, degraded at once their originals and themselves.

Johnson, of course, assumed that the translator wrote for a public that already possessed the original and consequently expected not a painstaking reconstruction but a recreation in contemporary poetic terms. When he called Pope's *Iliad* a "poetical wonder," he did not simply mean that it was a great translation; he meant that it was a great English poem. He was perfectly aware that Pope's *Iliad* is often very unlike Homer's and he knew how to defend Pope's liberties:

> In estimating this translation, consideration must be had of the nature of our language, the form of our metre, and above all of the changes which two thousand years have made in the modes of life and the habits of thought.

The situation is more difficult today when the languages and literatures the poet happens to know may be unfamiliar to the reader. Few can set Pound's Chinese versions beside their originals; many cannot even do as much for his versions from Greek or Latin. Nonetheless the poet-translator continues to claim the old freedoms, even if he defensively calls his work a "homage" or an "imitation." [1] Pound confronts his reader with far graver problems than Lowell who has done much of his work with nineteenth or twentieth century poets more or less familiar to most of us. In this respect, Lowell's relation to both his original and to his reader is similar to Pope's. The eighteenth-century public went to Pope's *Iliad* not primarily for Homer but for Pope; in the process they were given a great deal of what they wanted from Homer. We may approach Lowell's Villon or Baudelaire in the same spirit; and be similarly rewarded.

A translation, then, is something very different from a trot. And the process whereby an ordinary modern novel is transferred from one European language to another represents only a minimal exercise of the art. When the novel is by Proust, or by Joyce, then the full powers of translation are indeed required. But what prose sometimes demands, poetry almost always demands, and it is with poetic translation that I am concerned in this paper.

Translation, in this sense, means that two languages, two cultural traditions, grow into each other, making both demands and concessions, appropriating areas of foreign territory and ceding some of their own. And it involves the confrontation of two literary personali-

---

[1] Thus Pound was provoked by stupid criticism into denying that *Homage to Sextus Propertius* was a translation at all.

ties: Baudelaire remains Baudelaire and yet begins to resemble Lowell; Lowell is always Lowell, but a more Baudelairian Lowell than elsewhere. This dialogue, or tension, between the two texts, the two linguistic and cultural mediums, and between the two writers, is the differentia of true translation. It is a rare and richly rewarding art that allows us to see our own language and literary tradition as though we were foreigners, the foreign language and tradition as though we were natives. When it fails, it usually does so because the translator grants too much or too little. When Lowell translates the fifteenth canto of the *Inferno,* he allows Dante to overpower him: Dante's signals come through strong and clear, Lowell's are muted. When on the other hand he translates Ungaretti's fine poem "Tu ti spezzasti," there is some danger of Lowell's powerful rhetoric getting the better of Ungaretti's.

And there is a further critical point, depending on the distinction between translation proper and what the later seventeenth and eighteenth centuries called "imitation." The writer of an imitation, said Dryden,

> assumes the liberty, not only to vary from the words and sense, but to forsake them both as he sees occasion; and taking only some general hints from the original, to run division on the groundwork, as he pleases.

The distinction between translation and imitation is helpful so long as one does not try to draw the lines too closely. Pope's reworkings of Horace and Johnson's *The Vanity of Human Wishes* are imitations (though they include translation); Pope's *Iliad* and Pound's *Seafarer* are translations—creative translations which take a poet's proper liberties. It is easy to see why Lowell was drawn to the Augustan term, but in fact the majority of the versions in *Imitations* (in spite of the defensive title) are really translations. On the other hand his remarkable poem "The Ghost," in *Lord Weary's Castle,* begins as a translation (of Propertius 4.7), but then turns into an imitation. The twentieth-century revival of this genre is of the greatest interest and Lowell has done much to develop it. My main concern here is however with his *translations.*

The twentieth century has been a great age of poetic translation. Great in the intelligence and intensity of response to a wide range of literature, and great in the sense that translation has played a shaping role in the life of poetry. If Pound is the formal master of modern American (and to a lesser extent English) verse, his discovery of new forms—and revival of old ones—has been made through a series of encounters with foreign texts. The *Cantos* do not merely contain a great deal of translation; in a vital sense much of the poem *is* a translation—the translation into our idiom of earlier texts and documents and forms of experience which, as Pound sees it, contribute to the contemporary "tale of the tribe." (Virgil used the Greek classics, Milton the Greek and Roman and Hebrew classics in much the same way.)

But while the "original" poetry of our time has been accompanied by a great effort of the critical intelligence, translation has hardly yet come into our critical sights. The major modern critics have had curiously little to say about it and as a result the ordinary reader's response is muddled and uncertain. *Imitations,* Edmund Wilson remarked, has been "stupidly received." Lowell has been praised for writing what are essentially new poems of his own (sometimes he does so, but these are then imperfect translations), or criticized for not keeping close enough to the letter of the original. In discussing this neglected art, one has to start from first principles.

The root difficulty is perhaps that, as George Steiner remarks, although a translation can be read and responded to independently, "it is not ontologically complete." Much of the success of modern criticism has come from insisting that a poem (at least for practical purposes) *is* ontologically complete, an autonomous structure of words to which the critic must give all his attention, undistracted by sources or influences or the poem's irrecoverable occasion.[2] But in reading a translation we can never forget that it has, in the most obvious sense, an occasion, the parent text which begot it upon the translator's private experience. Our first response to a translation must be, "Yes, this is a good piece of writing." But we cannot go on to say, "This is a good translation," until we have made sure that it stands in a satisfactory relation to its original. Let me take an example. Towards the end of the second stasimon of the *Oedipus Rex,* the chorus, bewildered by the seeming impiety of their rulers, exclaim (in the version by Fitts and Fitzgerald):

> Though fools will honor impious men,
> In their cities no tragic poet sings.

As writing, I find this acceptable. Is it also good translation? We cannot say until we have looked at the Greek or, if we have no Greek, at a literal version:

> If conduct like this is to be honored, why should I dance?

This query does not make immediate sense to us and we turn for help to Jebb who provides a paraphrase and a gloss: "Wherefore should

---

[2] For the purposes of my argument, I describe a "pure" form of criticism, now little practiced. When criticism became an academic occupation, many of the old academic procedures returned by the back door.

we join in the sacred dance? . . . Why maintain the solemn rites of public worship?" David Grene, translating the play for the Chicago series, writes (with one eye on Sophocles and the other on Jebb):

> When such deeds are held in honour,
> Why should I honour the Gods in the dance?

Semantically, this is fair enough: culturally, it falls flat, since we do not honor our gods by dancing. As a rendering of the *poetry* of the original, it has little to commend it. The good teacher would at this point put down his book and start talking about the religious significance of dancing. He might quote to his class Aldous Huxley's remark that there are people for whom "ritual dances provide a religious experience that seems more satisfying and convincing than any other. . . . It is with their muscles that they most easily obtain knowledge of the divine." This is interesting and could keep class and teacher happily occupied until the bell rang. One point only has been ignored in this stimulating discussion: *Sophocles' lines have not been translated.* Mr. Grene's version makes no significant contact with the Greek text and therefore cannot be called a translation.

Fitts and Fitzgerald, in their version, have seriously faced the original and come up with a sensible solution to the problem it presents. What the chorus is asking for at this moment of moral perplexity (Jocasta has just urged Oedipus not to trust oracles) is the comfort of some familiar, hallowed usage in which a whole city can be at one. Sophocles, writing for fifth-century Athens, refers to the shared experience of sacred dancing; Fitts and Fitzgerald, writing for a civilization in which the dance has long been secularized, refer instead to the shared experience of tragic poetry. The sacramental quality of great art, the emotion, for instance, that unites an audience during a great opera—these are part of our culture and they therefore work for us as Sophocles' allusion to religious dancing must have worked for the Athenians. By the standard I am proposing, the Fitts/Fitzgerald translation is a good one: good because it moves at an acceptable level of style and because it has sought to meet the experience rather than the letter of the Greek. Mr. Grene's translation, by this standard, would still be inadequate even if it were better written, because it has obsequiously allowed the original to impose on it a weak or meaningless allusion instead of standing up for its own cultural rights.

Now for another example, this time from Lowell, that raises a different problem. In a love poem by Mandelstam which he has translated there is a line which reads "I stand at your threshold." The Russian word for threshold, *porog*, apparently also means "rapids" (of a river) and Lowell, taking this hint, translates

I stand on a steep cliff by the sea.

Mr. Avrahm Yarmolinsky (from whom, knowing no Russian, I derive this information, see *Encounter*, November 1966, pp. 90–91) calls the translation "totally impossible in the context" and therefore condemns Lowell's rendering. If Mr. Yarmolinsky is right, there are several critical points here or, rather, several critical positions to be resisted. First, as I have proposed, we should not say, "The poem reads well—what does it matter if it is free?", for this is to set aside the special relation to the parent text which constitutes translation. Second, we should not act like schoolmasters and give Lowell a bad mark for translating inaccurately—until we have made quite sure that in rendering *porog* as he does and rejecting the more obviously appropriate dictionary meaning he is not moved by his sense of the needs of the English language or cultural tradition: as Fitts and Fitzgerald were moved to translate *khoreuein* (to dance) as they did. In point of fact, I assume that Yarmolinsky is right and that Lowell has been led astray by his informant. But the theoretical point stands.

And there is a third position to be rejected. We should not say, "Oh well, Lowell doesn't claim to know Russian—how can he hope to translate Russian poetry?" It is desirable, certainly, that the poet-translator know the language of his original, *but it is not essential.* Christopher Logue's version of *Iliad*, XVI, is now rather generally recognized as a masterpiece of contemporary translation, yet Logue does not know a word of Greek. Working with a literal trot, he was able to find in Homer's narrative something that matched his own hard, rather contemptuous pity for man's condition. Narrative poetry, it is true, provides slightly less intransigent problems, but even lyric poetry can, on a lucky day, be approached through a prose crib.[3] There is something the translator needs even more than a knowledge of his author's language.

Lowell too has translated Homer. He knows a little Greek, but I imagine that he prefers to work mainly with prose versions. His treatment of the scene between Achilles and Lykaon at the start of *Iliad*, XXI, will take our enquiry a stage further. Even by Homer's standards, this scene is very powerful. Achilles, at the height of his daemonic war-lust, stands above the young man he is about to kill and realizes with a kind of metaphysical anguish that he who almost transcends the human condition is still as absolutely subject to the atrocity of death as poor Lykaon. Here are the key lines in Lowell's version:

[3] Mr. Ian Fletcher, for example, with very small Italian and no Greek, has produced magnificent versions of Tasso's madrigal "Nel dolce seno de la bella Clori" (*Nine* III, 2 pp. 132–33) and of the highly lyrical Euripidean ode at *Hippolytus* 732 ff. (*Motets*, University of Reading, 1962, pp. 29–30).

> You too must die, my dear. Why do you care?
> Patroklos, a much better man, has died.
> Or look at me—how large and fine I am—
> a goddess bore me, and my father reigned,
> yet I too have my destiny and death:
> either at sunrise, night, or at high noon,
> some warrior will spear me down in the lines,
> or stick me with an arrow through the heel.

What has happened? In an early essay (I quote from *Time* . . .) Lowell wrote of the *Iliad*: "Its magnitude and depth make it almost as hard to understand as life." Somewhere along the line this sense of Homeric poetry seems to have deserted him; at all events, it does not get into his translation. Lowell's sensibility, in his mature writing, is Christian: Jonathan Edwards' meditations on eternal torment yield, in his hands, a poetry of sombre magnificence. The Greek response to what Cafavy (a genuinely antique spirit) calls "the never-ending calamity of death" does not apparently much interest him—to judge from the bland movement of the verse. "The Killing of Lycaon" fails, or so it seems to me, not because of any infidelity to the letter but because Lowell has not taken possession of the experience of the Greek. I hear in these lines only the (for once) relaxed voice of Lowell: I do not hear the terrible speech of Homer.

To "take possession of the experience" of one's original may seem to be the minimal obligation required of every serious translator, but a glance at the evidence suggests that this is not so. There are other methods. One may, for instance, create a new (partly new) original and translate that. There is a sense in which one may say that Pope took a grand neo-classical author known to his world as Homer and turned him into grand neo-classical English.[4] Johnson arguably created a serious moralist whom he called Juvenal and made him speak to his own grave sense of man's nature. The real Juvenal, it has been proposed, was a writer who *used* moral attitudes to magnificent literary effect.[5] Another method is to do what Pound has done so often and sink one's identity into that of the author to be rendered. By a kind of inspired ventriloquism (demanding great formal virtuosity), Pound has contrived to write as though he were Li Po, Propertius, or an anonymous Anglo-Saxon poet of the eighth century miraculously

---

[4] Admittedly Pope realized, as his notes to the *Iliad* sometimes show, that Homer was a ruder and more remote figure than his own version of the *Iliad* would suggest, but these were perhaps piercing moments of intuition at odds with his everyday sense of the Greek.

[5] See the remarkable article by H. A. Mason, "Is Juvenal a Classic?" in *Arion* I:1 & 2, specially 1, pp. 20–21.

brought to life again in the twentieth. (But for Pound's name on the title page, would we know that *Cathay, Homage,* and *The Seafarer* were by the same writer?)

It remains true, nonetheless, that a temperamental affinity between the translator and his author is the usual prerequisite for fine work in this field. Certainly Lowell, a deeply private poet, needs to take possession of the experience of his original if he is to succeed. His finest translations are of poems which he might have written himself—which means, since Lowell is very much a man of our own time, that he is at his best with the poetry of the last hundred years. He lacks Pound's marvellous ability to make new the ancient or remote. (Lowell's Latin versions, in *Near the Ocean,* may seem to disprove this, but Latin poetry can be very "modern" in its sensibility, much more so than Greek—which is perhaps why we value it less.) I propose to spend most of the rest of this paper in dealing with Lowell's handling of two great modern poets both very close to him, Baudelaire and Montale, but first I want to look at one notable success he has scored with a poet remote from us in time, François Villon. Lowell's version of *Le Testament* is, I think, the finest modern account we have of a great medieval poem. Listen to these lines. Is this Lowell's voice, or Villon's? Or both in perfect unison?

> And there are women here,
> who used to bow and scrape,
> and struggle for earth's joys;
> some of them gave commands,
> and others served in fear.
> I see that none escape:
> bishops, laymen, or boys:
> they rot with folded hands.

I said Villon's *voice* advisedly, since there are not too many of Villon's *words* here. (The passage is a very free handling of stanza 163.) Yet in its place in Lowell's sequence, I would claim that this is a magnificent translation of Villon. Technically, the poem is of the school of *Homage:* Lowell rearranges the original, contracting and expanding, and he even includes some lines from *Le Lais.* Sometimes he works quite close to the French:

> What more have I to tell?
> I'm no arch-angel's heir,
> crowned with the stars and moon.
> My father (God have mercy!)
> is in the ground, and soon
> my mother also must die—

> poor soul, she knows it well,
> her son must follow her.

> Si ne suis, bien le considere,
> Filz d'ange portant dyademe
> D'estoille ne d'autre sidere.
> Mon pere est mort, Dieu en ait l'ame!
> Quant est du corps, il gist soubs lame.
> J'entens que ma mere mourra,
> El le scet bien, la povre femme,
> Et le filz pas ne demourra.

Again, the two voices in unison, a perfect symbiosis.[6] It is the Christian
strain in Lowell that has allowed him to capture this great medieval
theme: the struggle to achieve Christian resignation in the face of the
grim triumph of death. (Rhythmically I think he may have taken a few
suggestions from the solemn poignancy of Nashe's "Song.")

Lowell's Villon succeeds in a field where modern translators have
registered relatively few successes. With rather few exceptions (Pound
is the most notable, but then his voyages have been ecumenical), they
have felt more at ease with the Classics and modern poetry than with
medieval or Renaissance: because, I suppose, the Classics at best seem
"timeless," whereas the medieval or Renaissance poet belongs to our
own span of historical time. Lowell, too, as I suggested, is usually most
at home with the poetry of the last century or so, and of all modern
poets it is Baudelaire who meets him on the widest front and tests
him most searchingly. We would expect him to translate Baudelaire
finely, for the two poets have a good deal in common. A poem like
"The Flaw" is pure, perfect Lowell, yet it would not be quite as it is
had he not read *Les fleurs du mal.* One learns much about translation
by watching the two sensibilities, the two rhetorics, come to grips:

> Among the vermin, jackals, panthers, lice,
> gorillas and tarantulas that suck
> and snatch and scratch and defecate and fuck
> in the disorderly circus of our vice—

> Mais parmi les chacals, les panthères, les lices,
> Les singes, les scorpions, les vautours, les serpents,
> Les monstres glapissant, hurlants, grognants, rampants,
> Dan la ménagerie infâme de nos vices—

---

[6] I use the term in its exact biological sense, as defined in the *Shorter Oxford:*
"Association of two different organisms . . . which live attached to each other, or
one as a tenant of the other, and *contribute to each other's support.*"

The third line of the French is extremely violent: the cacophony of sounds produced by the bestiary of the first two lines (grouped according to a principle I do not quite understand) is intensified, to a kind of roar of rage and pain, by the furious rhythmic movement, and the syntactically unusual sequence of four adjectival present participles also plays its part. But if Baudelaire's third line strains against the decorum of style, Lowell's goes outside it altogether. At once, however, he pulls himself up: the steady, tragic control of line four is genuinely Baudelairian: "disorderly," though less powerful than "infâme," is arguably a more "classical" and hence more Baudelairian word here. ("Là, tout n'est qu'ordre et beauté . . .") [7]

What is remarkable about Lowell's versions from Baudelaire is that they stick so closely to the original, semantically and even rhythmically, without losing their own accent. Thus in "La servante au grand coeur," Baudelaire's grand, pathetic line

> Les morts, les pauvres morts, ont de grandes douleurs

becomes

> The dead, the poor dead, they have their bad hours.

This is not merely as good as the French line: it is good in the same way. Is this then an example of Gogol's definition of the perfect translator as one who becomes a pane of glass so transparent that the reader doesn't notice there is any glass? Or has the French original coaxed Lowell's line, very gently, into a fractionally un-English form of expression? Is there something slightly rhetorical—rhetorical in not quite the English way—in the repetition

> the dead, *the poor dead* . . . ?

There are certainly places in *Imitations* where Lowell has brought into English the very un-English (and un-American) quality of French rhetoric, as in

> Yesterday the Grand Army, today its dregs!

from his version of Hugo's "L'expiation" or, from the same poem,

[7] "Les Lices," in line one, are of course not "lice" but hound-bitches. Lowell shares, if to a lesser degree, Pound's seignorial disregard of mere dictionary meanings. There is a notable example in his version of the Brunetto Latini canto where "qual che si fosse, *lo maestro felli*" (line 12) becomes "on such a plan *the evil engineer*" (instead of "the master made them"). Such slips matter less than professors claim, but they are still blemishes.

one saw the picket dying at his post,
still standing in his saddle, white with frost,
the stone lips frozen to the bugle's mouth! [8]

And, more strongly, in his translation of Baudelaire's "Le Cygne":

I saw a swan that had escaped its cage,
and struck its dry wings on the cobbled street,
and drenched the curbing with its fluffy plumage.
Beside a gritty gutter, it dabbed its feet,

and gobbled at the dust to stop its thirst.
Its heart was full of its blue lakes, and screamed:
"Water, when will you fall? When will you burst,
oh thunderclouds?"

Et disait, le coeur plein de son beau lac natal:
"Eau, quand donc pleuvras-tu? quand tonneras-tu, foudre?"

An English swan, even an Irish Yeatsian swan, could not *address* the heavens in this grand way without a touch of absurdity. Lowell has mastered the French convention so completely that he makes us accept it in English. Minimally in my first examples, unmistakably in my last, he has extended the range of English poetic tone. This is *not* Lowell writing English poetry based on Baudelaire; it is Lowell speaking with Baudelaire's voice and yet remaining Lowell. (Equally, when we next read the French, we hear Lowell's voice as well as Baudelaire's. The two texts, henceforth, *"contribute to each other's support."*)

This readiness to be "violated" by foreign modes has been a characteristic of English verse for centuries and has contributed to the richness of our poetic tradition. The main alien presence working in the native texture has of course been Latin,[9] though Italian too has played

---

[8] My italics. Here is the French:

Hier la grande armée, et maintenant troupeau. . . . .
On voyait des clairons à leur poste gelés,
Restés debout en selle et muets, blancs de givre,
Collant leur bouche en pierre aux trompettes de cuivre . . . .

The last line provides an example of a translation greatly surpassing its original. In the first, did Lowell translate "troupeau" as "dregs" with the Latin *grex* somewhere in his mind?

[9] And not only in the Latin-nourished centuries but today, as in these elegantly Horatian verses of Auden:

Easily, my dear, you move, easily your head,
And easily as through leaves of a photograph album I'm led . . .

English literature has gained much from the fact that the Germanic structure of our language makes a Latinate turn of phrase or order of words stand out sharply. To create a comparable effect, a romance language has to go much further—as far,

its part with Chaucer and, much more strongly, Milton and today with Pound and Eliot. French poetry has played a very much smaller role; it is present, for example, at a superficial level, in the foppish versions of Verlaine by Arthur Symons and, more profoundly, in Wallace Stevens.[10] Stevens is sometimes almost a French poet writing in English. (This explains his well-known saying that "French and English constitute a single language.") Lowell, on the other hand, belongs profoundly to the English poetic tradition—as Jonson, for example, or Marvell did: and just as they enriched their English verse with effects derived from Latin, so Lowell (especially when he is working with a highly sympathetic poet like Baudelaire) has brought home new resources from French. One more example should provide whatever further illustration the point may need. Here is the final section from "La servante au grand coeur," first in French, then in English:

> Lorsque la bûche siffle et chante, si le soir,
> Calme, dans le fauteuil je la voyais s'asseoir,
> Si, par une nuit bleue et froide de décembre,
> Je la trouvais tapie en un coin de ma chambre,
> Grave, et venant du fond de son lit éternel
> Couver l'enfant grandi de son oeil maternel,
> Que pourrais-je répondre à cette âme pieuse,
> Voyant tomber des pleurs de sa papière creuse?

> The oak log sings and sputters in my chamber,
> and in the cold blue half-light of December,
> I see her tiptoe through my room, and halt
> humbly, as if she'd hurried from her vault
> with blankets for the child her sleepless eye
> had coaxed and mothered to maturity.
> What can I say to her to calm her fears?
> My nurse's hollow sockets fill with tears.

Baudelaire's verses are so masterly that one does not immediately see how complicated they are. After the initial temporal clause he moves

---

for instance, as Góngora's sumptuous hyperbaton, "mas, con desvíos Galatea suaves." By comparison, Milton's Latinisms are moderate: yet no less striking.

[10] George Steiner, in *Language and Silence* (New York, 1967), pp. 32–33, is less than just in suggesting that Stevens' use of French is mainly a matter of studding his verse with exotic French gauds. It reaches into the rhythms of his poetry and I fancy that his discovery of a new range of formal resources in the traditional blank verse line (at a time when critics were claiming that blank verse was finished) may represent a creative acclimatization of the rhythms of French verse no less significant than Pound's acclimatization of the Italian hendecasyllable. How French the movement of his poetry often is may be illustrated by the fact that one can read a poem like "Sea surface full of clouds" without realizing that the fourth tercet of each section ends with a line in French.

unexpectedly into a conditional sentence ("lorsque . . . si . . ."), skillfully concealing the symmetrical formation of the two cola of the protasis ("si le soir . . . je la voyais/si, par une nuit . . . je la trouvais") by setting them in different positions in the line structure. The period continues with the adjective ("grave") and the adjectival clause ("venant du fond . . .") of lines 5 and 6 and then, at last, runs into the relief of the apodosis in line 7, which in turn is prolonged by the attached participial clause. It would not be impossible to reproduce this construction in English, but it would be impossible, or nearly impossible, to make it sound as natural as it sounds in French. With perfect tact, Lowell has softened the complex hypotaxis of the original into a more relaxed paratactic structure: "The oak log sings . . . and . . . I see her tiptoe . . . and halt . . . as if . . . What can I say . . . ? My nurse's hollow sockets. . . . In the same spirit, he has eased the formality of Baudelaire's verses by letting the sense structure frequently run across and blur his couplets.

What of the "content" of this passage? We notice at once that Lowell has made some changes. The old woman, instead of crouching down in the corner of his room, tiptoes through it. Why? Perhaps because of the sound, the playful false echo of *tapie: tiptoe.* He has toned down the elevated phrase "venant du fond de son lit éternel" which in this exquisitely tender context would jar, in English; and he has removed the description of the nurse as "cette âme pieuse" which—in English, again—would not ring quite true. More important, he has simplified the action of Baudelaire's scene just as he has simplified the syntax. In the original, both the speaker and the nurse are placed in a double perspective. Where Baudelaire writes of the nurse "brooding over the grown-up child with her maternal eye," Lowell writes of "the child her sleepless eye/*had* coaxed. . . ." In the French, the adult speaks and at the same time sees himself, through his nurse's dead eyes, as a child (*enfant/grandi*); in the English, the speaker's childhood is entirely in the past. Similarly, Baudelaire presents two visions of the old woman: first, she appears *in the evening,* sitting down calmly in a chair by the fire; then, on a cold December *night,* she is seen (by the child rather than the adult?) crouching in a corner of the room. Lowell eliminates the first vision and presents only (his own slightly modified version of) the second. This consorts better with the poem's pathetic close, but I think we have to recognize that the pathos is won at some slight cost to the complexity of the original.

And yet (so far-reaching are the critical issues raised by translation) has Lowell, perhaps, in simplifying, made a more unified poem of it? It is not easy to see, in the original, how the vision of the nurse sitting calmly beside the fire arises from the desolate atmosphere of the first fourteen lines ("Vieux squelettes gelés travaillés par le ver") or prepares for its no less desolate close. The question cannot be pursued here. All that I think is certain is that, despite the modifications Lowell has introduced, this is true translation. We hear the great French poet speaking through the no less beautiful English verses.

The factors which operated in Lowell's favor in his translations from *Les fleurs du mal* (affinity of temperament, Baudelaire's seminal relation to all modern poetry) turned against him when he moved to another great nineteenth-century poet, Leopardi. *Imitations* includes three translations from *I Canti*. Here is the beginning of one of them:

> Sylvia, do you remember the minutes
> in this life overhung by death,
> when beauty flamed
> through your shy, serious meditations,
> and you leapt beyond the limits
> of girlhood?

> Silvia, rimembri ancora
> Quel tempo della tua vita mortale,
> Quando beltà splendea
> Negli occhi tuoi ridenti e fuggitivi,
> E tu, lieta e pensosa, il limitare
> Di gioventù salivi?

["Sylvia, do you still remember that period of your mortal life when beauty shone in your shy, laughing eyes and you, happy and thoughtful, mounted the threshold of youth?"]

I imagine that Lowell knows French better than Italian. The point is rather that Baudelaire's poetry and the traditions in which Baudelaire wrote belong to us in a way that Leopardi's poetry and its traditions do not. Dante we to some extent possess, but the arc of Italian lyrical poetry extending from Petrarch to Leopardi is now very little known in the English-speaking world and this presented Lowell with a grave initial obstacle. Leopardi, perhaps the last genuinely classical poet Europe has known, writes out of a long literary tradition, intimately known, exactly scrutinized. A single word or phrase ("occhi ridenti") may have behind it the living pressure of five hundred years of literature. No English poetry works in this way; the procedures of modern poetry are wholly different. Lowell, it seems to me, despairing of creating a formal equivalent for Leopardi, and finding it impossible to work with him, decided to work against him. Where Leopardi generalizes, confident that his generalization will carry the local significances he wants, Lowell particularizes; where Leopardi employs a vocabulary that seems effortlessly natural, Lowell heightens and dramatizes. Leopardi can write "quel tempo della tua vita mortale" with as grave and steady a sense of mortality as a Greek poet; Lowell must write "the *minutes*/in this life *overhung* by death." (My italics.) "Splendea" is intensified into "flamed," "salivi" into "leapt": the beautifully simple and exact "occhi . . . ridenti e fuggitivi" disappears— no doubt it would have seemed banal in the almost baroque climate Lowell has created. There are moments when his insistent need to present concrete particulars becomes almost ludicrous, as when Leopardi's phrase "le sudate carte" ("my laborious sheets") is expanded into

> and the heat
> of my writings made the letters wriggle and melt
> under drops of sweat.

What Leopardi meant by "sudato" is explained by a passage in a letter where he speaks of "quella sudatissima e minutissima perfezione nello scrivere alla quale io soleva riguardare." He is speaking, in other words, of a theory of composition. So in a way is Lowell (though the implied evocation of the temperature in Leopardi's study at Pisa is wholly unfortunate), but it is the wrong theory of composition. Leopardi's writing is not "hot" or molten; there is rather (in the cluster of unapproachable masterpieces to which "A Silvia" belongs) a poignant chastity of expression, a Greek simplicity.[11]

If Lowell's versions of Leopardi fail as completely as I think they do, the explanation is partly in Lowell's own temperament, partly in the distance of Leopardi's best manner from any English poetic tradition and from modern poetic as a whole. The relation between original and translation, between two linguistic and cultural mediums, which made the Baudelaire translations so impressive, is here completely absent. Steiner complained that Lowell's *Phaedra* "has an unsteady and capricious bearing on the matter of Racine," but at least it has some bearing; and the writing, whether or not we think it responsive to anything central in Racine, is often magnificent. But the matter of Leopardi resists Lowell's treatment altogether and his versions, even if judged as new poems by Robert Lowell, seem to me quite unsuccessful. I turn with relief to his dealings with a later Italian poet.

The ten versions from Montale included in *Imitations* constitute by far the most notable service yet rendered to this great poet in the English-speaking world. They are superb Lowell and, for all their radical and proper freedoms, superb interpretations of the Italian poet. Partly through temperament, partly through direct influence, Montale is (or seems to us to be) the most English (or Anglo-Saxon) of

---

[11] Cf. Nietzsche, *Wir Philologen* 162: "Ich empfehle an Stelle des Lateinischen den Griechischen Stil auszubilden, besonders an Demosthenes: Einfachheit! Auf Leopardi zu verweisen, der vielleicht der grösste Stilist des Jahrhunderts ist."

Italian poets, and if Lowell particularizes still further Montale's fierce particularities, he is only intensifying something that is emphatically present in the original.[12] Thus

> Libeccio sferza da anni le vecchie mura

("for years the south-wester has lashed the old walls") becomes

> For years the sirocco gunned the dead stucco with sand.

Another example:

> La sera che si protende
> sull'umida conca non porta
> col palpito dei motori
> che gemiti d'oche—

("Evening which stretches out over the humid bight brings only the throbbing of motors and the cry of geese.") Lowell's version:

> Night blanketing
> the fogging lake coves
> brings only the cat-calls of geese,
> the put-put-put of the outboards.

Here is an even more striking example of the way Lowell attaches himself with a kind of fury to the scenes and objects of Montale's world and turns them into his own substance:

> . . . e sugli spiazzi
> deserti, ove i cavalli incappucciati
> annusano la terra, fermi innanzi
> ai vetri luccicanti degli alberghi.

("And on the empty spaces where hooded horses [i.e. wearing sun-hats] sniff the ground, standing in front of the glittering windows of hotels.")

> . . . through the bald, distracted little squares,
> where a few senile, straw-hatted horses wheeze
> by the El Dorado of the rooming houses' windows in the sun.

In isolation such passages may suggest that Lowell is simply using a few suggestions from the Italian to make new poems of his own. Read in context, in the total strategy of each translation, the effect is different. What Lowell has done is *systematically* heighten and particularize the original; he may enlarge, but the proportions remain similar. Far from being wanton, his changes spring from a clear critical sense of the

---

[12] The question is intelligently discussed, from an Italian point of view, by Giorgio Morandi in his monograph, *Robert Lowell: Poesie di Montale* (Bologna, 1960).

difference between the English and the Italian poetic tradition. Even in the twentieth century, Italian is less metaphorical, less receptive to slang and neologisms than English; hence the translator, if he is to create a comparable effect, must heighten metaphor and employ a more colloquial, neologistic diction. One further example from the same poem ("Arsenio") may serve to show how brilliant Lowell's transpositions are. The Italian reads:

> . . . e lunge par la sera
> ch'è prossima: se il fulmine la incide
> dirama come un albero prezioso
> entro la luce che s'arrosa.

This becomes—surely one of the most powerful strokes in Lowell's poetry:

> . . . where the evening is already importunate.
> Like some delicate tree entering the reddening light,
> lightning etches a crash of pruned branches.

The Italian is highly compressed and suggestive. It is also difficult, and a literal version may help: "and far off seems the evening which is so near: if the lightning incises it, it branches out like a decorated tree within the light that turns pink." The fact that it is hard to be sure whether "sera" or "fulmine" is the subject of "dirama" suggests the strongly "esemplastic" quality of the poet's vision: either, the lightning branches out like a decorated tree; or (more likely), the evening sky, cut by lightning, is itself the branching tree. The Italian is extremely powerful, but turn it directly into English and most of the power goes. Here is the same passage in the hands of that gifted translator, Edwin Morgan:

> . . . and far far off seems the evening
> That is so near: if lightning comes to lance it
> It branches out like a precious tree . . .

What are the gains (and perhaps the losses) of Lowell's freer treatment? First, "*delicate* tree" for "albero *prezioso*": the English adjective is visually appropriate, but the Italian, suggesting a decorated Christmas tree, works more richly in the context. Lightning resembles a Christmas tree in being brilliant, brief, and inorganic. Moreover, in the plot of the poem, the storm heralded by the lightning brings the momentary promise of a new, almost miraculous (re)birth—which comes to nothing, as the promise of the Christmas birth has, for Montale, come to nothing. Next, "*reddening* light": this may be a mistake, a confusion between *arrosare,* "to turn pink or rosy," and *arrossare,* "to redden." It may simply be verbal tact: "rosy" is an impossible word ("pink," in this context, would not be much better) and if you compromise and write (like another translator, George Kay) "within the light flushing to rose," you produce something too decorative and pretty for this harsh occasion. Lowell's "etches a crash" is a superb stroke, wholly in context, wholly Montalian in its compression, even though such a phrase would I think be quite impossible in Italian ("schizza uno schianto"?). Lowell is using the greater poetic resources of English to complete what exists *in posse* in Montale's words.[13] Finally, "*pruned branches*": although "prune" is not *the* meaning here, it is one of the dictionary meanings of "diramare" and Lowell, wasting nothing, brings it in to make the image still more rich and precise.

Every language defines its own area of reality which for most of us most of the time is reality *tout court*. In reading or speaking another language we enter a different area of reality, which admits elements that ours excludes and excludes others that ours admits. But in so far as we read or speak the language well, we are to that extent enclosed within its special system of references; we have simply exchanged one set of limitations for another. The probing encounter between two linguistic and cultural mediums, which true translation creates, gives us the uniquely liberating experience of living within two areas of reality, two systems of reference. We see our own language and cultural tradition from the outside; we see the foreign language and cultural tradition from within. This, I take it, is what justifies the study of translation.

The assumption of this paper has been that translation offers an experience that is essentially bilingual and hence only open to those who read both texts. Approached in this way, it provides a unique literary perspective that reaches beyond literature into our life as articulate, sentient beings. What translation cannot do, except at a primitive level of communication, and what it is commonly supposed to do, is "give you the original," provide a means of access to work in languages that we do not know. In practice, of course, we have to pretend that it serves this purpose. Those of us without Russian claim that we have read Tolstoy: even though we know that we cannot go through a page of Stendhal or Flaubert in translation without being conscious at every turn of what we are missing.

In poetry, especially lyric poetry, the proportion of what will not come across increases vertiginously—so much so that I personally find

[13] This is quite a different relation from the one I proposed on page 162, note 8, where Lowell simply *improved* Hugo's rather undistinguished lines. It is more akin to what happens when Milton translates Virgil's "ingenti percussus amori" as "smit with the love of sacred song," raising and (from his Christian point of view) fulfilling the Virgilian phrase.

little value in reading verse translations unless I can also read the original. Contemporary Russian poetry is a case in point. Now that Russia grows fashionable, translations come thick and fast. When they are by Lowell or Auden, they are worth reading: because they are by Lowell or Auden. Written by men of lesser talents, they satisfy little except a purely journalistic or political interest: it is reassuring to learn that Russians feel as we do about sunsets, overcrowded cities, and going to bed with persons of the opposite sex. To suppose that a translation, divorced from its parent text, can do much more than quiet such innocent curiosities is damaging to the study of literature. To the practice, and the delectation, of the art of translation it is wholly disastrous.

Chronology of Important Dates

1917   Birth of Lowell in Boston, March 1. Only child of Robert Traill Spence Lowell and Charlotte Winslow Lowell; great-grandnephew of James Russell Lowell and a distant cousin of Amy Lowell.

1935–37   Student at Harvard. Left Harvard to study with John Crowe Ransom at Kenyon College in Gambier, Ohio.

1937   Spent three months at the home of Allen Tate where Ford Madox Ford, his wife, and secretary were already installed.

1940   Entered the Roman Catholic Church; marriage to Jean Stafford, author of *Boston Adventure* and *The Mountain Lion;* B.A. from Kenyon College, major in Classics. Graduated *summa cum laude.*

1940–41   Taught English literature at Kenyon College.

1941–42   Editorial Assistant, Sheed and Ward, New York City.

1943   Indicted for failure to obey the Selective Service Act; sentenced to serve a year and a day in a Federal prison; he was released after about six months.

1944   *Land of Unlikeness.*

1946   *Lord Weary's Castle.*

1947   Pulitzer Prize for poetry for *Lord Weary's Castle;* awarded American Academy of Arts and Letters Prize.

1947–48   Consultant in Poetry at the Library of Congress; Guggenheim Fellowship; divorced from Jean Stafford in June.

1949   Marriage to writer Elizabeth Hardwick, July 28.

1950   *Poems: 1938–1949* under the imprint of Faber and Faber; death of Lowell's father.

1950–53   First trip to Europe.

1951   *The Mills of the Kavanaughs.*

1954   Death of Lowell's mother.

1959   National Book Award; *Life Studies: New Poems and an Auto-biographical Fragment.*

1960   Given grant from the Ford Foundation for a study of the opera; received National Book Award "for the most distinguished poetry of the previous year."

1961   *Imitations; Phaedra and Figaro,* with Jacques Barzun.

1962   Bollingen Prize for translation.

1964   *The Old Glory* (plays); Obie award for the best off-Broadway play *(Benito Cereno); For the Union Dead.*

1965   In June, refused to participate in the White House Festival of the Arts in protest of American foreign policy.

1967   *Near the Ocean.*

Notes on the Editor and Contributors

THOMAS PARKINSON is Professor of English at the University of California (Berkeley). He is the author of *W. B. Yeats, Self-Critic: A Study of the Early Poetry* and *W. B. Yeats, The Later Poetry*. He has also written two books of poems, *Men, Women, Vines* and *Thanatos,* and has contributed to numerous critical and scholarly magazines.

WILLIAM ARROWSMITH, Professor of Classics at the University of Texas, is one of the most brilliant translators from Greek and Latin.

JOHN BERRYMAN, the distinguished poet and critic, is currently in Europe on a fellowship. His most recent publications are *77 Dream Songs* and *48 Sonnets*.

R. P. BLACKMUR, 1904–1965, is one of the founders of modern criticism.

DONALD CARNE-ROSS, critic and translator from many languages, is an editor of *Arion* and is currently associated with the National Translation Center at Austin, Texas.

RICHARD EBERHART, poet and critic, teaches at Dartmouth College. He has been Poetry Consultant at the Library of Congress, and has received many other honors, including the Bollingen Prize in 1962. The bulk of his work is in *Collected Poems, 1930–1960*.

IRVIN EHRENPREIS, Professor of English at the University of Virginia, has published one volume of his critical biography of Jonathan Swift.

ROBERT ILSON teaches in the English Language Institute at Queens College.

RANDALL JARRELL, 1914–1965, was a brilliant poet and critic. His last book of poems contains a moving appreciation of his work and person by Robert Lowell.

WILL C. JUMPER teaches English and Creative Writing at Iowa State University.

M. R. ROSENTHAL, editor, critic, and poet, teaches English at New York University. He is the author of *The Modern Poets,* and a book on contemporary poetry is currently in press.

FREDERICK SEIDEL is an advisory editor of *The Paris Review*. He is the author of *Final Solutions,* a book of poetry.

STEPHEN SPENDER is Professor of English at Northwestern University. His poetry, criticism, fiction, and autobiography have placed him at the center of the current literary imagination.

HUGH B. STAPLES published his pioneering study *Robert Lowell: The First Twenty Years,* in 1962.

ALLEN TATE is one of the most distinguished men of letters in the United States. His work is well represented in *Collected Essays* (1960) and *Poems* (1960).

WILLIAM CARLOS WILLIAMS, 1883–1963, is probably the greatest single force in contemporary American poetry.

Selected Bibliography

A bibliography of biographical and critical studies of Robert Lowell is found in Jerome Mazzaro's *The Achievement of Robert Lowell: 1939–1959* (University of Detroit Press, 1960). Below are listed studies made after 1959.

Alvarez, A. "A Talk with Robert Lowell," *Encounter*, XXIV, ii, 39–43.

Braybrooke, Neville. "The Poetry of Robert Lowell," *Catholic World*, CXCVIII, 230–237.

Calhoun, Richard J. "The Poetic Metamorphosis of Robert Lowell," *Furman Studies*, XIII, i, 7–17.

Cambon, Glauco. *The Inclusive Flame: Studies in American Poetry*, Bloomington, Indiana University Press, 1963.

Donoghue, Denis. *Connoisseurs of Chaos: Ideas of Order in Modern American Poetry*, New York, The Macmillan Company, 1965. ("Edwin Arlington Robinson, J. V. Cunningham, Robert Lowell," 129–160).

Fein, Richard. "Mary and Bellona: The War Poetry of Robert Lowell," *Southern Review*, I, 820–834.

Fein, Richard. "The Trying-out of Robert Lowell," *Sewanee Review*, LXXII, 131–139.

Gray-Lewis, Stephen W. "Too Late for Eden—an Examination of Some Dualisms in *The Mills of the Kavanaughs*," *Cithara*, V, ii, 41–51.

Hardison, O. B. "Robert Lowell: The Poet and the World's Body," *Shenandoah*, XIV, ii, 24–32.

Jones, A. R. "Necessity and Freedom: The Poetry of Robert Lowell, Sylvia Plath, and Anne Sexton," *Critical Quarterly*, VII, 11–30.

Martz, William. *The Achievement of Robert Lowell*, New York, Scott-Foresman, 1967.

Mazzaro, Jerome. *The Poetic Themes of Robert Lowell*, Ann Arbor, University of Michigan Press, 1965.

Mills, Ralph J. *Contemporary American Poetry*, New York, Random House, Inc., 1965 ("Robert Lowell," 134–159).

Ostroff, Anthony, ed. *The Contemporary Poet as Artist and Critic*, New York, Little, Brown and Company, 1964 ("On Robert Lowell's 'Skunk Hour,'" 84–113).

Rizzardi, Alfredo. *La Condizione Americana*, Studi Su Poeti Nord-americani, Bologna, Capelli, 1960.

Standerwick, Desales. "Pieces Too Personal," *Renascence,* XIII, 53–56.

Staples, Hugh B. *Robert Lowell: The First Twenty Years,* New York, Farrar, Straus & Cudahy, 1962.

Weatherhead, A. Kingsley. "Imagination and Fancy: Robert Lowell and Marianne Moore," *University of Texas Studies in Literature and Language,* VI, 188–199.

Wiebe, Dallas E. "Mr. Lowell and Mr. Edwards," *Wisconsin Studies in Contemporary Literature,* III, ii, 21–31.

Salmagundi, Vol. I, no. 4, is a special Robert Lowell issue.

TWENTIETH CENTURY VIEWS

American Authors